PHILADELPHIA'S
PENCOYD IRON WORKS

PHILADELPHIA'S PENCOYD IRON WORKS

• FORGING ALONG THE SCHUYLKILL RIVER •

KEVIN RIGHTER

THE History PRESS

Published by The History Press
Charleston, SC
www.historypress.com

First published 2020

Manufactured in the United States

ISBN 9781467143059

Library of Congress Control Number: 2020938501

This book is dedicated to:

Walter Righter, who worked at Pencoyd from his youth, was self-educated in motive power and all its facets and was a stabilizing force for the Righter family.

All the former employees of the Pencoyd Iron Works with diverse backgrounds and a multitude of skills—their incredible hard work should be remembered as a highlight of Philadelphia's history.

Contents

Acknowledgements

This project started as a low-key search for information about a company and piece of land that were connected with my family. As more and more information was collected and a rich story emerged, the sharper focus developed into a full-blown book. As it unfolded over a period of four years, many people helped out along the way.

Resources available for researchers are invaluable, and I benefitted from those at Rice University Fondren Library, University of Arizona Engineering Library, the Philadelphia Free Library, the Hagley Library, the Library of Congress, the Lower Merion Historical Society, Alpena County George N. Fletcher Public Library (Great Lakes Maritime Collection), Rochester Museum and Science Center, Denver Public Library, New Bedford Free Public Library, Historical Society of Pennsylvania, York County Historical Society, West Virginia University and articles archived through the Hathi Trust. In particular, Michael Sherbon of the Pennsylvania State Archives was extremely helpful, and his efforts uncovered many valuable photos of the iron works and surrounding areas.

Several years ago, fellow Haverford College cricketer and Main Line resident Doug Flieder suggested I contact the Neighborhood Club of Bala Cynwyd, which led me to Jerry Francis, the president of the Lower Merion Historical Society. Jerry has been a constant, unwavering and positive supporter with a desire to spotlight some of the fascinating history of Lower Merion. His generous and thoughtful nature is illustrated by bringing together people of various backgrounds (but with common interests) during visits to Lower Merion. Carole Strickland provided valuable comments and feedback on a book draft that improved numerous parts of the book. In this way, I became acquainted with Stephen Gibson, Glen Tomkinson, Sean McCloskey and Max Frieder of the Penn Real Estate group, as well as John Johnstone, Sylvia Myers, Barbara Cohen, Perrin Hamilton, and Ted Goldborough—all of whom share a passion for the several centuries of Lower Merion and Schuylkill River history.

I have also corresponded with several people with connections to or information about Pencoyd structures. Mike McCabe of Old American Golf Course in The Colony, Texas, shared information about the pony truss that was relocated to the golf course in 2010. Frank Griggs, Justin Spivey and Chris Marsdon, as well as bridgehunter.com and historicbridges.com, have provided information about various Pencoyd bridges.

Banks Smither of The History Press exhibited exceptional levels of encouragement for an amateur like me, with a constant level of constructive and positive advice. His disposition ultimately led me back to The History Press after some difficulty in identifying an interested press or publisher to carry this work. I am indebted to him and all of his generous advice.

Finally, my family's input and support have been invaluable. Cousin Steve Stocking taught me about the Boston molasses flood of 1920, which led us to many images of the Boston elevated railway, as well as a preserved Pencoyd-made Northampton Station now preserved at the Seashore Trolley Museum in Kennebunkport, Maine. Uncle Mitsuaki Goromaru—a civil engineer who contributed to the construction of the amazing Akashi suspension bridge between Kobe and Awaji Island—led me to detailed information about the Amarube viaduct where today there is a skylift and exhibit as a tribute to the original 1911 viaduct built by the American Bridge Company and steel parts made at Pencoyd. My father, Richard Righter, has encyclopedic knowledge of Philadelphia in general and especially the neighborhoods in west Philadelphia where the Righter family settled and flourished for hundreds of years. When we marveled over the oral history of Pencoyd's superintendent of motive power Walter Righter's narrow-gauge train running the length of the plant and realized the sparse information available about Pencoyd iron works, it became a small challenge for me to assemble some details for him as an offering of thanks for the decades of detailed, painstaking research. Maybe this work is a small step to closing a gap of information about this portion of local and family history. My mother, Eugenia Righter, has patiently endured many discussions of Pencoyd history and has her own gem of a connection to the

Fostoria glass company. All of my family members have tolerated Pencoyd references and trivia for several years now, and I thank them for humoring me and putting up with me for this long stretch. Finally, I thank my wife, Minako, for her exceptional patience and support of this project, which must at times have seemed dull and distant. The discovery that she traveled across Pencoyd bridges in her youth makes it all worthwhile!

1

Introduction

Oral Traditions and Interwoven Histories of Families and the Ironworks

Pencoyd Iron Works dominated the landscape of a portion of the Schuylkill River from 1852 well into the twentieth century, developing into one of the largest bridge builders and structural iron and steel producers in the world.[1] Starting as the A.&P. Roberts and Co., two cousins established a small forge that quickly developed into an industrial and engineering powerhouse, influenced by many preeminent civil, mechanical and chemical engineers of the time. Small parts of the history of the company have been presented in various places over many decades, but a single coherent history has not yet been assembled. The reasons for assembling this history are numerous.

First, the Pencoyd Iron Works played a major role in my family history. My great-grandfather Walter Righter was master mechanic in charge of motive power at Pencoyd from 1882 to 1932—50 years. And his uncle William Righter, a Civil War veteran who was captured at Spotsylvania and survived imprisonment at Andersonville, worked at Pencoyd after the war. Walter had other relatives who worked at Pencoyd: Harry Lentz Jr. was a crane operator at Pencoyd from the mid-1920s, and William Grennor held an administrative job at the plant from about 1915 to the 1930s. Although the ironworks obviously made bridges, the enormous number and diversity of mill buildings in the surveys and records make it difficult to know how and where my great-grandfather and other relations fit into the big picture. There are family oral traditions about Walter that are just enough to whet one's appetite for more information. My late uncle, the Right Reverend

Walter Cameron Righter, told stories of riding with his grandfather Walter in his own narrow-gauge locomotive at the ironworks—the track ran the length of the property and through buildings, too. Walter Cameron also recalled driving down Righters Ferry Road from Lower Merion with his father, Richard Righter, and as they approached Pencoyd, there were open vats containing a green liquid—what could this be? He further recalled that the green liquid was concocted by his grandfather and was useful in the processing of steel at the mill. The details of the green liquid remain elusive today, but these questions are essentially what initially got me hooked on learning more—what buildings were located along Righters Ferry Road in such a way that tanks of liquid would be visible, and what process may have occurred there? The green liquid may have been for pickling iron or steel, which would be a process involving weak hydrochloric acid that would turn green. The green liquid could also have been part of a process at the blacksmith shop. But Walter Cameron's trips with his grandfather occurred between 1925 and 1930; the wrought iron and traditional blacksmith operations were long gone, and steel would have been the dominant product. The green liquid likely has something to do with steel making or treatment. Walter kept a collection of books, many of which remain in our possession. Topics range from boilers to gearing to pumps and tell us that as master mechanic, he must have been knowledgeable in the many disciplines on which the mill relied—steam, electricity, gearing, engines. Basically, "anything that moves" was Walter's responsibility. He had learned much on his own by reading about technical and engineering topics in his spare time. He was known to have invented many household gadgets and was naturally inventive. Trying to learn more about the environment in which Walter worked (for 50 years) was a strong catalyst for this effort.

Second, I could not find, to my surprise, a detailed history of this company despite its fundamental and significant influence on the world. While assembling this information, it became clear to me that Pencoyd represented many classic elements of an American company, starting out small on the instincts of two adventurous cousins, steadily taking advantage of new technologies, acquiring unique character and capabilities, influencing the development of a major industry—and all before being acquired and consolidated under the roof of the American Bridge Company in 1900 and then the U.S. Steel Corporation in 1902.[2] Pencoyd president Percival Roberts Jr. was one of the first members of the board of directors of U.S. Steel. Records for the Pencoyd plant are more difficult to locate after 1905 because the American Bridge Company consisted of so many plants and

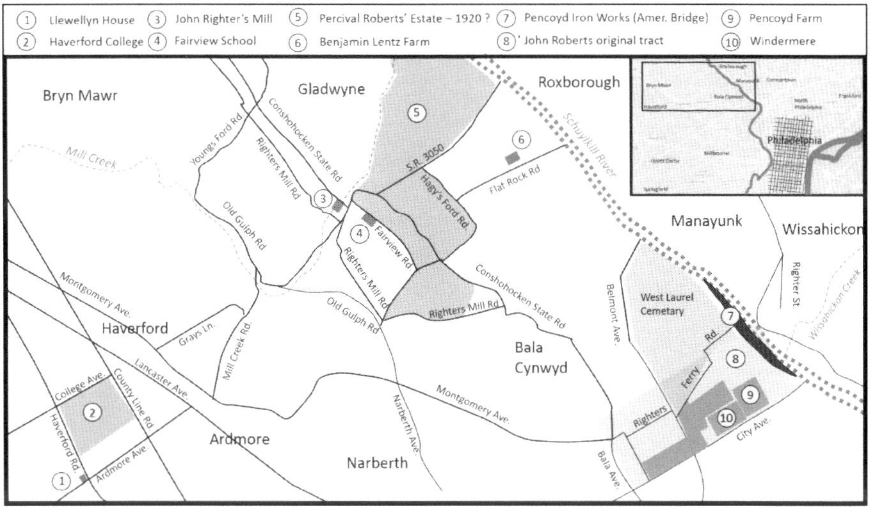

Map of the Lower Merion and Roxborough region showing nearby landmarks discussed in the introduction. *Map drawn by author.*

locations that when the company was credited with a bridge project, it is unclear which plants may have produced the steel or the components for the bridge. Rarely is that detailed information specified in engineering articles about the bridge or construction work. What I began to realize after digging into the history is that Pencoyd was an amazing company that was known all over the world for its great work and achievements.

Third, one of my great-grandmothers, Mary Wright Grow Lentz Bottomley, lived from 1874 to 1966 and was born on the Fairview Farm of Henry Grow and Mary Righter, whose daughter Elizabeth married Benjamin Lentz. Their son Henry Grow Lentz was Mary W.G. Lentz's father. The farmhouse is located on Flat Rock Road, above the banks of the Schuylkill River just upstream from the former location of Pencoyd Iron Works and adjacent to the property of Percival Roberts, the president of Pencoyd Iron Works. When I started to research the history of Pencoyd Iron Works, much of what I found initially concerned the Roberts family farmstead called "Pencoyd" near City Avenue[3] and the Mill Creek–area mansion and grounds of Percival Roberts called Penshurst (established about 1885).[4] Atlases from 1887 show Percival Roberts Sr. with a substantial portion of land and a cluster of houses labelled Penshurst. Penshurst is meaningful here because there is a family story passed down from my great-grandmother Bottomley. In the 1880s, she attended the Fairview School, one of the first local schools in the Lower Merion area, built in 1827 and organized by the Fisher-Keech-

Grow families. (The wives were all daughters of Bartel Righter Jr.: Elizabeth b. 1795+/-, Rebecca b. 1779 and Mary b. 1776.)[5] The site of the Fairview School was originally part of Bartel Righter Jr.'s property. The Penshurst property sat between the Lentz farm and the Fairview School, so a young Mary Lentz would walk through the Penshurst estate to go from one to the other. She told my father that she would frequently see the Robertses working in the gardens and found them to be very friendly and pleasant. It is perhaps surprising that the owner of a large and extensive industrial plant like Pencoyd, with an undoubtedly busy and hectic life, might nonetheless retain a down-to-earth personality.

Percival Roberts Sr. started purchasing property in Lower Merion in the 1860s, and Percival Roberts Jr. inherited property from his father, who passed away in 1898.[6] The Roberts family eventually amassed 571 acres of land in the Mill Creek area.[7] After Pencoyd Iron Works became part of the American Bridge Company and then U.S. Steel a few years later, Percival Jr. initiated construction of a well-known mansion at the Penshurst locality.[8] Penshurst required a significant number of support staff and included lavish gardens, grazing livestock (Argyllshire cattle) and spectacular views of the Schuylkill Valley. However, some portion of the land between Penshurst and the river, within view from the mansion, belonged to Lower Merion Township. When the township decided to build an incinerator plant, which would spoil the view from Penshurst, Roberts objected.[9] Ultimately, he could not stop the project, and instead of living with the ruined view, he decided to demolish Penshurst. He and his wife lived the rest of their lives in a hotel, and both had passed away by 1943. All that remains of this mansion are the original gates along Conshohocken State Road.

Finally, interest in the history of Pencoyd stems from the fact that the Righter family once operated a ferry from Roxborough to Lower Merion known as Righter's Ferry, located at exactly the same spot as the Pencoyd Iron Works. Righter's Ferry connected Roxborough and Lower Merion, with Righter's Ferry Road in Lower Merion at the west end of the ferry location.[10] Peter Righter Sr. emigrated from Germany to Philadelphia in 1699, joining the German Pietists led by Johannes Kelpius in Roxborough. Records of Peter's arrival and early years in Roxborough are sparse, but he bought land in 1724 and established himself as a farmer. Peter had four sons: Bartel, Peter (Jr.), Michael and George. Peter Jr. was likely born in the first decade of the 1700s, and in October 1741, he purchased land adjacent to his father's, fronting on the Schuylkill River, from Thomas Vickris.[11] In 1741, he applied for and was granted by Thomas, John and Richard Penn (proprietors) a patent for a ferry from his property on the east side of the Schuylkill River to the Lower Merion side.[12] This agreement forbade all others from transporting passengers from two miles above to two miles below his ferry. The original agreement was for seven years, but it was renewed in 1765 and extended through to the late 1700s.[13] It was noted that Peter Jr. had a plantation on his land, and he also built a stone house (sometimes referred to as the Righter mansion) just above the eastern end of current-day Pencoyd Bridge.[14] There was also a shad fishery here that was a lucrative business until the dam was built at Fairmount. The ferry, which was required to have a boat or boats that could transport passengers, horses, cattle and goods, became an important link between Lower Merion and Roxborough/Manayunk/Germantown.[15] Peter leased land from Thomas David on the western side of the river in Lower Merion but eventually purchased a small acreage for the ferry operations.[16] He operated the ferry until his death in 1776, when his sons Peter (III) and John became the operators.

The ferry, being in a strategic location for the area, became involved in military actions in the Revolutionary War. In 1777, Continental army general John Armstrong built redoubts along the Wissahickon Creek across from the Hessians encamped on the east side. The redoubts were located on the properties of Peter Righter Jr. and Michael Righter, not far from Righter's ferry house and ferry on the Schuylkill side. After this campaign in the Wissahickon, John Righter was allowed 68 pounds, 17 shillings and 6 pence for damage done by the Hessian raiders on his property.[17] John died in 1790 at the age of 37, and his estate was bequeathed to his daughter, Esther (1778–1808).[18] Because 12-year-old Esther was still a minor at that time, John named Algernon Roberts and Nathan Levering—two successful local businessmen—as her guardians. In 1786, the route of Ridge Road changed to its current location—the previous route utilized what is now Righter Street. Soon after John's passing, Esther's guardians filed a petition for damages due to residual traffic through her property—they collected twenty-nine pounds on her behalf.[19] In 1794, Righter's Ferry appeared in President Washington's travel plans and route from Baltimore to Germantown, indicating it was a well-known regional travel link.[20]

In 1801, when Esther was 23, she married Reverend Horatio Gates Jones, who was pastor of the Lower Merion Baptist Church. Her health became poor as early as 1805, and she passed away in 1808.[21] In the years after this, Horatio Gates Jones is listed as owner of the property that included the ferry.[22] But the ferry operations must have dwindled because of a new development in the Schuylkill valley—bridges. There was a bridge built at Flat Rock

(Domino Lane) in 1810—the first across the Schuylkill within the limits of Montgomery County.[23] Although it collapsed in 1823 due to overloading with a team moving marble, it was rebuilt. However, on September 2, 1850, a railroad bridge four miles upstream at Conshohocken gave way during a freshet, and the rails held the structure together as it became a battering ram and destroyed the bridge at Flat Rock.[24] This bridge was never rebuilt. In 1898, river access via Righter's Ferry Road was blocked when Pencoyd Iron Works purchased rights for the land, thus terminating Righters Ferry Road at the edge of its property.[25] Righter's Ferry was operated by members of the Righter family for roughly 60 years, and Righter's Ferry Road served as a major route connecting Germantown, Roxborough and Manayunk with Lower Merion and Montgomery County for around 100 years.

For all these reasons—family involvement, lack of comprehensive history of the mill, some family oral tradition and an even earlier family connection to the Pencoyd Iron Works property through the ferry—I have a deep-seated interest in knowing the history of the company, how it was born and why it flourished. Pencoyd is almost legendary in the iron and steel industry, yet little comprehensive has been written, and to my knowledge, this history is the most detailed. When I was a kid, my father introduced me to several books celebrating trades and crafts of the past. Eric Sloane wrote *A Reverence for Wood* explaining the trade of woodworking from the old broadaxe masters all the way through to the furniture makers.[26] His book is illustrated with beautiful detailed drawings of the various aspects of the art. Edwin Tunis wrote and illustrated a series of incredibly inspiring books about everyday life and skills of people in colonial times. By chance, Edwin Tunis is a distant relative of the Righter family, as discovered and documented by my father.[27] In 1754, Hannah Tunis married John Righter the Mill Creek grist miller and paper maker, from whom we descend. One of Edwin Tunis's books, *The Colonial Craftsman*, explains and illustrates the many hand trades of colonial times, including the earliest paper makers and iron workers, two industries that flourished in Lower Merion in the seventeenth and eighteenth centuries.[28] Another Tunis book, *The Tavern at the Ferry*, could easily have been about the many ferry crossings and taverns of the Schuylkill River Valley from Spring Mill inward to Philadelphia in the Belmont area.[29] Taverns were well known to the Tunis family—Anthony Tunis operated the Tunis Ordinary, remembered today as the General Wayne Inn. It is my hope that this book will bring to life the many levels of expertise that existed at Pencoyd Iron Works, the numerous industrial and technological advances and innovations as well as the working conditions that were associated with the company.

Presenting a history of Pencoyd for general readership is a challenge—it is not possible to present everything here, particularly all the details and photos from articles that are too numerous to show. I encourage interested readers to look up the many original articles cited here for a treasure-trove of additional information. In addition, if readers have a connection with the Pencoyd Iron Works—perhaps a family member or members worked there—share your history with the local historical societies. Some of the most important and meaningful information comes from the individuals who worked to help this company attain its prominent stature.

2

The Beginnings

AXLES, IRON BRIDGES AND PUDDLING MILL

The Roberts family has roots in Lower Merion all the way back to the late 1600s. John Roberts was part of the Welsh Edward Jones and Company, which purchased 5,000 acres of land in Pennsylvania from William Penn along what was called the Welsh Tract in Lower Merion.[30] The Lower Merion Welsh were Quakers, persecuted in England and Wales, and seeking religious freedom and tolerance in the Philadelphia area.[31] John Roberts, along with some fellow Quakers from Merionthshire, arrived in Philadelphia in November 1683. Roberts established a farm in Lower Merion,[32] just north of the Philadelphia city line and south of the locally notable Mill Creek district where so many mills were established in the seventeenth and eighteenth centuries.[33] Several subsequent generations of the Roberts family maintained the farm and the homestead referred to as Pencoyd by the family.[34] The Roberts family married other Welsh Quakers, including the Rees, Jones, Warner, Brooke and Williamson families, most of which were also original settlers with the Welsh along the mainline (Figure 2.1).[35] Isaac W. Roberts was the fourth generation, and he had several sons from his second marriage to Rosalind Evans Brooke, including Algernon (born in 1828), who would eventually co-found Pencoyd Iron Works (Figure 2.2), and George Brooke (born in 1833), who became the head of the Pennsylvania Railroad.[36] The Roberts family had four Algernons so the genealogy can be confusing. Isaac's younger brother Algernon S. (who lived in house called Windermere) had a son named Percival born in 1830 (Figure 2.3).

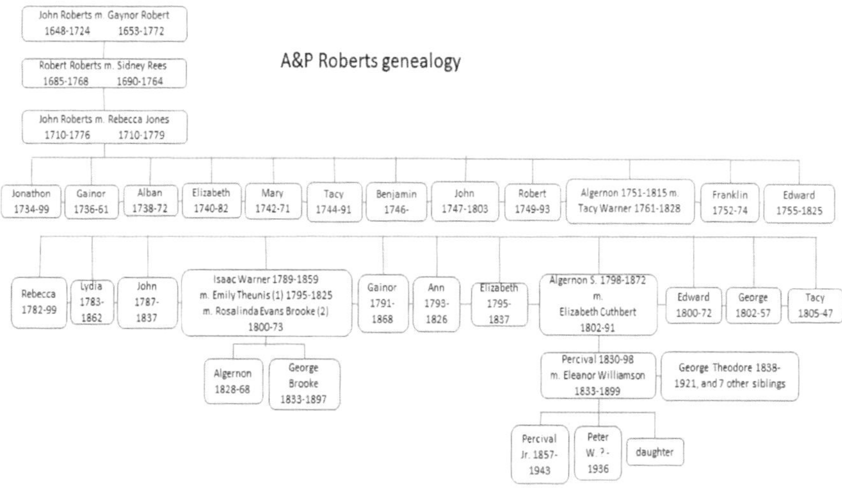

(2.1) Roberts family genealogy. *After Loth,* Pencoyd and the Roberts Family, *1961, and redrawn by author.*

The environment in which cousins Algernon and Percival were born and raised was culturally and educationally rich. We get a glimpse into their life as youngsters from Algernon's diary in which are recorded details of his daily life from 1846 to 1848.[37] Algernon was living in the city near Fifth and Race and had family living on Ninth Street (a gathering place for many aunts, uncles and cousins). He regularly walked, rode the train or took Westchester cars the six miles out to Pencoyd to visit with family and frequently attended Quaker meeting with family members. Even though streetcars were available, they were expensive.[38] Algernon worked at Price, Newlin, & Company, a hardware store; it became Newlin and Marshall when Price retired at the end of 1847. Borrowing library books for aunts and buying supplies for family were constant activities—such items included various pieces of clothing, shoes, pens, ink and various hardware items for his father and uncles. Items were delivered on a nearly daily basis out to Pencoyd or his other family members' residences. He wrote and received letters from cousin Percival, Uncle George (who was in New Orleans) and later his brother George, who, like Percival, attended Rensselaer Polytechnic Institute in Troy, New York. Algernon had many friends and acquaintances on whom he would call, such as Steven Byerly, Pennington Green, Isaac Sharpless and Thomas Yardley. His frequent visits to the library resulted in his reading a wide range of fiction such as *Letters of Lord Chesterfield*, *Don Quixote*, Homer's *The Odyssey*, the poetry of Shakespeare and nonfiction readings on bees, *Fruits and Trees of America*, *Washington and*

His Generals, chemistry, operative mechanics (Nicholson), Davy's *Agricultural Chemistry*, Millington's *Engineering*, Locke on education, the *Conquest of Mexico*, pictorial history of China, and Agassiz's book on geology. He also frequently attended lectures around town such as Gardner's lectures on science and art, Reid's lecture on Constitutional history, Gummere's book and lecture on astronomy (Gummere was professor of astronomy at Haverford College) and Booth's lectures on fluid mechanics.

Several events in his diary indicate his special interest in engineering and metallurgy, such as seeing iron being rolled in Kensington (in November 1847), discussions with his father about chemistry versus agriculture, viewing the progress of the Falls Bridge construction, a visit to see the steamship *Columbus* in Philadelphia and an exhibition at the Franklin Institute of a pump and hydraulic engine that impressed him in October 1848.

Top: (2.2) Algernon Roberts, co-founder of the Pencoyd Iron Works (daguerreotype). *The Library Company of Philadelphia.*

Bottom: (2.3) Percival Roberts, co-founder of the Pencoyd Iron Works (sketch) *From Roberts obituary in* Iron Age, *April 7, 1898.*

The rich environment extended into the arts and social circles. He wrote of hearing Lucretia Mott speak on women's rights in December 1848 at the Cherry St. Meeting, noting it was "very crowded." He also attended exhibitions at the Academy of Fine Arts, various plays and operas at the Arch St. Theatre and even dancing school, where he learned, among other dances, how to polka.

Percival Roberts attended Mt. Saint Mary's College in Washington, D.C., and then went to Rensselaer Polytechnic Institute, where he obtained a degree in civil engineering in 1847.[39] Upon graduating, he took a job as an engineer with the Pittsburgh, Fort Wayne and Chicago Railway, which was under construction.[40]

In this social and educational backdrop, Roberts cousins Algernon and Percival developed interests in the hardware industry and worked to establish a forge where they could manufacture anvils and hammers. The first generation to deviate from farming, Algernon and Percival were supported by their fathers in their business interests, which perhaps were perceived as a sign of the times; the future of farming was uncertain, but the developments in industry were compelling.[41] In 1852, the two cousins—Isaac W.'s son Algernon and Algernon S.'s son Percival—together founded the A.&P. Roberts Company and received their first order of axles that year.

PHILADELPHIA AND READING RAILROAD (PRRR) AND ACCESS TO NATURAL RESOURCES

Any history of the Pencoyd Iron Works must emphasize the development of the railroad in the Schuylkill valley because without it, coal, iron ore and pig iron could not have been delivered to the mill, and the products could not easily be transported when finished.

Railroads came to the Schuylkill valley via Reading, and the Philadelphia and Reading Railroad, which began in 1833, was completed in 1839 and opened for travel in 1842.[42] The Robertses' land extended from Lower Merion to the Schuylkill River banks, and the railroad ran along the edge of their property. The declining fertility of the land, coupled with the technological developments and ease of access to transportation (railroads), likely all led to the Roberts cousins' desire to start a foundry and mill along the river.

The railroad allowed access to the anthracite-bearing districts of central-eastern Pennsylvania, near Pottsville (Broad Top), and later to the bituminous coal mined in the western part of Pennsylvania. The hot- and clean-burning anthracite was used extensively in the furnaces at the mill, for heating iron or steel or for producing steam for powering equipment.

Many ironworks or steel mills had blast furnaces on site to produce pig iron, which is one of the basic ingredients for making cast iron, wrought iron or steel. Pig iron is made from reactions between iron ore and coke or coal occurring as:[43]

$$2\ Fe_2O_{3(solid)} + 3\ C_{(solid)} = 4\ Fe_{(liquid)} + 3CO_{2(gas)}$$

The liquid Fe (or pig iron) formed by this process contains 4 to 6 weight percent C, and when it solidifies it is very brittle. As a result, pig iron is further refined into a more useful or workable state to make wrought iron or steel.

Because Pencoyd Iron Works did not have a blast furnace to make pig iron, it would need to acquire pig iron from either the east (Philadelphia) or west (Reading) along the railroad. Pig iron was produced at a number of locations in the Schuylkill valley, making transport to Pencoyd easy with the PRRR line. If pig iron was not available, then scrap iron could be used to make wrought iron or steel. Pencoyd utilized a significant amount of scrap iron in its operations and received it from rail connections from the east and west as well.

GEORGE BROOKE ROBERTS AND COMPETITION WITH PRRR

Railroads were king of the day. Eventually, almost all of the products from Pencoyd Iron Works would be railroad-centric—car axles, turntables, bridges—with the railroads expanding from the 1850s onward. In addition to the Philadelphia and Reading Railroad that passed through the Robertses' riverside property, two other railroad systems served southeast Pennsylvania: the Pennsylvania Railroad (PRR) and the Lehigh Valley Railroad.[44] George Brooke Roberts, Algernon S.'s brother, would eventually become president of Pennsylvania Railroad.

George B. Roberts was born on January 15, 1833, to parents Isaac Warner Roberts and Rosalinda Evans Brooke. The Roberts family was one of the best known of Montgomery County. George was born at Pencoyd Farm, on which he resided all his life. He graduated from the Rensselaer Polytechnic Institute in 1849, taught there for two years and then became immersed in field activities related to the expansion of the railroad westward.[45] He immediately began life as a railroad engineer, working himself up to the highest position, which he attained by incessant diligence and superior ability as a civil engineer and railroad manager. He began work as a rodman on the mountain division of the Pennsylvania Railroad and, in 1852, while he was only 19 years old, was made assistant engineer of the Philadelphia and Erie Railroad, aiding in the construction and location of the Sunbury and Erie, the North Pennsylvania and other important lines, being employed as chief engineer on several of them.[46] In 1862, he returned to the Pennsylvania Railroad as assistant to President J. Edgar Thomson, continuing in this position for seven years. While under Thomson's guidance, Roberts oversaw the construction of bridges and other engineering work, including the Connecting Railway Bridge over the Schuylkill River, which connected the railroad's southern and northern lines.[47] While Roberts's professional life was developing well, his personal life had suffered a tragedy: George married Sarah Brinton, whom he lovingly called "Sallie," in 1868, but a year later she died after giving birth to a son named George Brinton Roberts.[48]

George's service with PRR was so valuable that he was made fourth vice-president of the road in 1869.[49] He was soon afterward made a second vice-president, and on June 3, 1874, when Colonel Thomas A. Scott succeeded J. Edgar Thomson in the presidency, George Roberts was promoted to the post of first vice-president. This was a vastly important position, with great interests and responsibilities being confided to his care. When Colonel Scott died in May 1880, Roberts was chosen to succeed him, and he held the position by annual reelection until his death in 1897.[50]

There was, for a period of time, significant competition between the Philadelphia and Reading Railroad and the Pennsylvania Railroad, which must have seemed awkward to the Roberts brothers, each of which was heavily involved in these competing railroad systems. Part of the competition related to railroad access to the north and south of the Schuylkill River. George Roberts was primarily responsible for construction of the Broad Street Station, a major landmark in Philadelphia history (see chapter 3).[51] Prior to the Broad Street Station project, railroad locomotives could not cross the Schuylkill River but instead delivered passengers at West Philadelphia Station (at 32nd Street), and then horse-drawn streetcars took them into Center City. Construction of the new bridge and a 10-block viaduct (also called the "Chinese Wall") elevated the railroad tracks above street level and routed them into the new Broad Street Station. This new innovation started the migration of Philadelphia's business district to Broad and Market Streets, which made passenger commuting possible and thus increased suburban growth, for example, on the Main Line to the east (PRR).[52] By 1886, the station was being used by 1 million passengers a month.[53]

George and his wife, both of Welsh descent (from Welsh colonists dating back to 1680s), named several of the stations along the PRR, including Bala and Cynwyd. Because George's ancestry was Welsh, and specifically his ancestor came from Bala, in Wales (more than two centuries previously), he gave the name to the railroad station near the homestead.[54] These names would ultimately also become associated with the Pencoyd Iron Works, which was located in Bala Cynwyd. Although the PRR did not serve the Pencoyd Iron Works directly, the PRR would benefit from bridges built by Pencoyd

Iron Works late in the nineteenth century. The intertwining of businesses of the Roberts family had an enormous influence on the development of Lower Merion and this part of Philadelphia, as will also be seen in the later chapters on bridge building and the specialized equipment that was developed locally for use in the mills.

BEGINNING OF THE PENCOYD IRON WORKS

In June 1852, the A.&P. Roberts Company officially opened.[55] Algernon and Percival initially invested $8,000, but they also received loans from their fathers (Isaac and Algernon S., respectively).[56] Originally, there were four people working at the mill. The forge was established, allowing them to make wrought iron, but they also wanted to be able to shape the iron into hardware. They arranged to have part of an old-fashioned trip-hammer delivered from James Rowlands & Company (an ironworks in Kensington, Philadelphia).[57] Although the company had started making anvils and other hardware, the founders quickly realized the potential for railroad axles and centers, which formerly had to be imported and were thus expensive.[58] The first order—for 10–20 axle hubs and centers—came from the large railroad car axle company A. Whitney and Sons.[59] In 1853, production was a respectable 304.4 tons. In 1854, A.&P. added a rolling mill to its capability, and in 1855, the mill started making rolled scrap axles. Growth was rapid in this industry, increasing from the 12-axle order of 1852 to the production of 80,000 axles in 1869 and 45,390 axles in 1872.[60] As described later, Pencoyd also developed an axle testing protocol that became an industry standard. This growth is even evident in the sketch of the mill from 1863 (Figure 2.4) showing a cluster of buildings that must have included the hammer mill, rolling mill and puddling mill.[61]

In 1856, an 18″, 2 high, bar mill was added to the capabilities to work scrap into bars. The "2 high" refers to a rolling mill with two rolls of a specific size, with "3 high" meaning 3 rolls, and so on. (This continued until 1895.) In 1859, a 2 high rolling mill and puddle furnaces were added for production of puddled iron. The mill was driven by a 24″ x 36″ Corliss steam engine.[62] As a historical side note, the Corliss engine was one of the main pieces of technology featured in the 1876 centennial celebration, which occurred not far away from Pencoyd, just downriver at Fairmount Park.[63] But more about the connection between Pencoyd and the centennial in chapter 4.

(2.4) Lithograph of Pencoyd Iron Works, 1863. *Courtesy of Historical Society of Pennsylvania, HSP medium graphics collection [V64], call number: Bb 38 R 235.*

The explosion of bridge building to come in the 1860s required an ample supply of wrought iron. Wrought iron is produced by a process known as puddling, and the puddling mill at Pencoyd was located in the old stone building to the east of Righters Ferry Road.[64] According to an 1881 plan of the mill, there were 18 puddling furnaces in this building.[65]

Puddling is a process that transforms high-carbon pig iron into more workable and useful wrought iron, and it was developed in the 1780s by Henry Cort in England.[66] Cort also developed the rolling process that takes blooms or billets of wrought iron and transforms them into sheets or bars. Puddling involves taking the pig iron and subjecting it to an oxidized atmosphere that allows the carbon in the pig iron to become oxidized to CO_2; the resulting product has a lower carbon content and eventually becomes wrought iron. The pig iron is heated in the reverberating furnace and then flowed out into a trough where either silicon-rich slag is pulled off at one end (thus reducing the Si content of the iron) or Fe bar is used to stir iron oxide or scale into the puddled iron (Figure 2.5); either of these cause the iron to be more pure, reducing the C and Si contents to make it useful for structural shapes or construction.[67]

The process of making puddle balls of iron is a special art that deserves description.[68] To begin, white cast iron or refined iron (for dry puddling) or scrap iron or iron oxide (wet puddling) is placed in the hearth of a furnace, a process otherwise known as charging. The charge is heated until the top starts to melt and the oxides begin to mix, usually after about 30 minutes. Then the mixture is exposed to a blast of air and stirred by long puddling bars (or rabbles) through doors in the furnace (Figure 2.5). This step encourages oxygen from the oxides to react with the impurities Si and Mn (to form slag) and S and P (to form gases that are exhausted) in the pig iron. Then, additional fuel is added and the temperature increased so that the iron completely melts and the carbon starts to burn off as CO_2, as well. During wet puddling, the CO_2 formation produces bubbles, giving the appearance of boiling, and causes the slag to puff up on top. These visual signs give the puddler an indication of the progress of the process. Furthermore, as the C burns off as CO_2, the melting temperature of the increasingly Fe-rich residue increases from around 1,150°C (2,100°F) to 1,540°C (2,800°F), so the furnaces have to maintain this heating level by continuous feeding. Eventually, C is almost totally removed or burned off, and the iron acquires a spherical spongy mass. At this point, the process has completed, and the puddle ball can be removed by using the hook on the end of a puddling bar or a pair of tongs. Puddle balls typically weigh 35 to 40 kilograms (70–80 pounds) and measure 30 to 38 centimeters (12–15″) in diameter.

In 1859, the bridge company commenced with the manufacture and erection of wrought-iron bridges. A.&P. Roberts employed civil engineer John W. Murphy to design and construct Whipple-Murphy truss bridges (or a double intersection Pratt truss; see chapter 7, Figure 7.6).[69] John Murphy graduated from Rensselaer Polytechnic Institute in 1848 and likely met George and Percival Roberts there, as they both attended RPI in the same period. Before becoming associated with the Robertses, Murphy had worked

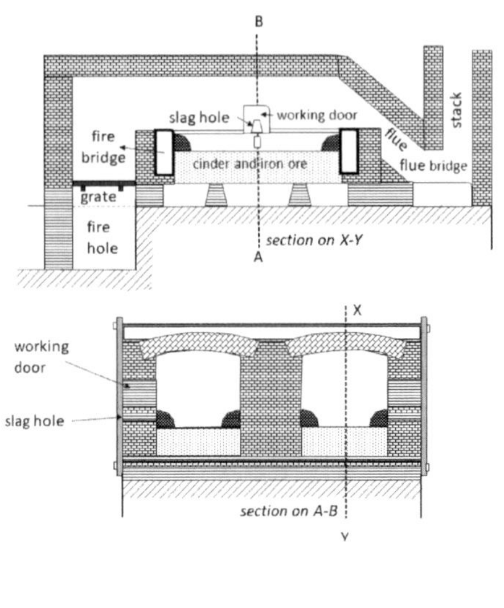

(2.5) Puddling furnaces (double) for making wrought-iron billets and blooms. Puddling bar accessed iron through the working door. After Steelmaking: 1850–1900 *(London: Institute of Materials, 1990), 27–35, and redrawn by author.*

with Squire Whipple, one of the United States' most innovative bridge engineers, in the Erie Canal region.[70]

An appreciation of this early connection between Pencoyd and Whipple-Murphy truss structures requires some background about their origin and designer. Squire Whipple was born in 1804 in Hardwick, Massachusetts.[71] His father designed, built and ran a cotton-spinning mill in Greenwich, Massachusetts, and then the Whipple family moved to Otsego County near Cooperstown, New York, for farming. He attended Hartwick and Fairfield Academies in central New York and then graduated from Union College in Schenectady, New York, after one year of study in 1830.[72] He started out his career with an apprenticeship working on the Baltimore and Ohio Railroad and then the Erie Canal enlargement, the New York and Erie Railroad and several other railroads. He had an interest in inventing and tinkering: he designed, built and sold mathematical instruments such as transits and engineer's levels and drafting equipment, and in 1841, he designed and built a 300-ton-capacity weigh lock scale to weigh the canalboats on the enlarged Erie Canal in Utica—the largest weighing device in the country at the time.[73]

While working on the Erie Canal, Whipple realized that the wooden bridges crossing the canal had a short life. He became interested in designing and building the even longer span bridges that would be necessary on the newer, wider canal. What resulted was his bowstring iron truss arch design—issued patent No. 2,064 on April 24, 1841—for the "construction of iron truss bridges."[74] Whipple's first bridge built to his patent was in 1841. The wooden bridge across the canal at First Street in Utica had failed, and the canal commissioners approved the construction of his bridge after he built an example in a vacant lot in Utica.[75] Hundreds of Whipple bridges were built in the Erie Canal region, as well as seven short span iron bridges for the New York and Erie Railroad near Newburgh and Binghamton, New York. He also developed the first successful long span trapezoidal railroad bridges on New York Railroads in West Troy and Utica. This was a double intersection truss design that eventually became one of the most common railroad truss bridges until the 1890s and built over western rivers with spans over 500′.[76]

Perhaps Whipple's major accomplishment was a book he wrote and published in 1847, titled *A Work on Bridge Building Consisting of Two Essays, The One Elementary and General, the Other Giving Original Plans and Practical Details for Iron and Wooden Bridges.*[77] This book, updated in 1869, and in print until 1899, presented methods of analyzing and designing a truss bridge and was influential worldwide in the use of basic mathematical principles in the design of bridge structures. It was for this work that he was honored by the American Society of Civil Engineers (ASCE). Even though he retired in 1860, he continued to design swing and lift bridges, building many swing bridges over the Erie, Portland and Welland Canals, including the first vertical lift bridge in the United States over the Erie Canal in Utica in 1874.[78]

The interested student of bridges can see restored Whipple bridges at Union College in Schenectady, over the Enlarged Erie Canal at Vischer's Ferry, New York; one at Boonville, New York over the Utica and Black River Canal; and one in Central Park, Schenectady, New York, the restorations all overseen by civil engineer Frank Griggs. In addition, a Whipple change bridge originally built in 1858 for the Erie Canal in Rochester has been recently restored in Palmyra, New York, and other known Whipple trusses are in Claverack, New York; over the Normanskill Creek in Albany, New York; one in Tokyo, Japan, in a historic park; and one on the campus of Ohio State University.[79] Whipple was clearly an important figure in early bridge design in America.

This association of Murphy and the Robertses would ultimately lead to the construction of a number of wrought-iron bridges, as A.&P. Roberts apparently bought the rights to the patent of Squire Whipple for the Whipple-Murphy truss design,[80] which was a variation of the standard (at the time) Pratt truss.[81] Pencoyd's insight to build Whipple bridges with the help of John Murphy was easy to understand—these were innovative structures and established the ironworks' ability to make wrought-iron bridges. As early as 1858, a North Pennsylvania Railroad wrought-iron Whipple-Murphy bridge was built by Pencoyd near Bethlehem over the Saucon Creek (Figure 2.6).[82] In the same time frame, a similar bridge at Mauch Chunk, Pennsylvania, was featured in catalogue of bridge-making companies.[83] Finally, a 165′ span bridge over the Morris Canal at Phillipsburg was built in 1859,[84] and some images of this bridge may be seen in the Historic American Engineering Record study of the Morris Canal.[85] This bridge was in service there until 1869, when it was moved to Towanda, Pennsylvania, and then moved again in 1879 to a crossing of the Cayuta Creek in Sayre, Pennsylvania.

More bridges were to follow:

> *In 1859, in company with Levi Line, George B., Algernon and Percival Roberts, under the firm name of A. & P. Roberts & Co., he being the Chief Engineer, and I.P. Morris & Co. the builders of the iron work, he erected for the U.S. Government seven bridges for Beale's Wagon Route: on the Plains, four of which were 100 feet, and three 50 feet spans, on the*

(2.6) Whipple-Murphy bridge built for the North Pennsylvania Railroad in 1858. *From the* Journal of the Society of Industrial Archeology *19 no. 2 (1993): 17–47, 1993.*

> *Whipple plan, with cast iron arches. Also one of 65 feet span, with draw, over Frankford Creek, Bridesburg; one of 50 feet span on the Foglesville Railroad, one of 165 feet span on the Murphy-Whipple plan over the Delaware at Easton for the Lehigh Valley Railroad; one of 160 feet span, for the Illinois Central Railroad, under Gen. McClellan; two of 125 feet span over the Jordan Creek, at Allentown, for the Lehigh Valley Railroad Co., and one of 50 feet span, for A. Campbell & Co., over the canal at Manayunk. This bridge, when finished, was remarkable for its lightness, being sent to its location in a furniture car, but they refused to receive it, as they did not believe it would answer the purpose intended. The bridge was, nevertheless, erected, and is standing at this present time in as good condition as when erected, and for the first six years carried a 4-inch line of shaft, which transmitted over 50-horse power to the opposite side of the canal; also a 4-inch water main, and the carriage of the products of their large mill, of 20,000 spindles.*[86]

The Illinois Central Railroad bridge was featured in the magazine of the ICRR in 1921.[87]

The association with Murphy was the first of many connections between innovative bridge designers and the company (see chapter 7). Whipple and Murphy developed, in 1849, what is called the pin connection design. This ultimately dominated bridge design in the United States. It would be one of the predominant designs used by Pencoyd in future bridge-making enterprises; Pencoyd would become one of the country's leading makers of eye-bars (see chapter 9).

The early bridge making was interrupted by the outbreak of the Civil War in 1861, with Philadelphians enlisting in great numbers in 1862.[88] The A.&P. Roberts Company had an interesting and perhaps unexpected attitude toward military service (given the founders' Quaker heritage). During the summer of 1863, employees of the works were drilled every afternoon by Algernon Roberts on the site that would ultimately be occupied by the 12″ and 20″ mills.[89] A number of these men enlisted in the service of the state, the firm paying the men a bounty and monthly pay equivalent, in addition to the sum paid by the state. The firm also cared for their families during their absence in the army.

After the war, the company continued to expand, and by late 1869, railroad axles were the main product of the mill, for which it had achieved widespread and solid reputation. "The business has been steadily increasing, until it has reached a product of 30,000 axles a year; and they have earned a reputation for their axles, both rolled and hammered, that is second to none in the country."[90] The 1872 survey of the company grounds shows the well-developed forge (Figure 2.7) with co-located furnaces, puddling mill and hammers, as well as a new rolling mill building on the up river side of Righters Ferry Road.[91] The Pencoyd Iron Works consumed mainly scrap iron, which was thoroughly cleansed from dirt and rust using revolving cylinders before use in piling and rolling. The rolled axles were further improved by having the journals hammered in; after the axle was made, the ends were placed in a heating furnace, brought to a white heat and then placed under a heavy hammer; this served to clean and condense the iron, giving a cleaner and better-wearing surface.[92]

The company experienced a major loss in 1868. Algernon Roberts died on November 8, 1868, at the young age of 40, as a result of blood poisoning

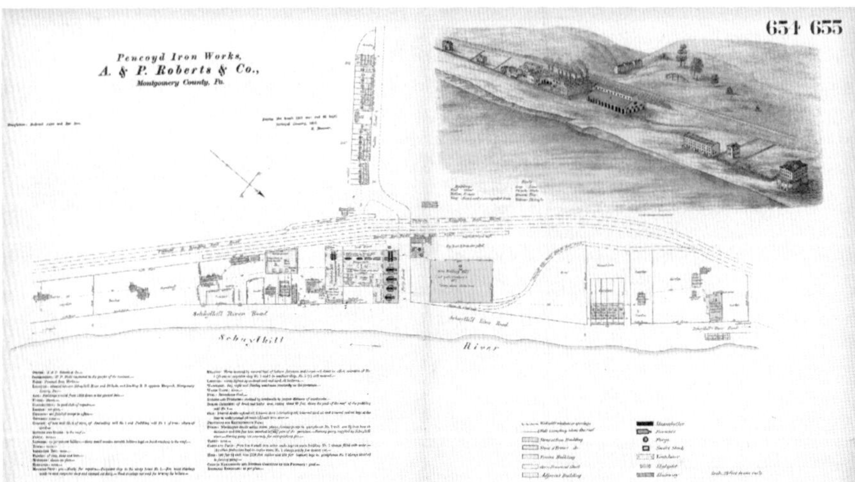

(2.7) Hexamer survey of Pencoyd Iron Works from 1872, showing puddling mill location (near center of the map). *Free Library of Philadelphia, Map Collection.*

(2.8) A 20-ton steam hammer with cranes on each side and furnaces in background. Photo taken in Hammer Mill. *From the* Railroad and Engineering Journal *60, no. 12 (December 1889): 568–70.*

after lancing a carbuncle.[93] This shocking development had two immediate effects. First, it gave Algernon's younger brother George B. Roberts of the PRR full title to the ancestral home at Pencoyd Farm.[94] And second, it initiated the involvement of G. Theo. Roberts in the business, together with the continuing involvement of original co-founder Percival.[95]

Steam hammers were used to work the billets into bars, and by 1889, Pencoyd even had a 20-ton steam hammer (Figure 2.8)[96] with specially designed cranes to move blooms ingots and other pieces of work.[97]

Tests were routinely done and helped Pencoyd to establish its reputation. According to *Van Nostrand's Engineering Encyclopedia* (1869),

> *They have lately engaged in the manufacture of Bessemer steel axles, and are now executing an order of some 200, for the Pennsylvania railway, under a guaranteed test of a drop 1049 pounds, falling 20 feet, the axle to stand five blows, reversing at each blow. The axles are made four feet longer than required in use, to give a trial piece. They are also making bridge bolts, piston rods, etc., of Bessemer steel, and lately rolled bridge bolts for*

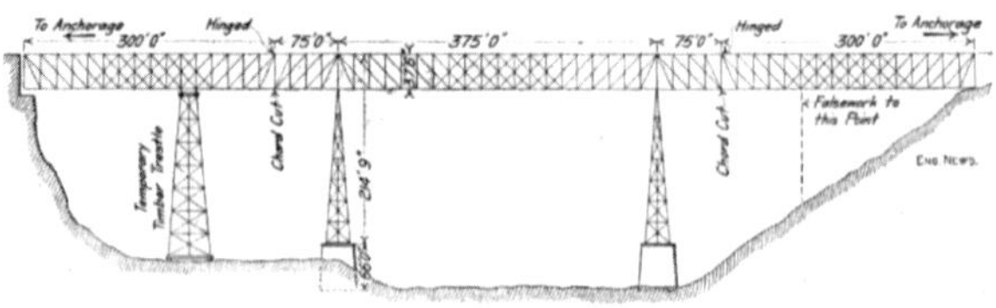

FIG. 1. ELEVATION OF KENTUCKY RIVER BRIDGE FROM ERECTION DRAWINGS.

Top: (2.9) Kentucky River High Bridge, built in 1876–77 by the Baltimore Bridge Company. The wrought iron was rolled at Pencoyd, and then the bridge was fabricated at Edge Moor Iron Works. *From* Engineering News *53, no. 12 (March 23, 1905): 312–14.*

Bottom: (2.10) Sketch of Kentucky River High Bridge. *From* Scientific American, *October 27, 1877, 1,503–5.*

> *the Philadelphia, Wilmington and Baltimore railway, of this steel, 35 feet long, 24 inches in diameter. In addition to the axle business, which is their specialty, they manufacture bar iron, bridge bolts, guaranteed to stand 60,000 pounds tensile strain to the square inch, and Pencoyd shafting.*[98]

Testing related to axles continued into the twentieth century (1907), even though Pencoyd had stopped producing axles a few years before that. Over nearly a half century, it had built a strong reputation in making and testing axles.[99]

A notable bridge of historic significance was built in Kentucky in 1877. The Kentucky River bridge was designed and built by the Baltimore Bridge Company under the supervision of engineer C. Shaler Smith. The cantilever design over the Kentucky River about 100 miles south of Cincinnati illustrated a major advantage of this approach—eliminating the need for falsework during construction (Figures 2.9, 2.10).[100] This was a wrought-iron bridge, and most of the iron was rolled at Pencoyd Iron Works, then moved to Edge Moor Iron Works for fabrication. The rolling took place between 1874 and 1875, just before Pencoyd installed its next rolling mill in 1876. This new mill would produce structural shapes for construction.[101]

Pencoyd's immersion in the manufacturing of axles is exhibited by advertisements from railway journals in the mid- to late 1870s.[102] The fledgling company, stabilized by this extraordinary business of iron axle and bridge making, would soon undergo another transformation with the influence of Percival Roberts Jr. and installation of additional rolling mills that would increase production of structural wrought iron and steel.

3

STRUCTURAL SHAPES, THE CENTENNIAL EXPOSITION AND PERCIVAL ROBERTS JR.

The focus on iron bridges and railroad car axles broadened to include structural wrought iron (and eventually steel) for construction. The expansion of the rolling mills and capabilities, as well as materials testing, led to Pencoyd becoming a leader in this field by the mid-1880s.

In 1875, a 23″ 3-high roll train—supplied by three heating ordinary furnaces—was erected at Pencoyd specifically for the manufacture of structural shapes.[103] The mill was located in one of the company's original stone buildings, dating to the 1850s (Figure 3.1).[104] Initially, the mill produced 250 to 400 tons per week, but by 1901, output had increased to 700–900 tons per week.[105] Blooms, slabs, billets and bars from the puddling and hammer mills could now be worked and rolled into structural shapes, and in the case of Pencoyd, this would be beams, angles and tees, along with the many other shapes for which Pencoyd would become renowned.

As early as 1870, planning for the Centennial Exposition had begun, with the request to use Fairmount Park as the location for the enormous fair.[106] Commemorating the 100th anniversary of the United States, the Centennial Exposition was to be a national and international draw. Nearly 200 structures were ultimately built for the exhibition, including the Main Building, Agricultural Hall, Horticultural Hall, Machinery Hall, Memorial Hall and the Women's Pavilion. Lasting from May to November 1876, the exposition was opened by President Ulysses S. Grant, along with Pedro II, the emperor of Brazil, starting a large Corliss engine (see Figure 5.1)

(3.1) View of workers in the rod mill (probably 12/23 inch mill because top of window frame is rounded like those in the 12/23 inch mill building). *From the Collection of Philadelphia Commercial Museum, Pennsylvania State Archives, collection MG 219, folder 6, box 2.*

in the Machinery Hall.[107] This engine would provide much of the power required for the exposition.

Machinery Hall would be a showcase for technology—in addition to the Corliss engine, there were precursors to dynamos, electric lights, specialized tooling machinery and more from local Philadelphia companies such as William Sellers and Co. (see chapter 9).[108] The Women's Pavilion emphasized the many achievements and influence of women both domestically and in areas such as industrial and fine arts, woodworking, furniture making, ceramics, clothing and woven goods, philanthropy, science and medicine, education, literature and more.[109] One can only imagine young Walter Righter—who was 11 years old in 1876—walking the grounds of the Centennial Exposition, a short distance from his house in Roxborough across the river, marveling at his future.

This event had an undeniable effect on American industry and marked a new chapter in the history of the young A.&P. Roberts Company. In 1876,

A.&P. Roberts received a contract for structural elements of Centennial Exhibition buildings.

> *The cost of the Main Building was $1,580,000. The engineers and architects were Henry Pettit and Joseph M. Wilson. The wrought and cast-iron work was manufactured by William Sellers & Co., of the Edgemoor Iron Works; the wrought-iron was furnished by A&P Roberts, of the Pencoyd Rolling Mills; the cast-iron was furnished by Morris, Tasker, & Co., of the Pascal Iron Works; and the iron work was erected by the Watson Manufacturing Co. The foundations of the building were begun in the autumn of 1874. On the 8th of May, 1875, the erection of the iron work was begun, and was completed on the 21 of December 1875. The other work was carried out with rapidity, and the building was completed early in February, 1876, and on the 14th of that month was delivered by the contractor to the Board of Finance.*[110]

The Main Exhibition Building (Figure 3.2) encompassed 21.5 acres, and with that total area, it was the largest building in the world.[111] It would ultimately be disassembled and sold in 1881.[112] The only remaining building at the exposition grounds is Memorial Hall, which became an art museum. As of this writing, it is a fine children's museum, the Please Touch Museum. Despite the brief lifespan of these buildings, the exposition gave Pencoyd Iron Works a jolt to its structural shape capabilities. The ironworks would soon be leading the country in this respect.

(3.2) Main Exhibition Hall for the 1876 Centennial Exhibition, under construction in Fairmount Park, 1875. *Library of Congress.*

(3.3) Percival Roberts Jr. *From* Cassier's Magazine, *March 1903, 679–80.*

The year 1876 also marked another milestone in the history of the Pencoyd Iron Works. Percival Roberts Jr.—19-year-old son of company founder Percival Roberts and fresh out of Haverford College—started working at the mill. The 18″ mill was running, but the 12″ and 23″ mills were idle. Sometimes, the mill crews switched back and forth from one to the others. Percival Roberts Jr. started with shearing iron and then got involved with the puddling mill. He soon took up residence at 2 Rolling Mill Lane, just south of the mill across the railroad tracks.[113]

Percival Roberts Jr. (Figure 3.3) was born in Philadelphia in 1857 and educated at the Episcopal Academy, the University of Pennsylvania and Haverford College, graduating from the latter in 1876. During that year, he was for several months a volunteer assistant in the Geological Survey of Pennsylvania. In November 1876, he entered the Pencoyd Iron Works as a mill clerk and, the next year, took a postgraduate course in chemistry and metallurgy at the University of Pennsylvania, subsequently returning to the Pencoyd service, which became his life's work.[114] He eventually served in every branch of the plant, learning every detail of the business of making iron, structural forms and bridge building. After the company's role in preparation of the girders and other structural material for the buildings of the Centennial Exhibition of 1876, the scope and character of the Pencoyd Works were extended under the care of Percival Roberts Jr. It was under his direction that a special bridge department was added. Meanwhile, the business completely reorganized with electrical and other modern appliances.[115] As will be seen in chapters 4, 6, and 7, Pencoyd became a worldwide leader in steel making, structural steel in construction and bridge building. Pencoyd would ultimately merge (with 27 other companies) into the American Bridge Company, of which Percival Roberts Jr. was made the president. He was elected director on January 9, 1900, and then several years later, the American Bridge Company was absorbed by U.S. Steel Corporation.

In 1881, the company's most distinctive building and one of the landmarks in Lower Merion Township was completed: the office building that is at the end of Righters Ferry Road near the Schuylkill River.[116] The office building is not in the 1872 Hexamer Survey drawing (Figure 2.7), but it is on an 1881 map of the Pencoyd plant (Figure 3.4).[117] Some have speculated that the office building was designed by the famous Philadelphia architect Frank Furness, who planned many distinctive buildings in the Philadelphia region in that period, including an addition to the Roberts family ancestral Pencoyd farmhouse.[118] It remains unclear who the architect was, but the office building has beautiful and unique brickwork that is not unlike that used in some of Furness's designs (Figure 3.5.)[119]

Rolling mills became a critical component to the Pencoyd Iron Works. In 1876, a 12″ 3-high roll train was built for guide iron, small bars, angles, tees and so in. It was supplied by two ordinary heating furnaces; these were not removed until 1896, when a new type of continuous heating furnace was erected. This mill produced 500 to 570 tons per week in 1901, and it also appears in the 1881 sketch of the plant with the label "bar mill" (Figure 3.4).[120] This new roll train was housed in the same building as the 23″ 3-high mill

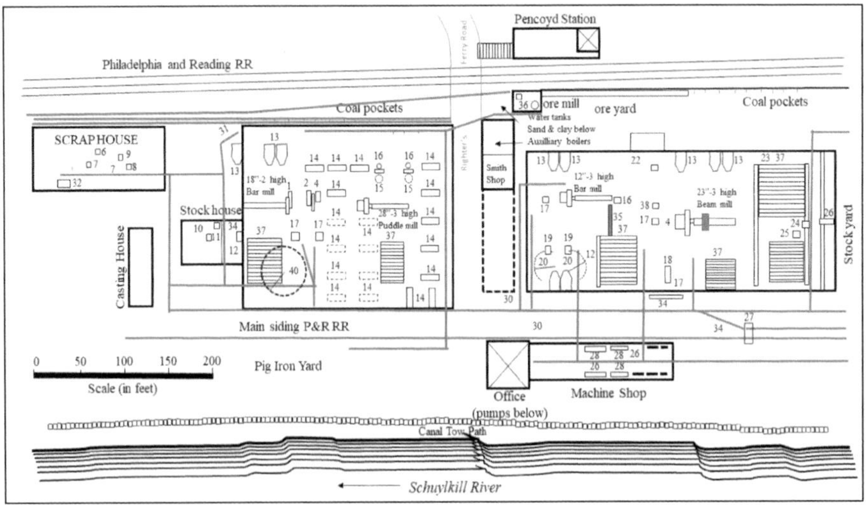

(3.4) 1881 sketch of plant with items numbered as follows: (1) engine, 19"x48"; (2) engine, 12"x36"; (3) engine, 18"x22"; (4) engine, 32"x48"; (5) engine, 24"x36"; (6) fan blower; (7) cleaning barrel; (8) scrap shears; (9) engine, 10"x24"; (10) engine, 8"x12"; (11) straightening rolls; (12) hot saw; (13) heating furnaces; (14) puddling furnaces; (15) squeezers; (16) engines, 16"x24"; (17) piling shears; (18) cropping shears; (19) steam hammers; (20) cranes; (21) steam crane; (22) engine, 10"x12"; (23) pulling engine; (24) straightening rolls; (25) engine, 14"x14"; (26) straightening press; (27) shipping crane; (28) roll lathes; (29) engine, 14"x16"; (30) scales; (31) shipping crane; (32) plate shears; (33) steam hoist; (34) engine, 10"x12"; (35) cooling bed, small iron; (36) ore crusher; (37) cooling beds; (38) cold saw; (39) pulling machine; (40) crane. *Redrawn by author from original reference,* Engineering Record, *March 25, 1893, 334–36.*

(3.5) View of the Pencoyd Iron Works office building. *Photo by the author.*

installed in 1875 for structural shapes. The latter initially had an output of 250 to 400 tons per week, but this had increased to 700 to 900 per week by 1901.[121] This mill is also called "beam mill" in an 1881 sketch of the plant, indicating that beams could be made at two different rolling mills at the plant (Figure 3.4).[122] These two rolling mills were upriver from Righters Ferry Road in a large stone building. Downriver from Righters Ferry Road was the 18″ 2-high bar mill. Built in 1856 and in operation until 1895, this was one of the oldest rolling mills at the plant. Co-located with the puddling furnaces, it was originally used for puddled (wrought) iron, but then later also used for steel.[123] With this addition, Pencoyd had three rolling mills; as rolling was central to its operations, more explanation is justified.

Iron (and later steel) products from the puddling mill could be worked in the hammer mill to produce slabs, blooms and billets—all of which could be rolled into various shapes (Figure 3.6). Rolling mills consist of 2-, 3-, or 4-high rolls, with some of the rolls being reversed, which means that a piece could be rolled in one direction with the first and second rolls and then rolled back in the opposite direction with the second and third rolls (Figure 3.6). Some processes required multiple passes through the rolling mill to get from a raw bloom, billet or slab to intermediate roughing shapes and then to a final product shape such as an angle or channel (Figure 3.7). Blooms could be rolled into beams using combinations of various roughing and then finishing shapes (Figure 3.8).

By 1882, a small shop had been erected at Pencoyd, at the upper end of the 23″ mill building, for punching beams and channels for structural purposes (Figures 3.9, 3.10).[124] The plant had a yearly capacity of about 10,000 tons of iron bars up to 12″ wide and shapes up to 15″ beams and channels, and it employed about 800 people. Pencoyd had become a leader of wrought iron (and later steel) in construction and published a book, frequently updated, that became an industry standard.[125] In this book—the first edition of which was published in 1884, with nearly annual updates—one could see the range of products available for construction needs (Figure 3.11), as well as the theory used to derive the dimensions (and associated strengths) of each piece.[126]

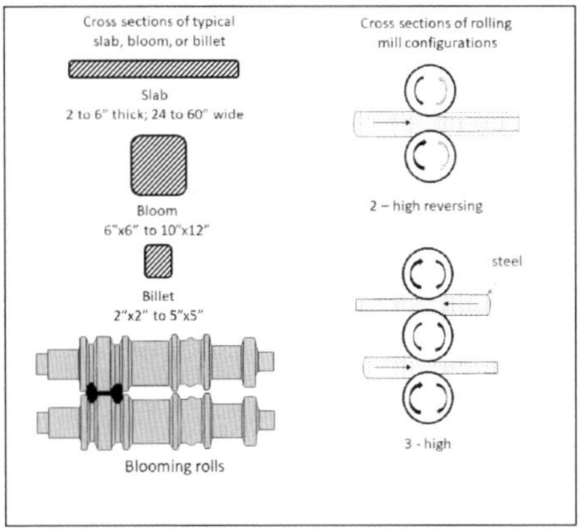

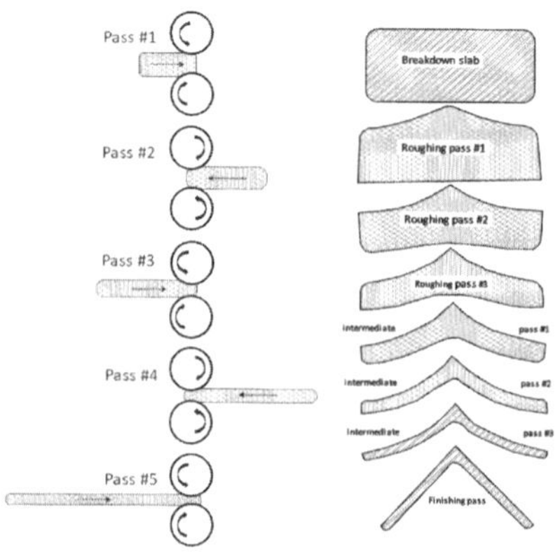

Top: (3.6) Illustration of rough forms used to create various structural shapes—slabs, blooms and billets (*left*), example of roll configurations for rolling blooms into beams, and illustration of 2 high and 3 high reversible rolling mills. *From* After Making and Shaping of Steel, *1951 impression, 421, 423 and 464, redrawn by author.*

Bottom: (3.7) Schematic illustration of multiple passes of work piece through a two high reversible mill. Such a sequence could be used with a slab to create, for example, the angle illustrated on the right. *From* After Making and Shaping of Steel, *1951 impression, 465 and 536.*

In addition, there are many example calculations of loads—both even and uneven—that various structural elements can bear.

The material presented in the Pencoyd book was derived from a series of experiments carried out by James Christie, chief engineer, and published in the journal *Transactions of the American Institute of Mining Engineers* in 1884.[127] Christie used a lever-style Fairbanks testing machine to study the strength of a wide range of structural shapes of various lengths made of both wrought iron and then steel.[128] He combined his measurements at Pencoyd with results of tests done at the U.S. Army facility in Watertown, Massachusetts. A commonly used parameter in engineering to assess strength or tendency to buckle is the least radius of gyration. A plot of pressure applied to the strut versus length divided by the least radius of gyration demonstrated this relation for the various structural shapes (tees, angles, channels, beams) made at Pencoyd (Figure 3.12). In general, hinged and round-ended shapes were not as strong as the flat and fixed-ended shapes. Together these experiments

(3.8) Large rolls and transfer tables for a hot bloom in Pencoyd's blooming mill. *Courtesy of Philadelphia Commercial Museum, Pennsylvania State Archives, collection MG219.2, box 15.*

demonstrated the relative strength of shapes made from wrought iron, and a second paper demonstrated the superior strength of steel compared to wrought iron (see chapter 5).

James Christie (Figure 3.13) was born on August 28, 1840, near Ottawa, Canada.[129] His family was Scottish, and he was first employed in the United States with a railroad construction corps, then as an apprentice in a Detroit locomotive works machine shop. After spending one year in Missouri as an assistant to engineers and contractors on the Pacific Railroad of Missouri, he went to Philadelphia to work for the I.P. Morris Company as a machinist. In 1865, he took a job as superintendent and engineer of the Fulton Foundry in Pittsburgh, then moved on to Phillipsburg, New Jersey, where he became superintendent of the Phillipsburg Manufacturing Company and engaged in construction of iron bridges.[130] In 1876, Christie became construction engineer with the Pencoyd Iron Works, and he stayed until after Pencoyd became part of the American Bridge Company in 1902. At Pencoyd, he carried out many important studies, including his experiments on the strength of wrought iron and steel; his measurements of steel composition using the Talbot process; and his organization of machinery, personnel and workflow to make Pencoyd one of the most efficient ironworks in the eastern United States.[131] Upon his retirement from the company, he established a consulting practice of his own. In addition to his contributions to the ironworks, Christie also had an inclination to public service, having served in the Antietam campaign of the Civil War and holding several political offices, including mayor of Phillipsburg in

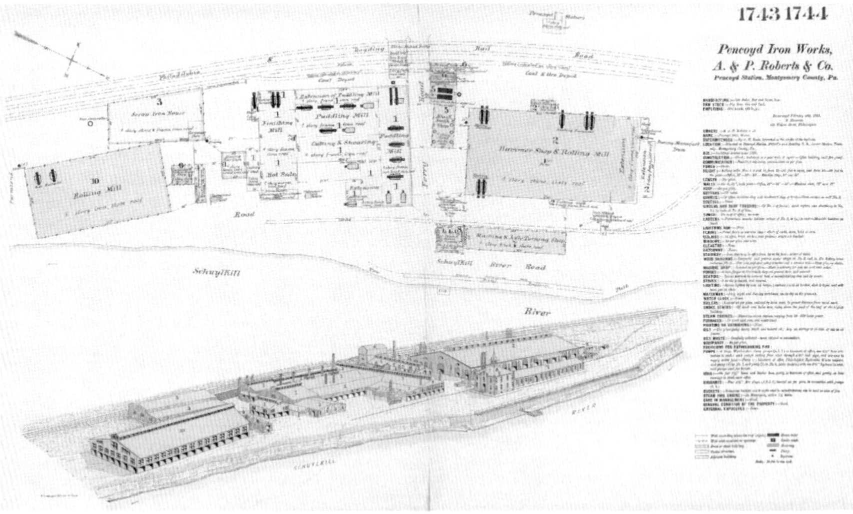

Top: (3.9) 1883 Hexamer Survey of A.&P. Roberts Company. *Free Library of Philadelphia, Map Collection.*

Bottom: (3.10) View of A&P Roberts Company from across Schuylkill River in Manayunk, circa 1885. *From Christie,* Wrought Iron and Steel in Construction, *1892.*

1870. He was active in a number of societies: vice-president of the ASCE from 1902 to 1904, president of the Engineers Club of Philadelphia, a member of the Franklin Institute and the American Philosophical Society and fellow of the American Association for the Advance of Science.[132]

Christie's papers and the subsequent theory derived from them and presented in the Pencoyd construction books set the stage for the expansion of this company in 1880s and 1890s. Christie won the Norman Medal of the American Society of Civil Engineers for this work in 1884.[133] The Norman Medal was instituted and endowed in 1872 by George H. Norman,

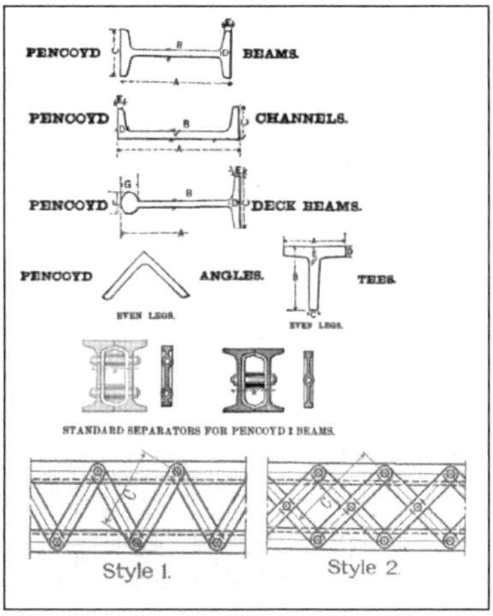

Left: (3.11) Examples of Pencoyd beams, channels and angles. Bottom two drawings show two styles of lacing used in structural elements. *From Christie,* Wrought Iron and Steel in Construction, *second edition, 1884.*

Below: (3.12) Strength of wrought iron of various geometries and sizes. *Drawn by the author using data reported by Christie (1884).*

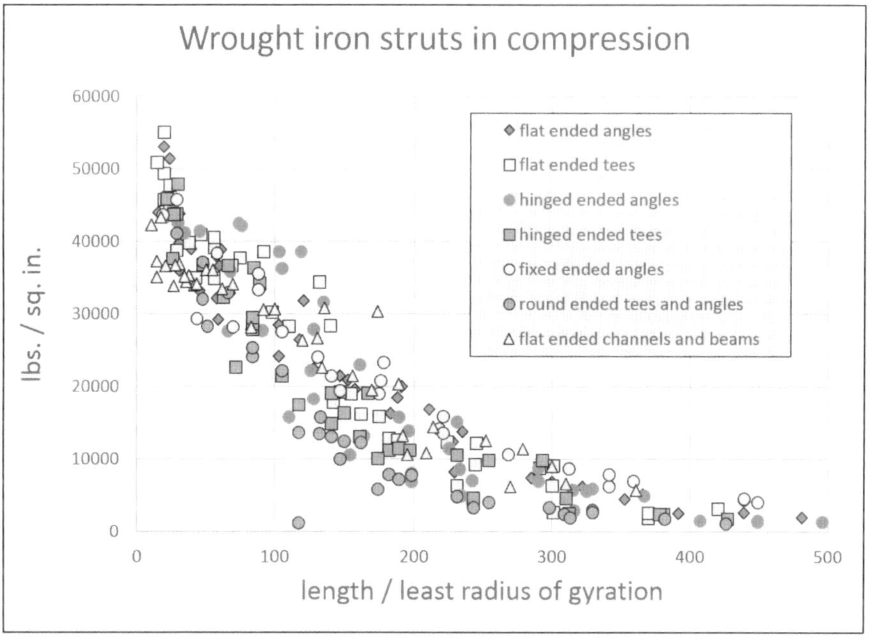

member of the ASCE, and recognizes a paper that makes a contribution to either practical or research aspects of engineering disciplines. The practical value of a contribution and its effect on engineering practice are important considerations.[134] Christie's reputation in structural engineering was evident in an exchange published in *Engineering News* in 1898; a criticism was leveled against handbook publishers such as Pencoyd, Cambria and Carnegie-Steel for their I-beam spans. The only reply was provided by Christie, who explained and dismissed the criticism by citing experience and test results on materials tested at Pencoyd.[135] Pencoyd's ability to test materials led the company to engage in testing of steel structural elements for steamships in 1896—this was shortly after it had furnished beams for two new lake steamers, as described later.[136] In this same time frame, it announced the capability to produce 18″ beams, filling a void between the 15″ and 20″ beams, and provided testing results and specifications to convince new customers.[137]

(3.13) James Christie. *From* Journal of the Franklin Institute *172, no. 1031 (1911): 512–14.*

Pencoyd purchased a Tinius Olsen and Company testing machine of 300,000-pound capacity in 1893.[138] Testing at Pencoyd continued into the twentieth century, as the company obtained a 600-ton press from the Union Bridge Company of Athens, Pennsylvania, sometime around the turn of the century.[139] This press was capable of much higher pressures/loads than the Fairbanks testing machine and no doubt led to increased understanding of steel being produced in this busy period in the company's history.

A final noteworthy and extensive study of the strength of nickel and carbon steels was carried out in part at Pencoyd.[140] Engineer John Waddell (see also chapter 7), organized and published an extensive study of the strength and physical properties of nickel steel (containing about 3.5 percent Ni), because of its demonstrated higher strength than standard steel. Tests were carried out over several years, including yield strength tests in 1903–4 and bending, drifting and punching tests in 1906. Along with testing at Pencoyd, materials were tested at other companies in Pittsburgh and Ohio. The extensive array of tests established an important baseline for understanding the optimal use of nickel steel in the rapidly growing bridge-building industry.

By the mid-1880s, Pencoyd was poised to expand. It had established the ability to produce wrought-iron bars, beams and structural shapes. It had established a name in the markets of axles, bridges and construction. James Christie and Percival Roberts Jr. created a productive, cutting-edge plant whose productivity was about to increase by nearly a factor of ten. In the next chapters, it becomes clear how Pencoyd transitioned to steel making, boosted power capabilities and experienced an explosion of building and bridge construction.

4

Transition from Wrought Iron to Steel

While Pencoyd had perfected wrought iron making, had an extensive puddling mill and was producing structural shapes with the 12″ and 23″ rolling mills, it was apparent that the volume of wrought iron produced could not keep up with the demand developing for steel. Several individuals, including Percival Roberts Jr., James Christie, Benjamin Talbot and Samuel Wellman, helped steer Pencoyd through the technical innovations that shaped this industry.

As early as 1880, Percival Roberts Jr. wrote that wrought iron would ultimately yield to steel, although it was not clear whether Bessemer or open-hearth steel-making processes would be advantageous. Roberts realized that either wrought iron, Bessemer, or open-hearth steel could all be the best for any particular company, depending on each company's abilities and expertise, the product of interest and the market.[141] His 1880 paper on this topic indicated Pencoyd's recognition of this issue far ahead of the time.

Superior Strength of Steel

A fundamental property of steel that makes it desirable over wrought iron in most applications is its increased strength. Pencoyd had a direct and important role in establishing the strength of not only various wrought-iron shapes but also a comparison of shapes made of wrought iron versus steel.

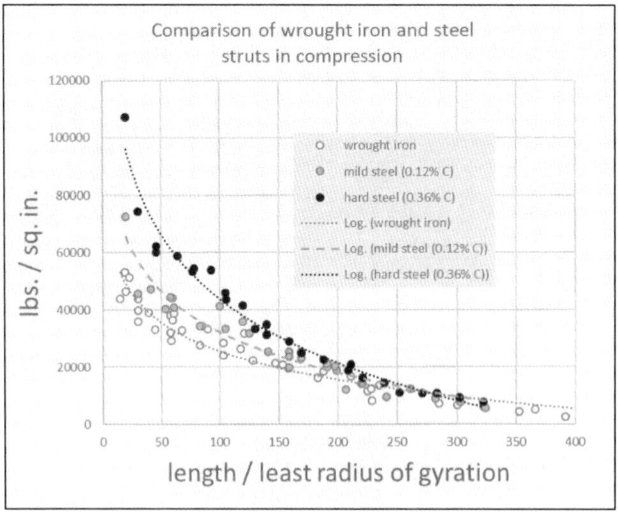

(4.1) The strength of flat-ended wrought iron, mild and hard steel struts. Dashed lines are logarithmic fits for each material. *Diagram by author using data reported by Christie (1884) in* Transactions of the American Society of Civil Engineers *13, no. 286 (1884): (253–300).*

This work, as well as measurements of the composition of the steel, was carried out under the supervision of James Christie. As mentioned earlier, Christie published an extensive study of the relative strengths of various wrought-iron shapes.[142] His follow-up work comparing steel and wrought iron demonstrated the greater strength of steel; he presented this work at meetings of the American Institute for Mechanical Engineering in 1884.[143] Careful measurements on steel struts of various shapes allowed him to demonstrate that hard steel and mild steel were both stronger than wrought iron; comparison was made with struts of equal geometry (Figure 4.1).[144]

Christie's second paper demonstrated that steel had approximately 20 percent greater strength in tension than wrought iron. The pieces tested were made and rolled at Pencoyd and then tested either at the Watertown (Massachusetts) testing machine of the U.S. arsenal or at Pencoyd using a Fairbanks lever testing machine.[145] Hundreds of experiments were involved in these tests, and the resulting work guided construction projects ranging from bridge design to skyscraper architecture.

Open-Hearth Steel

Christie's work guided the recognized need to transition to steel, but the kind of steel was the next question. Pencoyd became well known for its basic open-hearth steel making, but the path to that position involved decades of development. Steel making in Europe and the United States was dominated initially by the Bessemer process, developed by Sir Henry Bessemer in 1856.[146] The Bessemer process involves passing air through the liquid steel, and the oxygen oxidizes the carbon in the steel, making it low in carbon and thus stronger. When steel started replacing wrought iron in construction, one particular event transformed structural steel use to nearly exclusively open-hearth steel.[147] Structural beams made by the Bessemer process (Homestead plant) for the Leiter II Building in Chicago in 1889 arrived on site, and one was completely fractured in two pieces.[148] This event, along with other aspects of open-hearth steel, such as a slower pace of melts allowing quality control by chemical testing, led the market toward open-hearth steel. Many architects and contractors began specifying open-hearth steel for their structural work.[149] Open-hearth quickly took over, and there were no incidents with failure or other problems.

The open-hearth approach was developed by William Siemens, a German metallurgist working in England, and implemented by Pierre and Emile Martin of France.[150] Siemens redirected the exhaust heat of the furnace through a brick checkerwork; when air was mixed in with the exhaust heat, it was preheated and helped to heat the liquid iron. This was the major innovation of the open-hearth process.[151] Acidic and basic refer to the linings used in the crucibles in which the liquid steel was prepared and produced. An acidic lining, usually silica, was used first by the Martins and subsequent designers.[152] Although this worked fine for most purposes, the slag produced was acidic in nature, being rich in SiO_2, Al_2O_3, Na_2O and K_2O. Iron ores available in continental Europe and the United States were largely phosphorus-bearing, and a problem with the acidic open-hearth furnaces is the P would remain in the steel, and P causes steel to be brittle.[153] A Welsh metallurgist Sidney Thomas (and his cousin Percy Gilchrist) developed an alternate furnace lining made of a basic material such as dolomite ($CaMg(CO_3)_2$), magnesite (MgO) or limestone ($CaCO_3$). The major advantage offered by the basic open-hearth technique (called the Thomas-Gilchrist method) is that the phosphorus in the liquid steel reacted with the furnace lining and was removed into the slag as $CaPO_4$.[154] This technique proved to be important to U.S. steel-makers such as Pencoyd.

In 1887, Pencoyd established a regenerative furnace of 15-ton capacity for the manufacture of acid open-hearth steel.[155] On July 12, 1887, the first heat of 8,270 pounds of steel ingot was cast; the second furnace was completed shortly thereafter. In 1889, the first furnace was rebuilt and changed to 20 ton capacity. Steel furnace no. 3 started operations on October 30, 1891, and no. 4 on May 10, 1892, both of 20 ton capacity. Output at this time amounted to 615 tons per week. In the late 1880s and early 1890s, Pencoyd was experimenting with steel making and had initially used open-hearth furnaces with acidic linings. However, due to the high phosphorus content of iron ores available in the United States, they would move to basic linings to produce steel of optimal composition. At this point, some explanation is required for the difference between acidic and basic.

Although Pencoyd had established four steel furnaces in 1891 that had acidic linings, by 1893, it had begun to transform these to basic linings. In 1893, furnace no. 1 was rebuilt to arrange for making basic open-hearth steel, and the first melt of basic open-hearth steel ingots was cast on September 18, 1893. Furnace no. 2 was also changed from acid to basic.[156] No doubt they had discovered the advantage of basic linings, which was to allow removal of P into the slag and easier separation of slag from the steel by tilting. The basic linings were working well enough that some specific characteristics were patented by Talbot in 1899.[157]

Steel was obviously advantageous for strength in structural elements such as beams and girders, but it had started replacing other items as well. In 1893, the first solid steel sleeve nuts were forged to take the place of wrought iron for bridge work. The bolt and rivet department also manufactured miscellaneous forgings for bridge work and machinery.[158]

By 1895, with demand for steel rising, four additional thirty-ton basic open-hearth steel furnaces were completed and put into operation: no. 5 on April 11, 1895; no. 6 on April 26, 1895; no. 7 on September 26, 1895; and no. 8 on November 8, 1895. In 1896, furnace no. 3 was rebuilt with its lining changed from acid to basic and the first melt cast on July 25. Then, in 1897, furnace no. 9 was completed, with its first melt cast on January 22, 1898. Finally, on March 11, 1898, furnace no. 4 was rebuilt with lining changed from acid to basic, and its first melt was cast that day. In 1900, furnace no. 11 was erected and the first melt cast on March 12.[159]

Furnace no. 10 was of a special design and of engineering significance—a tilting furnace of 75 tons with a hydraulic ladle crane for tapping (Figures 4.2 and 4.3).[160] Along with the necessary cupolas for melting pig iron, gas producers and other appliances, installation was complete and first steel cast on September 3, 1899. It was experimentation by Benjamin Talbot using this furnace that led to the breakthrough of making steel by the continuous open-hearth process.[161]

Talbot and Pencoyd chemist and later superintendent of the steel works Anson W. Allen carried out extensive studies of the steel chemistry that led

Top: (4.2) Action from adding carbon to the molten steel in ladle, after which the steel is poured into the ingot molds in the foreground. *Courtesy of Philadelphia Commercial Museum, Pennsylvania State Archives, collection MG219.2, box 15.*

Bottom: (4.3) Hydraulic ladle crane used with the 75-ton tilting furnace. *From* Scientific American, *December 12, 1903, 421–40.*

to the improvement of the open-hearth process.[162] Allen studied at MIT from 1881 to 1885 and was instrumental in establishing the chemical laboratory near the steel plant. That active research was carried out in this lab is evident in various scholarly works at the time. In 1890, Pencoyd's G.L. Norris published a paper in the *Journal of the Franklin Institute* demonstrating a superior technique for measuring phosphorus in steel.[163] Near the turn of the century, Allen and Talbot carried out an extensive study to understand the evolution of steel composition during the continuous open-hearth process.[164] In 1907 and 1909, Allen patented aspects of the open-hearth process that led to more efficient de-phosporization and prolonged furnace lining lifetime.[165] Even after leaving Pencoyd in 1913, Allen went on to be superintendent of a steelworks in Alabama, where he filed additional patents perfecting the open-hearth process.[166]

Pig iron or cupola iron contains high sulfur, phosphorus, carbon and manganese. These elements all give steel certain properties—some desirable and some not.[167] Carbon, for example, is a hardening agent. Steel with 0.1 weight percent C is still ductile and can be worked and flattened without any cracking. If C is near 0.2 weight percent, the steel becomes more brittle and can sometimes crack during working. Steel with 0.25 weight percent C will always crack, while steel with 0.4 weight percent C or higher can be used for tools. So, the control of C content allows steels of a broad range of properties to be made. Manganese also has properties of strength and can add 1000–2000 psi per 0.1 weight percent Mn added, and structural steel typically has 0.4 to 0.8 weight percent Mn. Manganese is thought to be of chemical import and can eliminate or neutralize certain oxides that are otherwise a nuisance. A very small amount of silicon is known to reduce the tendency of molten steel to bubble violently, and as little as 0.1 weight percent Si added can have the desired effect. At Pencoyd, SiC (silicon carbide) was being added to steel as early as 1897; the advantageous compound provided both silicon and carbon to the steel, both of which allowed for more manageable molten product.[168] In addition, Si-bearing steel was eventually used for stiffer steel members in bridges, with a notable example being the Bessemer and Lake Erie railroad bridge near Cheswick, Pennsylvania.[169] Sulfur and phosphorus, even at very low levels, tend to make steel brittle and levels are typically kept as low as possible. If they are not removed to low enough levels, steel will easily crack when forged. Finally, nickel was added to steel to increase its strength while not affecting its ductility—Pencoyd became involved in an extensive set of experiments and measurements comparing nickel and carbon steels that was described in more detail earlier.[170]

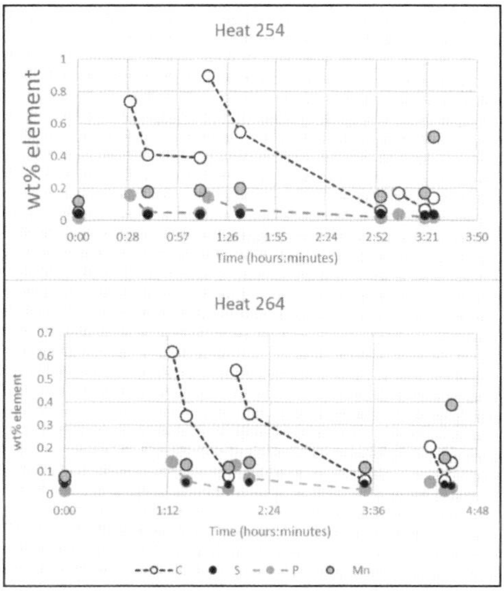

(4.4) Two examples of open-hearth steel heats prepared at Pencoyd by the Talbot process, illustrating the overall evolution of the steel C, S, P and Mn content as batches of pig iron are added, slag removed and overall C, S, P and Mn content drops to the levels desired. Note Mn rises at the end of the process due to addition of Mn-bearing material. *Diagram by author using data from* Engineering, *June 22, 1900, 832–36.*

The Bessemer process, in which the air is passed through the molten steel relatively rapidly (minutes) can be effective, but it is difficult to control the levels of these ingredients, especially if the grade of steel needed to be fine-tuned, as was common for structural steel. The open-hearth process took longer than the Bessemer but allowed opportunity to fine-tune the steel composition while also allowing sampling during the process to verify the chemical composition.[171] Talbot's innovation built on this and made the process longer and continuous, with the advantages of easier removal of slag, tapping of molten steel and utilization of some of the residual liquid for the next batch, thus eliminating down time between heats or batches of steel. His continuous process allowed the steel makers to sample and analyze as needed to determine when the steel was exactly of the composition required. The slow reduction of C, S, P, Si and Mn from the levels of the initial pig iron is demonstrated from some Pencoyd steel heats (Figure 4.4).[172]

Benjamin Talbot was born on September 19, 1864, at Hadley, near Wellington, Shropshire, England, the son of an engine millwright, Benjamin Talbot.[173] After schooling and an apprenticeship in south Wales, he worked for his father at the Castle Ironworks at Wellington. In 1890, the ironworks ceased operations, and Talbot came to the United States, where he became superintendent of the Southern Iron and Steel Company in Chattanooga, Tennessee, and developed a basic lined gas-heated mixer for the preliminary refining of high-silicon pig iron. Then, in 1893, he was hired as superintendent of the steel works at Pencoyd. It was there in

1899 that he applied the tilting furnace concept used by Campbell and Wellman to develop a "continuous" process for making basic open-hearth steel. Talbot's process involved charging and tapping a tilting vessel at frequent intervals. The furnace contained molten steel into which liquid iron was poured and which quickly decarburized on coming into contact with the highly oxidizing slag floating on top of the steel bath. Refining was completed in just four hours (in contrast to about twelve hours in a fixed furnace using cold metal practice) and 20–25 percent of the finished steel was then tapped into ingot molds and allowed to cool before rolling.[174] Talbot's approach was criticized by H.H. Campbell of the Pennsylvania Steel Company in Steelton, Pennsylvania, who had developed open-hearth steel making techniques as well.[175] Campbell pointed out that he had the tilting furnace concept earlier than Talbot and questioned the effective role of the hot gas in the regenerative furnaces used by Talbot.[176] Talbot and others involved in the discourse countered that the Talbot tilting design was more successful and economically viable in practice and had several advantages over Campbell's design. And metallurgists both agreed and disagreed with Talbot's arguments for the role of the gas chemistry in controlling the heat in the furnace, but again the important factor is in the final products—Talbot's approach was being implemented and used successfully across the world.[177]

Talbot returned to England in 1900, and his new process spread quickly due to its ability to handle the large volume of slag associated with P-rich ores, and its reliable and constant supply of steel to rolling mills increased output while lowering labor, fuel and repair costs.[178] Basic open-hearth steel accounted for 18.2 percent of output in the United Kingdom in 1906 and 36.7 percent by 1914. Overall, his process lowered operating expenses by 20 to 25 percent and was quickly adopted by firms with access to low-grade ores, such as Frodingham Iron and Steel Company, Cargo Fleet Iron, Palmer's Shipbuilding and Iron and South Durham Steel and Iron. Talbot served as director at Cargo Fleet and then South Durham Steel in 1906, becoming managing director in 1919 and chairman from 1940 to 1947. After the First World War, South Durham adopted a hydrocarbon lining process that Talbot invented for pipe making. Talbot was a solid manager with sound organizational skills, coupled with effective sales and marketing plans. Talbot had advisory roles in the British steel industry during, between and after World Wars I and II, and he was a critic of nationalization of the industry just before he passed away in Yorkshire in 1947. He received many medals and awards for his innovations and contributions to the industry, including the Bessemer gold medal of the Iron and Steel Institute, the Elliott Cresson gold medal and the John Scott medal of the Franklin Institute. He also served as president of the Iron and Steel Institute and the National Federation of Iron and Steel Manufacturers.[179]

By 1900, the Pencoyd steel plant consisted of ten open-hearth furnaces each of around 30-ton capacity and one tilting furnace of 75-ton capacity, giving a total output of 4,600 tons of ingots per week (compared to approximately 600 tons per week in 1892).[180] This configuration would remain for several decades under the auspices of U.S. Steel, which purchased the American Bridge Company in 1902.[181]

CHARGING MACHINES, CARS AND GAS PRODUCERS

Several other pieces of the puzzle fell into place for Pencoyd due to two of Samuel Wellman's innovations: the charging machine and car and the regenerative gas producer. Both of these would be essential in Pencoyd's path to steel productivity—unmatched in the eastern region. Because of the central role Wellman's inventions played in Pencoyd steel making, Wellman's life and contributions are here described in some detail and illustrate the many connections between industries in Philadelphia, Pittsburgh and Cleveland.

Wellman was an inventor, engineer and manufacturer and one of the most important figures in the development of modern iron and steel manufacturing. During his career, he was associated with the development of more economical, efficient and safe equipment used in the making of steel, such as the electric charging machine and the electric magnet for handling of materials.[182] Wellman was born in 1847, in Wareham, Massachusetts, but later moved to Nashua, New Hampshire, where his father, Samuel K. Wellman, was superintendent of the Nashua Iron Company, which specialized in rolling locomotive tires from hammered steel blooms imported from England. Wellman earned a bachelor's degree from Norwich University, Vermont, and from 1864 to 1865, he served in the Civil War as corporal in the First New Hampshire Heavy Artillery (Company F).[183]

After gaining some experience at the Nashua ironworks, he became familiar with the specific operations that changed the blooms to finished tires. Wellman's knack for mechanical work was evident. In the early 1860s, he was given the drawings for a new regenerative gas furnace that was to be used for heating blooms and told to build it according to the plans. The

(4.5) Wellman high design open-hearth charging machine in use at the steel mill at Pencoyd. *Courtesy of Philadelphia Commercial Museum, Pennsylvania State Archives, collection MG219.2, box 15.*

English designer of the furnace, C.W. Siemens, sent an engineer to build the furnace and discovered that Wellman had already built and installed it successfully.[184] The engineer then took Wellman to Pittsburgh's Anderson Cook & Company to assist with a new completed crucible steel melting furnace. Siemens kept him employed building two crucible furnaces for Singer, Nimick & Company (Pittsburgh) and a furnace for the Chrome Steel Works in Brooklyn. Wellman left Siemens in 1870 to build an open-hearth furnace at the Bay State Iron Works in South Boston, Massachusetts—the first installation of its kind in the United States to be commercially successful—and took this experience back to Nashua, where he built an open-hearth furnace and a plate and bar mill.[185]

Wellman's career flourished at Otis Steel Company in Cleveland, where he was engineer and superintendent from 1873 to 1889.[186] Here he developed the open-hearth charging machine and cars (Figure 4.5) and an electromagnet for handling pig iron and scrap steel. He later installed these systems in 1890 in the plants of the Wellman Steel Company in Thurlow, Pennsylvania, and the Standard Steel Works of Burnham, Pennsylvania (both low type), and four high-type machines for the Homestead works of the Carnegie

POURING SIDE OF 20-TON OPEN-HEARTH FURNACES, WITH FORE HEARTH IN POSITION.

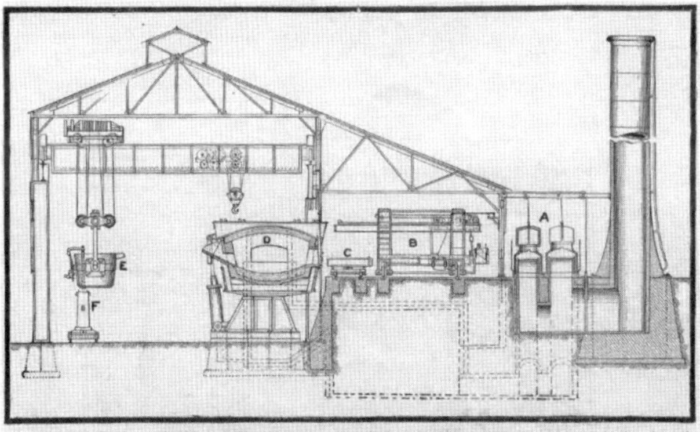

To extreme right is the chimney; then follow: A, air and gas reversing valves; B, charging machine; C, buggies from which charger picks up boxes of "mixture," thrusts them into furnace and empties them; D, Wellman rolling furnace, showing charging door, pouring spout, and hydraulic cylinder for pulling over; E, ladle crane, with its crane in position over a mold for pouring an ingot.

SECTIONAL VIEW, SHOWING RELATIVE POSITIONS OF PARTS OF A WELLMAN OPEN-HEARTH PLANT.

Top: (4.6) Pouring side of 20-ton open-hearth furnace—of which Pencoyd had 10 at peak operations in late 1890s. *From* Scientific American, *December 12, 1903, 421–40.*

Bottom: (4.7) Wellman open-hearth system. *From* Scientific American, *December 12, 1903, 421–40.*

Steel Company in 1895. In 1896, Wellman organized the Wellman, Seaver Engineering Company.[187] Pencoyd installed high-type charging machines in its steel plant, reducing labor needs and saving substantial costs (Figure 4.5).

The high-type charging machine and charging cars were just small parts of the overall Wellman-Seaver open-hearth systems that were put into operation at Pencoyd (Figures 4.6 and 4.7). These systems included the cupola for a source of liquid iron, the charging machines, the twenty-to-thirty-ton furnace with charging door and hydraulic system for tilting to pour off slag or steel and the overhead crane system for pouring ingots (Figure 4.7).[188]

Another innovation was the gas producer. Gas producers were an integral part of open-hearth systems because they provided both the reducing atmosphere and a heating medium within the furnaces.[189] Direct heat in

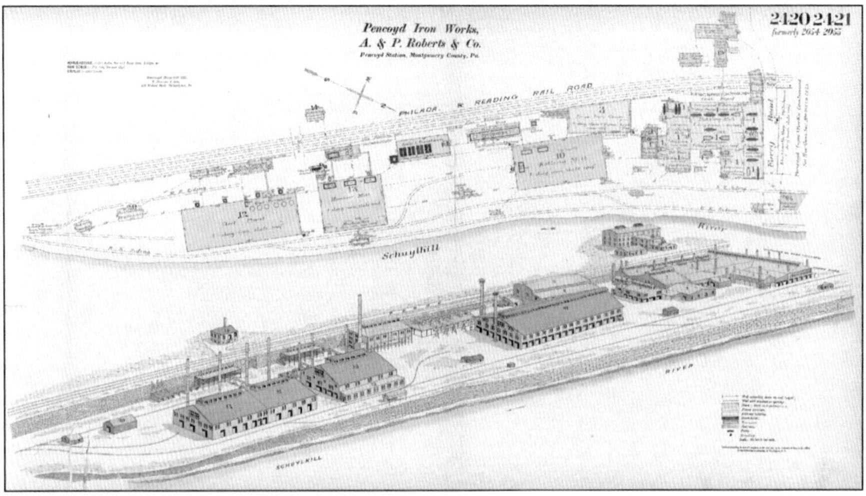

This page, top left: (4.8) Hughes Gas Producers. *From the* Industrial World, *March 23, 1907, 341–44.*

This page, top right: (4.9) View of Pencoyd steel plant on the uphill side of the plant, showing the coal bins immediately adjacent to the railroad tracks between the tracks and the mill. *Courtesy of Lower Merion Historical Society.*

This page, bottom: (4.10) An 1891 Hexamer Survey of Pencoyd Iron Works, A.&P. Roberts Company, showing downriver half of the plant. *Free Library of Philadelphia, Map Collection.*

Opposite, top: (4.11) Cross-section through the Pencoyd gas producers showing the funnel where coal is added (A), the motor and mechanism for driving the mechanical radial stirrer (G and H) and the piping and valving for the gas near the bottom (E and F). *From* Le Genie Civil *41, no. 22 (September 1902): 345.*

Opposite, bottom: (4.12) Interior view of the length of the steel mill, showing ladles tilted on side for maintenance. *Courtesy of Philadelphia Commercial Museum, Pennsylvania State Archives, collection MG219.2, box 15.*

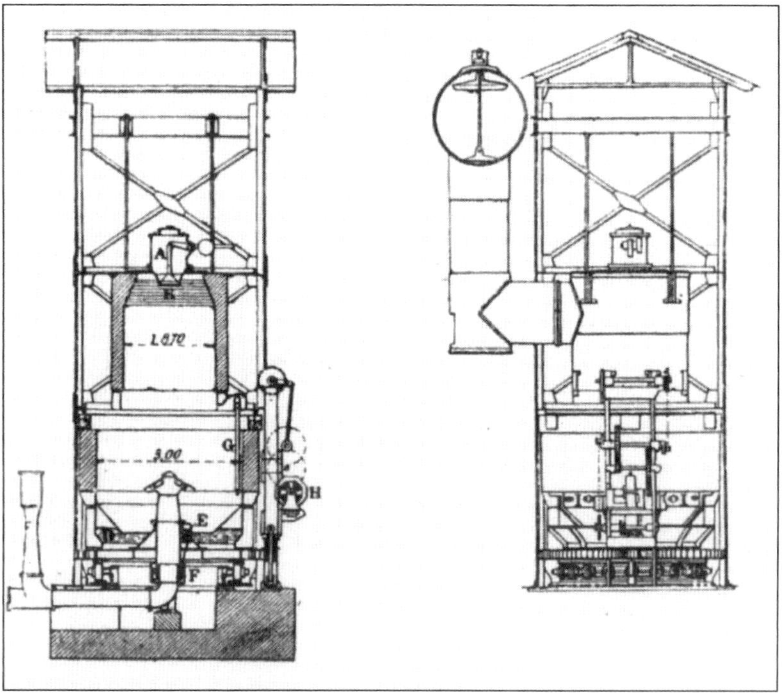
A
3.00
G
H
E
F

the furnace was not very efficient, as much heat was lost in such efforts. However, gas is a more uniform and continuous medium whereby heat can be evenly applied in the furnace. A typical gas analysis from a gas producer was 3–6% CO_2, 25–35% CO, 6–15% H_2 and the balance N_2, with the fuel comprising variable proportions or mixtures of coal, coke and lignite from nut- to pea- to dust-sized particles.[190] The gas producer was usually located at the side of the furnace and coupled closely to air ducts such that the air and gas could be mixed and/or the two could be valved and flow direction reversed if necessary depending on the step in the process and nature of the work. Gas producers had a variety of designs, differing mainly in geometry of fuel containers and introduction of air. U.S. plants used the Forter-Trump, Hughes, Morgan or Talbot producers. The Hughes was used at Pencoyd and could gasify 25 pounds of coal per hour per square foot of producer area.[191] Six men were required to operate a battery of eight producers, where coal was fed into the hoppers from overhead bins. The first Hughes mechanically poked continuous gas producer was built in 1897 for Pencoyd, and afterward the Wellman-Seaver-Morgan Co. obtained the rights to manufacture them.[192] The mechanical poker allowed the fuel (coal) to be poked or agitated in a radial fashion to keep it fed evenly from above, while also keeping the fuel bed of homogeneous distribution and porosity (Figure 4.8).[193] By 1920, Pencoyd had 15 such gas producers, and large banks of gas producers are evident parallel to and outside the steel and rolling mills and coal bins along the rail lines on the Hexamer Survey from 1891 (Figures 4.9 and 4.10).[194] The Pencoyd gas producer design was apparently unique enough that it was featured in a Spanish engineering journal in 1902, replete with sketches showing the geometry (Figure 4.11).[195]

Percival Roberts recognized the potential for the transformation from wrought iron to steel in 1880, and steel making started to take over at Pencoyd. However, the enormous growth of the company and expanding output are apparent in the statistics and summary provided by Percival Roberts.[196] Pencoyd had perfected the art of puddling and wrought-iron production and could produce 330 tons of puddle bars a week using one single and 15 double puddle furnaces, two sets of 20.5″ 3-high rolls and one rotary squeezer added between 1859 and 1895.[197] However, this operation could simply not keep up with the demand for structural steel. The expansion of the steel plant to 11 furnaces (Figure 4.12) led to the eventual abandonment of wrought-iron manufacturing and the removal of the puddling furnaces and supporting equipment in 1895.[198]

(4.13) Interior of the blooming mill, showing ingot (lifted by crane) being heated in the ingot furnace before rolling. *Courtesy of Philadelphia Commercial Museum, Pennsylvania State Archives, collection MG219.2, box 15.*

BILLETS AND BLOOMS AND SHEARS

At the end of the steel mill, immediately upriver, were the hammer mill, where ingots could be worked into useable shapes such as billets and blooms, and then the blooming and beam rolling mills, where the billets and blooms could be rolled into shapes that could then be used for production—rods or beams, respectively. In 1891, a 36″ 2-high mill with double reversing engines, power-driven roller tables, manipulators and heating furnaces was completed to prepare steel for the finishing mills (Figure 4.13). This 36″ blooming mill (but used for both blooms and billets) could produce 3,800 tons per week by 1891.[199] The next building was the 20″ finishing mill, which had a capacity of 500 tons per week between 1884–94 and was then replaced by the 23–28″ mill (28″ 2 high roughing and 23″ 3 high finishing) achieving an output of 2,000–2,600 tons per week.[200] The mill was supplied with electrically driven roller tables, a 40-ton overhead crane for changing rolls and housings, three regenerative gas heating furnaces with necessary gas producers and two electric charging machines. Angles could be rolled

Left: (4.14) Hydraulic billet shears (probably between 36″ and 23–28″ mills). *From the* Engineering News Record, *September 29, 1898, 194–97.*

Below: (4.15) Angle-straightening roll. *From the* Engineering News Record, *September 29, 1898, 194–97.*

up to 190′ long and beams to 100′ long; the blooms used for that purpose were from 1,150 to 6,000 pounds.[201] Near the end of the finishing mills, there were some specialized pieces of equipment for handling and trimming rods and beams, such as the hydraulic billet shears (Figure 4.14) and angle straightening mill (Figure 4.15).[202]

The new 36″ blooming mill and the 23–28″ mills, combined with the other three mills, brought the total number of rolling mills to five. The five roughing and finishing mills were spread across four different buildings, partly by necessity of the shape of the property along the river but also due to the specialized nature of each mill for handling pieces of various sizes, shapes and lengths. Even by 1891, the length of the operation from steel mill at the southeast end to eye-bar forging at the northwest end of the plant stretched for 3,000′—an impressive industrial operation.[203] This diverse array of milling capability also contributed to Pencoyd's great success. Pencoyd's expertise in rolling structural shapes of great size was recognized by Thomas Matthias of the Lackawanna Steel Company in Buffalo, who noted, "At Pencoyd, a 24-inch beam was rolled on a 23-inch mill. In this case the shaped bloom was reheated, thus making it possible to roll a large section of this weight and size on rolls of so small a diameter."[204] The importance of diversity was recognized by rolling mill superintendent Henry James, who wrote, "There are different conditions to be met at each plant and they require individual thought to produce the best results.…The more perfect the equipment, the better the service, and so it would seem that a knowledge of the mills, an understanding of the furnaces and heating of bars, ability to run the lathe and turn the rolls, a mechanical drawing-room experience, an eye open to the percentages of waste, which can be decreased by skillful roll designing, and, above all, a personal supervision of the rolls, make the all-around designer of today."[205]

The production of bridge parts became the main driver for production, and the combination of design, engineering and specialized equipment focused on bridge-making is described in chapters 6 through 8, but first we look closely at how the power and water needs and requirements changed as the mills evolved.

5

Electricity, Steam and Power for Iron and Steel Production and Construction

From its beginnings in 1852 through to the turn of the twentieth century, Pencoyd experienced a revolution in technological advances that included the specialized machinery for steel making, rolling, cutting, bridge part making and hydraulic forging, all of which required increasingly more power. This period spanned the use of steam, the beginning of electric light and the development of dynamos and later electric engines; it even bridged the DC versus AC electrical competition. Pencoyd was leading innovation in this industry during the latter decades of the nineteenth century, and a look at the detailed expansion of power sources and design is worthwhile and enlightening. Some effort is also spent in this chapter highlighting parallel industrial inventions and inventors, without which the many technical capabilities of Pencoyd would not have been achieved.

The modest start of this company is illustrated by its power and water needs. In 1852, one 50-horsepower engine drove the tilting hammer and a blower for furnaces and provided all the power required.[206] Primitive hand torches supplied light at night—this would be the case until 1882. A small creek emptying into the river close to the mill supplied about 50 gallons of water per minute, which was more than enough for steam and other purposes of the works.[207]

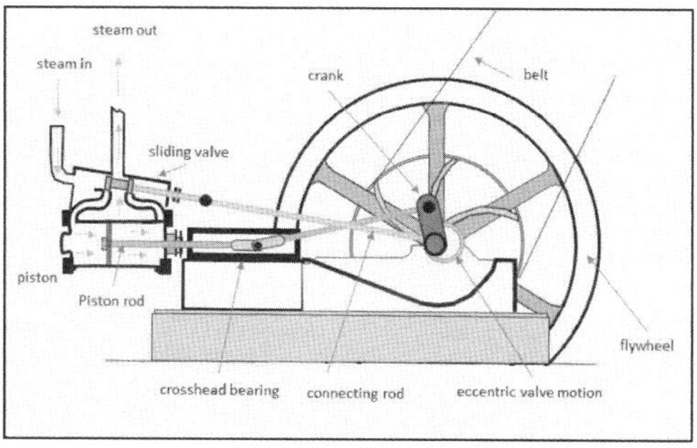

Left: (5.1) Photograph of the Corliss engine displayed at the 1876 Centennial Exhibition in Fairmount Park. *Free Library of Philadelphia, Centennial Exposition, Print and Picture Collection.*

Right: (5.2) Components of a steam engine. *After Things to Make, 1913, redrawn by author.*

STEAM ENGINES

By 1872, four steam engines were distributed within the puddling mill and scrap house.[208] Power in the mills was provided entirely by steam, with either heat from the regenerative furnaces (boilers located above furnaces) or bituminous coal as the fuel for the boilers. The only light was provided by enclosed coal and lard oil lanterns.[209]

An 1881 plan of the mill indicated 13 engines in use in various locations in the mill.[210] Steam engines were most commonly used in industrial plants in the nineteenth century, and Pencoyd had an abundance even at this early phase of its history.[211] The Corliss steam engine had been displayed at the Centennial Exhibition in 1876 at Fairmount Park—a local attraction for the young Pencoyd Iron Works company. The Corliss engine stood nearly 20′ high and provided power to all the buildings of the exhibition (Figure 5.1).[212] It was even the starring attraction of the opening ceremonies. Although this display of technology must have been inspirational to any Pencoyd employee attending the exhibition, Pencoyd already had a smaller Corliss engine that drove the 18″ 3-high rolling mill.[213]

Because the steam engine was so fundamentally important to the power needs at Pencoyd and required for the shafting and later electrical generation, some description of its advent seems necessary. George Corliss was born in Connecticut, where he established a general store in Greenwich before delving into more mechanical ventures.[214] In 1842, Corliss obtained a patent on a machine for sewing boots, shoes and heavy leather. Corliss moved to Providence, Rhode Island, in 1844 hoping to find funding that would allow him to perfect his sewing machine and found work in the shop of Fairbanks, Bancroft & Company as a draftsman. It was there that he become more interested in making improvements to the stationary steam engine, which was then only a supplement to water power. It is also interesting to note that this company was where Philadelphia engineer William Sellers worked early in his career (see chapter 9). In 1848, Corliss, Nightingale & Company, a partnership between Corliss, John Barstow and E.J. Nightingale, built the first engine utilizing Corliss's improvements. This engine design was fitted with rotary valves and variable valve timing and patented in 1849, becoming known as the Corliss steam engine (Figure 5.2).[215] This new company built a factory in Providence that would expand greatly; by 1888, the plant would cover about five acres and employ over 1,000 people.[216]

Corliss engines were commonly used as stationary engines to provide power to line shafting in mills and to drive dynamos to generate electricity. Many were large, standing meters tall and capable of hundreds of horsepower. Because of their high efficiency and low maintenance requirements, many remained in service even after newer technology was developed.[217]

ELECTRICITY AND DYNAMOS

In 1882, the first dynamo was installed overhead in the lower end of Pencoyd's machine shop and provided current for ten arc lamps.[218] This dynamo and accompanying lights were built and provided by the Thomson Houston Electric Company, which was founded by Elihu Thomson and E.J. Houston in 1879 in Philadelphia.[219] Thomson had invented the three-coil arc dynamo (Figure 5.3), which, along with its automatic regulator, became the basis of the lighting system the company marketed in 1882 and onward.[220] The carbon arc lamp (Figure 5.4) was one of the first lighting systems available with which ten or more lamps could be powered with one of the dynamos.[221] The company also marketed a 250-horsepower generator in 1891.[222] It eventually moved to Lynn, Massachusetts, and then in 1892 merged with the Edison Electric Company to become General Electric.[223]

Dynamos were in widespread use at the end of the nineteenth century but are rarely discussed today. Dynamos generate direct current (DC) electric power using two magnets, one of which rotates around the other. The rotating magnet, the rotor, moves around an axis within the magnetic field of the static magnet, or stator. As the rotor crosses the magnetic field lines of the stator, electricity is generated (Figures 5.5).[224] Because the rotor causes the current to reverse every half turn, early inventors devised the commutator, which keeps the current in the same direction and produces direct current. Brushes were added to the commutator to help conduct electricity.[225] Dynamos were first implemented in France in 1831, and by 1880, they were a full-fledged industry supplying electricity all around the world. The reason we don't hear about dynamos much anymore is because DC electricity was surpassed by alternating current (AC) electricity due to its ease of long-distance transport.[226] DC-producing dynamos could only be used locally in settings with high electricity requirements such as a building or an industrial plant. They were perfect for Pencoyd, and the ironworks eventually established several dynamos, as did many other large electric light companies and industrial companies in the United States.[227] For example, dynamos were featured at the World Columbian Exposition in Chicago in 1893.[228] But by the turn of the century, electricity would be almost exclusively supplied by AC generators taking over the market.[229]

Thomas Edison and General Electric were champions of direct current. When electric power came into widespread use, and there was demand in geographically widespread areas, DC was at a disadvantage because the system Edison had devised was based on relatively low voltage, which could not be efficiently transported across long distances from a power source. (Low voltage lines lose too much heat and are thus inefficient.)[230] Instead, what was needed to transport electricity across long distances was higher voltage, and Westinghouse and Tesla teamed up to develop alternating current and transformers to be able to transport electricity across long distances by stepping the voltage up before transport and then back down at the destination.[231] Ultimately, AC would win out in the application of electricity beyond industrial use and into residential applications. The diverse Westinghouse company also provided "junior engines" (20–25 horsepower)

(5.3) An early Thomson-Houston dynamo. *https://ethw.org/w/images/2/22/Thomson-Houston_arc-lighting_dynamo_0228.jpg.*

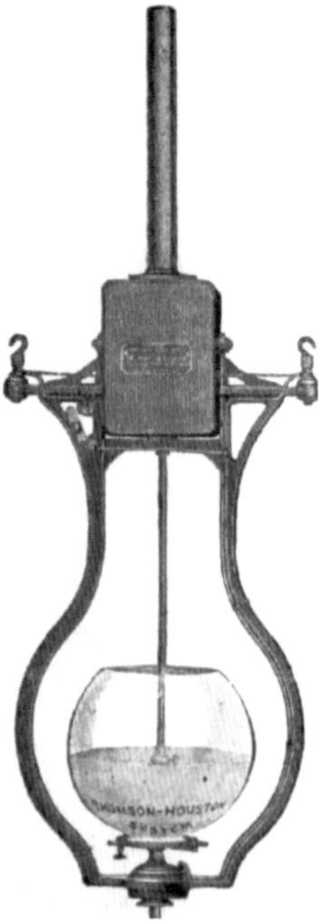

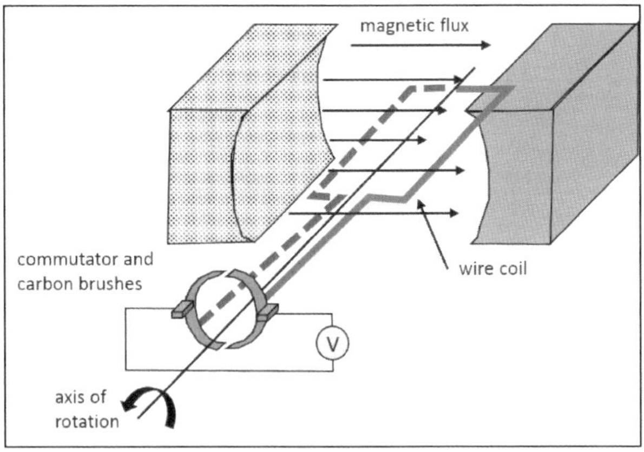

Left: (5.4) Carbon arc lamp, Thomson-Houston system. *From the Thomsen-Houston Electric Light Company catalogue, 1885.*

Above: (5.5) Schematic diagram of how dynamo generates electricity. *http://edisontechcenter.org/generators.html*, redrawn by author.

that could be used with steam to generate electricity and many of these were used at Pencoyd, as well (Figure 5.6).[232]

The Hexamer survey of 1883 (Figure 3.9) shows a large boiler house along Ferry Road and indicates lighting was enclosed coal, lard oil and electric, with gas proposed in offices.[233] The boiler house was the first of many to be built at Pencoyd.

In 1884, the 20″ and 23–28″ mills were driven by two 30″ x 36″ double reversing engines; the mill was supplied with electrically driven roller tables and also had two electric charging machines.[234] Clearly, electricity was beginning to change the way the mill operated. In January 1884 an electric light station was established at one end of the blacksmith shop, a second dynamo placed therein, and 25 additional arc lamps distributed throughout the ironworks.[235] Between 1884 and 1886, a third dynamo was installed to provide 300 incandescent lights for the offices, machine and bridge shops.[236] In the 1887 Hexamer Survey, the dedicated dynamo room is indicated in the same building as the blacksmith shop, near Righters Ferry Road (Figures 5.7 and 5.8).[237]

By 1889, the electric light station had been moved to a new building and an additional 85 arc light dynamo installed.[238] The location of this light station is indicated on the 1891 Hexamer Survey (Figure 4.10) and was on

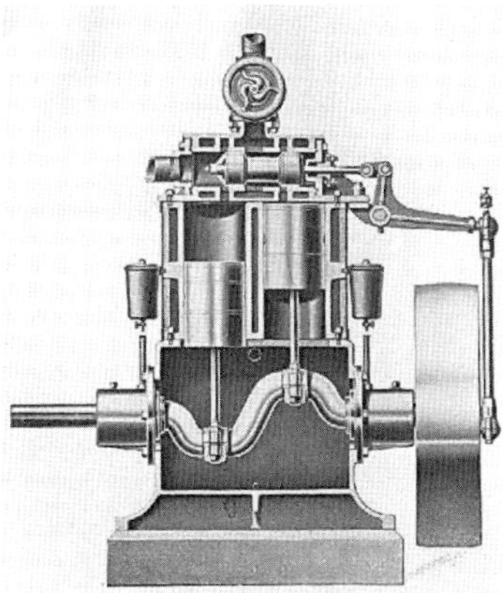

Left: (5.6) Westinghouse junior steam engines; Pencoyd had purchased more than a dozen such engines. *From* Locomotive Engineering *5, no. 9 (September 1892): 318.*

Middle: (5.7) 1887 Hexamer Survey of the A.&P. Roberts Company. *Free Library of Philadelphia, Map Collection.*

Bottom: (5.8) Panorama view of Pencoyd Iron Works in 1887. *From* Wrought Iron and Steel in Construction, *1888.*

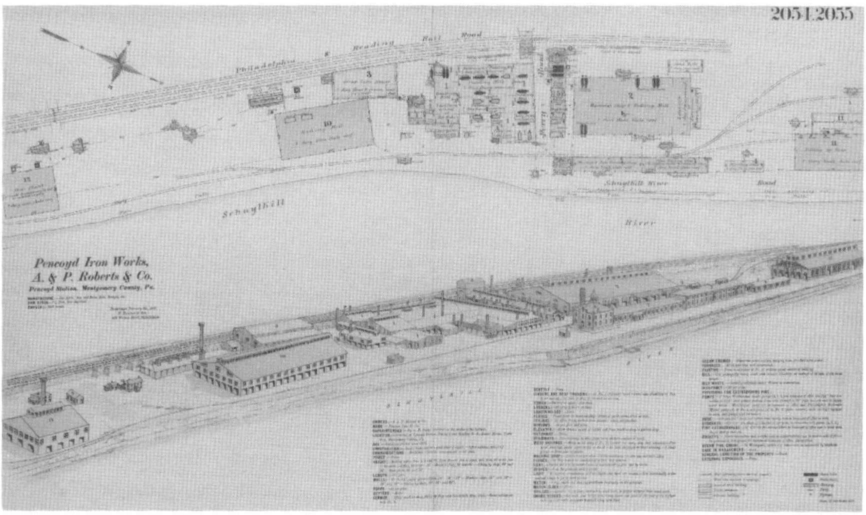

the Lower Merion side of the railroad tracks just uphill from the mill along Righters Ferry Road.[239] Crocker-Wheeler Company built this new dynamo and had also outfitted lighting for the famous U.S. Government Printing Office, Grand Central Station and Columbia University.[240] Pencoyd was clearly on the cutting edge for lighting capabilities and was one of the first industrial companies to utilize this new technology.

The lighting system undoubtedly provided additional productivity for Pencoyd and was installed at a key time for the company when the volume of projects was increasing annually. How these dynamo systems developed and how they attained an integral role in Pencoyd's evolution can be appreciated with some knowledge of the inventors and the post–Civil War era in which they flourished. Francis Bacon Crocker and Schuyler S. Wheeler were influential engineers who had a significant role in developing electricity in the United States. Crocker was born in New York in 1861 and had a childhood interest in electricity; he even built telegraph and telephone lines as a boy.[241] He graduated from the School of Mines of Columbia University in 1882 and received a doctorate in electrical engineering in 1895. In 1899, he founded Columbia's department of electrical engineering and remained head of it for 20 years. In the 1880s, Crocker and associate Charles G. Curtis invented and developed various electrical applications and ultimately the "C.&C." electric motor. When Curtis became ill in 1888, Crocker formed a new company with Wheeler that would ultimately become the Crocker-Wheeler Company, an important electrical motor company. Crocker was a director of the company until the time of his death in 1921.

Schuyler Skaats Wheeler was also born in New York, on May 17, 1860, and attended Friends' Seminary, Keble Hall, Columbia Grammar School and Columbia College.[242] Wheeler left college in 1882 (when his father died) and was employed as assistant electrician of the Jablochkoff Electric Light Company until it dissolved in 1883, when he joined Thomas Edison's staff at the United States Electric Lighting Company. He became electrician in charge of the Edison's Pearl Street station in New York. After various other works supporting Edison's company, in 1886, he joined the C&C Electric Motor Company and established, organized and became electrician and manager of its factory. The Crocker-Wheeler Company of Ampere, New Jersey, employed 500 at that time. Wheeler invented and patented many electrical devices, such as the direct application of electricity to driving tools, development of the electric motor and its application to driving machinery and the portable electric fan. He jointly authored (with F.B. Crocker) *The Practical Management of Dynamos and Motors* in 1894.[243]

As electricity was applied to individual machines rather than groups of machines and moved away from the mills being belted to one main power source, electricity needs became greater and greater. Electricity for power was first used at Pencoyd, for example, when a 20 horsepower, 110 volt generator and a 10-horsepower motor were installed in the bridge shop to drive the eight head multiple drill gantry.[244] The extensive application of electric motors in the works led to many examples of electricity being used in hot, dirty and/or dusty areas with surprisingly little problems.

The general plan of the electrical system in 1898 consisted of a 220 volt distribution used for power purposes, for incandescent and enclosed arc lights and a constant current system used in the series arc lighting.[245] The electrical generating plant contained one 200-kilowatt, 220-volt generator direct connected to a 12 x 22 x 42″ tandem compound condensing Greene engine, and two 100-kilowatt, 220-volt generators, each direct connected to a cross compound condensing vertical engine 10 x 19 x 16″. The series arc lighting lamps are of 2,000 candlepower (nominal) and supplied with current by three 50-light and one 35-light General Electric dynamos belted from Westinghouse engines. The 1898 power plant was subsequently enlarged with addition of a 500-kilowatt generator and direct-connected engine.[246]

The switchboard routed electricity to five distinct circuits: the bridge shop, beam mill, beam mill yard, steel mill and the 20″ mill, each with separate automatic circuit breakers. On these circuits were over 200 motors summing to 2500 horsepower, including 74 (860 horsepower) in the bridge shop (32 of which were on cranes), 66 (930 horsepower) in the beam mill, 27 (356 horsepower) in the steel mill and 16 (100 horsepower) in the 20″ mill.[247] In addition, there were about 10 other motors in miscellaneous areas such as the boiler house, repair shop, laboratory and blooming mill, two 50 horsepower motors (part of the Ward Leonard system used to control the tables for the 23″ mill) and a 50-horsepower motor for the gantry in the bridge shop carrying the work through the 100-ton riveter. At the stockyards at the extreme upper portion of the works there is a 15-kilowatt generator, with other motors comprising an additional 35 horsepower. There were numerous other small motors throughout the works in addition to what is described here.[248] The infiltration of electricity throughout the mills operations is astonishing but, at the same time, in accord with the incredible output of the plant in both steel making and finished bridge products (see chapter 6). The intensive lighting capabilities are illustrated with a World War I–era photo of Pencoyd taken at night from across the Schuylkill River in Roxborough (Figure 5.9).

The incandescent (1,000 lamps in two series) and enclosed arc (40 arc lamps) systems of lighting were also run using the power circuit. The incandescent arc system was used in the central area of the works, and the enclosed arc lamps used in the outlying areas driven locally by dynamos connected to the main power system.[249]

(5.9) Photo of steel mill portion of Pencoyd taken at night, from across the Schuylkill River, circa 1917. *World War I special collection photos, National Archives, https://catalog.archives.gov/id/31489273.*

The last comprehensive snapshot we have of Pencoyd's electrical system is from 1902. Trends continued, with power increasingly connected directly to more machines and supplied from the central plant. The original 30-kilowatt unit was by 1902 expanded to five 220-volt generators (1100-kilowatt total capacity). These generators provided power to 67 cranes equipped with 159 motors, 6 charging machines with 20 motors, 300 arc lights and 2000 16 candlepower incandescent lamps, in addition to 387 motors distributed throughout the works, for a combined 4,645-horsepower of motors (from 1/6 to 125 horsepower).[250]

Steam and Boilers

Although electricity had become a huge portion of the motive power at the ironworks, steam was also critical to many aspects of the operations, outgrowing the initial approach of steam production utilizing excess heat over the puddling furnaces.[251] By 1898, there were three principal steam boiler plants at the works (Figure 5.10): boiler house no. 2 consisted of a dozen 156-horsepower Babcock & Wilcox boilers, boiler house no. 3 contained four 250-horsepower, four 140-horsepower and four 156-horsepower Babcock & Wilcox boilers.[252] These two boiler houses were connected by a 16″ steam pipe and supplied steam for all parts of the works (with the exception of the bridge department) and were located downriver from Righter's Ferry Road. Boiler house no. 4 had one 250-horsepower and two 156-horsepower Babcock & Wilcox boilers and supplied all steam used for power purposes at the bridge department, the prominent uses being that demanded by air compressors and hydraulic pumps.[253] The curious reader might wonder about boiler house no. 1: there was a boiler house near the eye-bar forge (and evident on the 1891 Hexamer Survey drawings) that was probably no. 1, but it was likely replaced by no. 4 in the late 1890s.

All boilers throughout the works used bituminous coal, with each boiler house area designed for ease of access to coal bins and (with conveyor belts) resupplying coal, as well as removal of ashes, with both supply and removal involving railcars.[254] Babcock-Wilcox boilers were provided in 1889 (124 horsepower) and expanded by 1898 to 3,840 horsepower in one of Pencoyd's boiler houses (Figure 5.11).[255] Pencoyd's boiler house was featured in a 1901 German technical book that shows a detailed cross-section of the boiler house and its design (Figure 5.12).[256] The boiler house also featured the support of eight Westinghouse, Church & Kerr Company automatic stoking machines (bring the total number of such machines at Pencoyd to 38) to provide for the new approximately 4,000-horsepower boiler.[257]

Like developments in electrical generation, steam boilers achieved widespread success and application in the post–Civil War period. In 1867, Stephen Wilcox and his partner George Herman Babcock patented the Babcock & Wilcox Non-Explosive Boiler, which used water-filled tubes and boiling to generate steam more safely than either under-fire or fire-tube boilers. The boiler safely generated high-pressure steam and was more efficient (as an energy to steam converter) than existing designs.[258] The Babcock & Wilcox boiler of 1867 was the first to combine the sectional construction with a free circulation of the water in one continuous round. Wilcox, originally from Rhode Island, and Babcock, who moved from New York

(5.10) Inside a boiler house at Pencoyd. *From the Babcock and Wilcox Company catalogue, 1898, 94 and 132.*

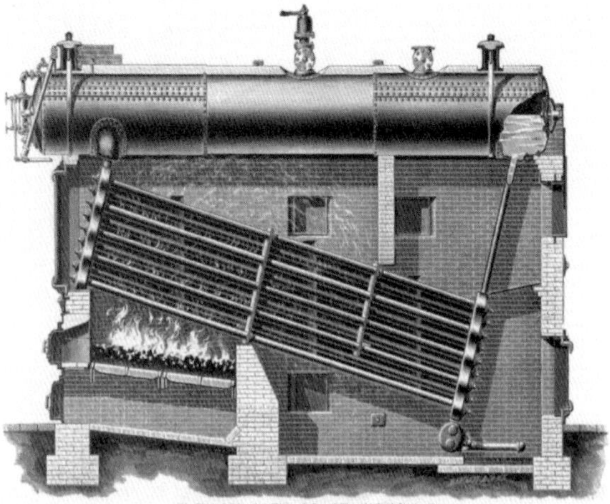

Top: (5.11) Schematic cross section of boiler design. *From the Babcock and Wilcox Company catalogue, 1898, 94 and 132.*

Bottom: (5.12) Perspective and cutaway view of Pencoyd's boiler house showing the boilers at ground level, coal bins above and a conveyor belt system to deliver coal to the system. *From M.W. Buhle,* Technische Hülfsmittel zur Beförderung und Lagerung von Sammelkörpern (Massengütern), *1901, 69.*

to Rhode Island, teamed up after the Civil War to perfect the boiler design, for which they anticipated a strong market with high demand for steam power. It was, for example, a Babcock and Wilcox boiler that Thomas Edison used to drive a dynamo in an 1881 demonstration of incandescent lighting.[259] They had developed this boiler technology at just the right time, and these became in demand in many industries. The Babcock and Wilcox Company continue to develop boiler technology adapted to innovations and change in power.

WATER NEEDS, PUMPS, COMPRESSORS AND CONSERVATION

An enormous water supply was required for all the operations of the plant. The water supply for the steam boilers was largely acquired from dams constructed in the adjoining hills—collection of surface drainage and spring water yielded an ample supply for the boilers.[260] By 1901, the total power of steam engines used at the plant had already increased to 12,000 horsepower, in addition to the 4,000 horsepower of electric motors.[261] In 1901, descriptions of the plant's water needs included 8 million gallons of water every 24 hours, drawn from the river by 37 pumps of various sizes.[262]

Water and hydraulic pressure for the plant operations were split into the lower and upper portions and designed for the specific needs of the equipment and operations in each place. The hydraulic pressure required at the lower portion of the works was obtained from a pumphouse located between the steel mill and the gas producers (for example, Figure 5.6). This system worked at about 500 pounds and required two pumps, both compound duplex pumps with two 18″ x 10′ accumulators. From this station, the pressure was taken down the river to the steel mill, where the ladle cranes, furnace doors and the gas- and air-reversing valves were operated by it and up the river through the blooming mill, beam mill and stockyards, where it actuated furnace doors, manipulators, transfer tables, turntable, screws on mill boxes, shears and so on.[263]

The upper portion of the works (bridge shop and eye-bar forge) above the storage yard had air compressors and pumps supplying the air and hydraulic pressure required at this part of the works. The hydraulic power was supplied at two pressures of 600 pounds and 1,300 pounds, respectively. Where required at the individual machines, intensifiers were used to increase the pressure to the desired value. The pumps were all of the duplex Worthington type, with compound condensing steam cylinders.[264] In 1898, Pencoyd added a Worthington triple expansion pump.[265] There were also pumps in the basement of the office building and a number of other pumps distributed as needed in the mill buildings.

The rise of pump technology paralleled that of Pencoyd's birth and evolution in the mid-1850s. Worthington pumps were used extensively at Pencoyd and offer a cogent representative of that critical industry. Born in Brooklyn in 1817, Henry R. Worthington developed into an important mechanical engineer largely due to on-the-job training and practical experience. He improved steam-driven, direct-acting pumps for steam-powered vessels and invented one of the first practical water meters.[266] Worthington started thinking about pumps and power when he entered a New York State–sponsored competition to design a steam canalboat for use on the Erie Canal in place of mules and horses. Although the competition did not pan out, Worthington's design, a steam-driven feed pump, was direct-acting and operated independently and automatically from the boat engine. Worthington continued to work on the pump and joined with William H. Baker to found Worthington & Baker to manufacture the pump in 1845. The company's first pump sales were to the U.S. Navy in 1850 for the USS *Susquehanna*, but the pump was also sold for use in hotels, factories, mines and quarries. Worthington developed many designs and patents for a water meter, boiler feed, oil pipeline and hydroelectric uses, but in 1857, he invented a duplex direct-acting pump, considered the most significant development in steam-powered pumps at the time (Figure 5.13). Due to reliability and low operating cost, these pumps were used for many decades in waterworks and for pumping oil through long pipelines in oil fields. For these reasons, Pencoyd utilized Worthington pumps in its iron works for operating ladle cranes, furnace doors, gas- and air-reversing valves, actuating furnace doors, manipulators, transfer tables, turntables, screws on mill boxes, shears and more.

(5.13) Worthington duplex pump. *From A.M. Greene,* Pumping Machinery, *1919, 75.*

There were two supplies of compressed air: one of 10 pounds pressure used in oil furnaces and the other of 80 pounds pressure for riveters, chippers and reamers in the bridge shop. Air was compressed by a number of piston engines of various makes. The Norwalk machines are used for the high pressure and have both steam and air systems compounded.

Water conservation was important at the mill given the huge volumes required for operations, and two approaches were used.[267] There was a main line for exhaust steam throughout the works, which collected in a main line and conveyed it to water heaters and/or for heating purposes in winter. Secondly, most engines of the works were outfitted with condensers for water recovery and reuse.

The diverse array of machines at the mill included Corliss steam engines, Westinghouse engines, Crocker-Wheeler and General Electric dynamos, Babcock-Wilcox boilers and Worthington pumps. The list of machinery reads like a who's who of industrial innovation and change. Indeed, it was this industrial capability that allowed Pencoyd (and many other industrial companies like Pencoyd) to become a leader in its field, expanding productivity and output while also adapting to new technologies as they became available in the ever-changing world of inventions. The industrial equipment might seem rather mundane to the general reader, but this author wanted to spend some time on all the innovative machinery that made it all possible and hopes that a greater appreciation of these capabilities is possible without plunging into too much detail. Walter Righter was superintendent of motive power. After compiling all of these detailed capabilities utilized at Pencoyd and the numerous machines and trades required to connect them all in an efficient way, it seems he had his work cut out for him. His bookshelf—handed down to children and then grandchildren—included Grant's treatise on gearing and works on valves, steam turbines, boilers, pumps, shafting, belting, governors and electrical engineering—and now we can understand why.

6

Construction

The construction projects undertaken by Pencoyd included some of the tallest buildings and widest spans at the time of their building. Pencoyd was also involved in building the first elevated railways in New York, New Jersey, Boston and Chicago. Pencoyd's projects were of a wide diversity, but they fall into three general categories: transportation-related buildings (train sheds, pier sheds and rail stations), skyscrapers and steel skeleton buildings, and large government buildings. Their influence on each of these categories is described in this chapter.

Transportation Related

The first major transportation building undertaken was the structural steel for the B&ORR Philadelphia Depot, which was designed by Philadelphia architect Frank Furness and built in 1886 (Figures 6.1 and 6.2).[268] This building remained in operation until 1958, when the service to Philly was discontinued; the building was ultimately destroyed in 1963.

Pencoyd next constructed the Brooklyn elevated railway.[269] The date of construction is about 1887, and while it was one of the earliest elevated systems, much attention was also focused on the design of the traveling crane that allowed the elevated tracks to be extended during construction.[270]

By 1891, Pencoyd was contracted to build the new PRR terminal and train sheds in Jersey City, New Jersey. This project was one of eight different

Top: (6.1) B&ORR Station in Philadelphia, built in 1886. *From Baltimore & Ohio Railroad Station, Philadelphia, HABS PA-1220.*

Bottom: (6.2) Interior stairway of B&O RR showing the steel beams used in construction. *From Baltimore & Ohio Railroad Station, Philadelphia, HABS PA-1220.*

lines that came from the west into the Jersey City and New York area right to the Hudson River (Figure 6.3).[271] These structures were unique at the time, as they spanned nearly 300′, and the train tracks had portions that were elevated above street level.[272] At most locations (although some were train sheds), there were ferry terminals at the river that could take passengers across to Manhattan. Bridges were few then, and the perceived passenger traffic was high. As a result, there was steep competition for both the access to the river and for the various rail lines feeding the area and the ferry lines providing river crossing service. The span of the Jersey City Trainshed was 252′8″, which made it the largest trainshed in existence and the second largest span after that of the 1889 Machinery Hall of the Paris Exposition.[273] The terminal and trainshed were used for about 30 years, until 1922, when they were dismantled. The dismantling was a natural consequence of the diversion of the main stream of PRR passenger traffic to the 33rd Street terminal on Manhattan.[274]

In 1893, Pencoyd built a similar structure for the PRR at Broad Street station in Philadelphia. The train shed roof was slightly larger and a longer span than the Jersey City structure, but of a similar design and appearance (Figure 6.4).[275] The train shed contributed to the complete redesign of the Broad Street Station area in Philadelphia, which led to the transition of most traffic through this station and opened access to suburbs for commuters working in downtown Philadelphia.

Pencoyd next built a portion of the Chicago Union Elevated railway. In 1897, it was involved with the Randolph/Wabash Avenue station on the Loop Elevated railway.[276] The architect was John Alexander Low Waddell (1854–1938), consulting engineer of Kansas City, Missouri.[277] Construction materials were acquired from the Pencoyd Iron Works.[278] A set of original plans for the Randolph/Wabash Avenue Station was developed in 1896 by John Alexander Low Waddell for the Northwestern and Union Elevated Railroad in Chicago.[279] Pencoyd was one of several companies building sections of the Loop as it was constructed over the course of several years.

Pencoyd also participated in other notable structures such as the White Star Line pier shed in New York City in 1898.[280] This is the line operated by Cunard and berthed the *Titanic* and its sister ship *Britannic*. Parts of this shed structure are still there, including a metal gate. Back Bay Station in Boston was built in 1898,[281] but it had a short lifespan due to a fire that destroyed the building in 1928.[282] Shortly thereafter, Pencoyd, along with the Carnegie Company and Pennsylvania Steel Company, built the Boston Elevated railway in 1899–1900 (Figure 6.5), including terminal stations at Dudley Street in Roxbury and Charlestown.[283] In 1900–1901, Pencoyd also worked on an extensive project for the city of Richmond that involved a train station, train shed, viaducts and long elevated rail line along the James River (Figure 6.6).[284] Most of these structures are still in operation in Richmond, and the station and train shed have been recently revitalized.

Pencoyd's work on elevated railways continued in Philadelphia and Newark. In 1903 and 1905, Pencoyd fabricated steel for the Atlantic Avenue and Newark Viaducts, and in 1906, it helped complete the Market Street Elevated Railway near city hall in Philadelphia.[285] In 1909, the company built the Trenton Ave. Elevated Railway in the Kensington neighborhood of Philadelphia.[286] At nearly the same time, and together with the Trenton

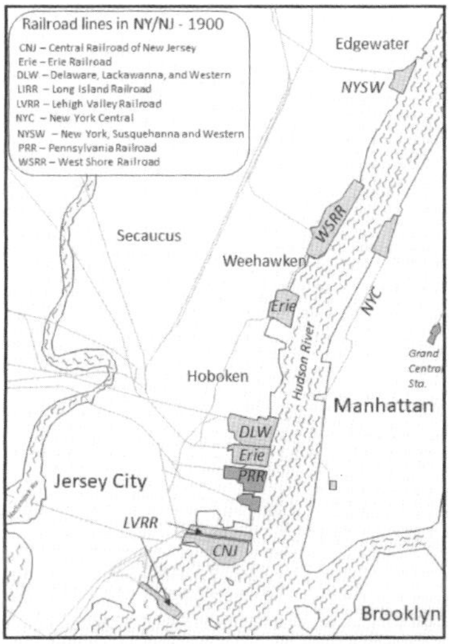

Left: (6.3) Map of Manhattan and Jersey City showing the locations of railroad terminals and stations along the Hudson River. *https://upload.wikimedia.org/wikipedia/commons/f/f2/New_York_City_Railroads_ca_1900.png and redrawn by author.*

Below: (6.4) Broad Street Station interior photo showing the steel structure. *Free Library of Philadelphia.*

plant of the American Bridge Company, Pencoyd fabricated 25,000 tons of structural steel for the Hudson Terminal Buildings in Manhattan (Figure 6.7).[287] These twin tower buildings offered the largest office space in the world (by floor area, about 880,000 square feet).[288] The towers were completed in

Left: (6.5) Northampton Station of the Boston elevated railway. *Library of Congress.*

Middle: (6.6) Terminal, station and railway project in Richmond, Virginia, built in 1900–1901, and for which Pencoyd rolled all the steel viaduct and structural shapes. *From* Engineering News, *November 29, 1900, 379–80.*

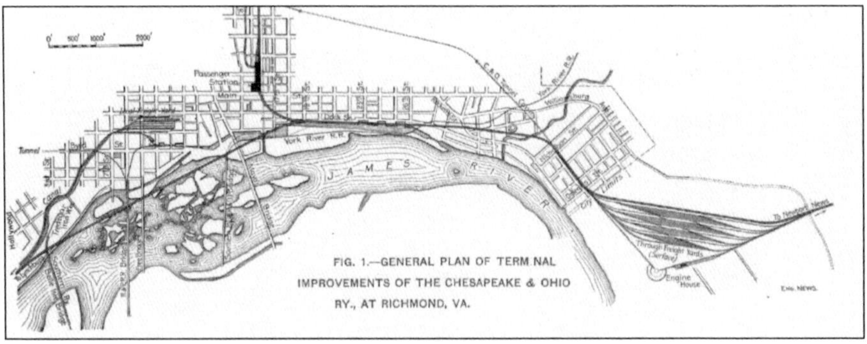

(6.7) Hudson Terminal Buildings (*on right side of image*) built in 1909 at the eventual site of the World Trade Center Buildings near Cortlandt and Dey Streets. *Library of Congress.*

1909 and in use until the mid-1960s, when they were sold and then destroyed to make space for the World Trade Center built in the 1970s.

Two final examples of transportation-related structures are the most western of all in these categories. Downtown Denver grew considerably near the turn of the century and redesigned the area near 14th and Wazee Streets.[289] The 14th Street viaduct took traffic over the South Platte River, city streets and rail lines from Blake Street to Platte Street. The viaduct crossing the Platte River was composed of two riveted Warren girder spans (Figure 6.8), each 102′ long and made of Pencoyd steel. The total length of steelwork was 2,576′ and total earth embankment approaches were 2,084′ long, making a total length of the viaduct 4,660′. The approximate total weight of steel was 2,100 tons.[290] The viaduct project was a joint venture between the cities of Denver and Highlands. Pencoyd also provided steel for several truss bridges for street traffic at each end of the viaduct.[291] With its 63 spans of steel stringers, the viaduct is the only long steel bridge in Denver that does not have trussed spans over the river or the railroads and serves an example of an elevated roadway erected before the introduction of the automobile in Colorado.[292] Several decades later, Pencoyd provided the steel for a hanger building at a Hawaiian airport. The John Rodgers Airport, Hangar no. 2, at Honolulu International Airport was built in 1929. It has historical significance in that it is "associated with the oldest commercial airline company in Hawaii, represents distinctive characteristics of a type,

(6.8) 14th Street viaduct in Denver, built in 1898–99. *From Denver Public Library, Western History Collection.*

(6.9) Hotel Walton (1892) constructed with steel made by Pencoyd Iron Works. *Library of Congress, HABS PA-1091.*

period, and construction methods important to Hawaii's aviation history, and has retained integrity throughout periods of major expansion" of the airport in Honolulu.[293] For these reasons, it recently became part of the historical American Buildings Survey.

SKYSCRAPERS AND STEEL IN CONSTRUCTION

While completing these enormous railroad projects in Philadelphia and New York City, Pencoyd also expanded into structural iron and steel in some of the tallest buildings of that period in Philadelphia, New York, Chicago and Buffalo. Pencoyd fabricated the structural steel for Philadelphia's Hotel Walton (later John Bartram Hotel, see figure 6.9) in 1892, Girard Estate Building (1896), America Baptist Publishing House (1896), Land Title and Trust Building (1897), West End Trust Building (1898), UGI Building (1898), Real Estate Trust Building (1899), Wanamaker Building (1899–1900)[294] and the Bellevue-Stratford Hotel (1905).[295]

In New York City, many taller buildings were constructed with structural steel fabricated by Pencoyd, including the Metropolitan Life Insurance Company (1893),[296] Manhattan Life Insurance Company (1894),[297]

Central Syndicate Building (1896), Vincent[298] and Gillender[299] Buildings (1897), the Franklin Building (1897)[300] and the B. Altman Department Store building at 34th Street and 5th Avenue (1905).[301] The Metropolitan Life Insurance Company later added the enormous tower that became a well-known landmark in New York City.[302] Several of these buildings deserve some extra description.

In 1894–95, the Manhattan Life Insurance building was constructed in Manhattan (Figure 6.10). Kimball and Thompson were the architects for the original building, and Chas. O. Brown was the consulting engineer. Sooy Smith & Company were the contractors for the foundations, and the Pencoyd Bridge Company was the contractor for the structural steel work.[303] The Manhattan Life building, which cost about $2 million, occupied a lot about 67′ by 122′ in size, and the 18 stories rose 350′ above the pavement to the foot of the flagstaff. The building had an iron-and-steel framework for floors, roof and dome and independent outer main walls of stone, brick and terra cotta, with steel skeletons and iron or copper sheathing for some of the auxiliary construction.[304] It was the first skyscraper to pass 330′ (100 meters) in Manhattan, was the tallest building in the United States in 1894–95 and remained the tallest building in New York until 1899. After the Manhattan Life Insurance Company, the building was owned by the Manufacturer's Trust Company and Central Union Trust Company, but it was finally demolished in the early 1960s for an annex to the Irving Trust Company Building (now One Wall Street) in 1965.[305]

The Gillender Building, completed in 1897, was a 20-story, 273′ tall skyscraper on the northwest corner of Wall and Nassau Streets, measured only 26′ by 73′ and was one of the tallest structures in New York.[306] Despite its attraction as a tall building with a small footprint, it did not do well financially, and by 1910, it had been demolished to be replaced by the 41–story Bankers Trust tower at 14 Wall Street. The Gillender Building had the distinction of being the first skyscraper in New York City to be torn down and replaced by another.[307]

Despite this demolition, numerous other buildings sprang up in the city made with Pencoyd steel. The United Express Company Building is a 22-story building at the corner of Rector and Greenwich.[308] This steel-cage construction also features a brick and terra-cotta exterior, granite and marble walls and hollow tile floors on the interior; the 1907 building is still in use today. Several years later, in 1912, Pencoyd built the steel structure for the Guaranty Trust Building, an 8-story steel-frame structure that was not especially tall for its time but contained large open spaces on the first,

(6.10) Manhattan Life Insurance Building, Manhattan, built 1894–95, on the right side of image. *Wallach Division Picture Collection, New York Public Library.*

Above: (6.11) Heavy girder being installed at Bonwit-Teller Building with gantries. *From* Engineering Record, *March 16, 1912, 290–91.*

Left: (6.12) Bonwit-Teller girder being transported by rail from Philadelphia to New York. *From* Engineering Record, *March 16, 1912, 290–91.*

second and third floors that required some specially designed trusses.[309] This building at 140 Broadway was ultimately demolished in 1964 to build the 52-story Marine Midland Building.[310]

The widely recognized "House of Morgan" or Morgan Building at 23 Wall Street is a New York City landmark. This building was erected in 1914 and, like the Guaranty Trust Building, is not a tall structure, but it contains open space without any columns in the first floor. The Morgan Building has three upper floors supported entirely by the wall columns and a series of very heavy long-span trusses and 29′ long plate girders in the roof.[311] Post & McCord were the contractors for the steel work, and the fabrication was done at Pencoyd as part of the American Bridge Company. This

Left: (6.13) Guaranty Building in Buffalo, New York, built in 1895 with Pencoyd's structural steel cage design. *From the* American Architect and Building News, *July 11, 1896.*

Right: (6.14) Fisher Building under construction in 1895 showing the steel cage construction. *From W. Birkmire,* Planning and Construction of High Office Buildings, *1898.*

concept was popular at the time: the 11-story Bonwit-Teller Department store building in New York City had an open storefront with no window columns in the first few floors. It used two enormous girder beams on the third floor to support the loads (Figure 6.11).[312] The beams were produced at Pencoyd and then loaded onto railcars for transport to New York (Figure 6.12).

Several important buildings were also built in Chicago and Buffalo. The famous Guaranty building in Buffalo, New York, was designed by Louis Sullivan and built in 1895.[313] This building is most well known for its unique decorative terra-cotta interior and exterior, but all of the structural steel of the skeleton framework was fabricated by Pencoyd (Figure 6.13).[314] The Fisher building on Dearborn Street in Chicago was built in 1895–96. This building still stands today—it was originally 18 stories with interior structural steel elements. Construction photos reveal the steel skeleton—fabricated by Pencoyd—that was typical of many of these skyscrapers (Figure 6.14).[315]

LARGE GOVERNMENT BUILDINGS

In addition to the transportation structures and urban buildings and skyscrapers, Pencoyd supplied structural steel for many large government buildings, most of which are still in use today. In 1898, the U.S. Mint Building was built on Spring Garden Street (Figure 6.15).[316] The building is now part of the Community College of Philadelphia. Also in 1898, the National Export Exposition buildings were constructed for the 1899 exposition (Figure 6.16). Pencoyd provided the steel for these buildings in an amazing time frame—30 days from date of order.[317] The National Export Exposition was nearly the same scale as the 1876 Centennial Exposition, in which Pencoyd had also participated. In addition, for its exhibit at the exposition, Pencoyd received the Cresson Medal of the Franklin Institute:

> *The exhibit consisted of a very creditable and interesting display of steel structural shapes, girders, bridge materials, etc., and a full-sized model of one of the expansion ends of the Delaware River Bridge, with its roller bearings. Apart from the high quality of the articles exhibited and the exceedingly interesting display made, the attention of your subcommittee was called to some special features in the construction and erection of several important bridges recently built by the company, namely, the Niagara and Clifton bridge at Niagara Falls; the Atbara River Bridge over the Atbara River for the*

(6.15) The U.S. Mint, which is now part of the Community College of Philadelphia. *AIA T-Square Yearbook, 1900, 151.*

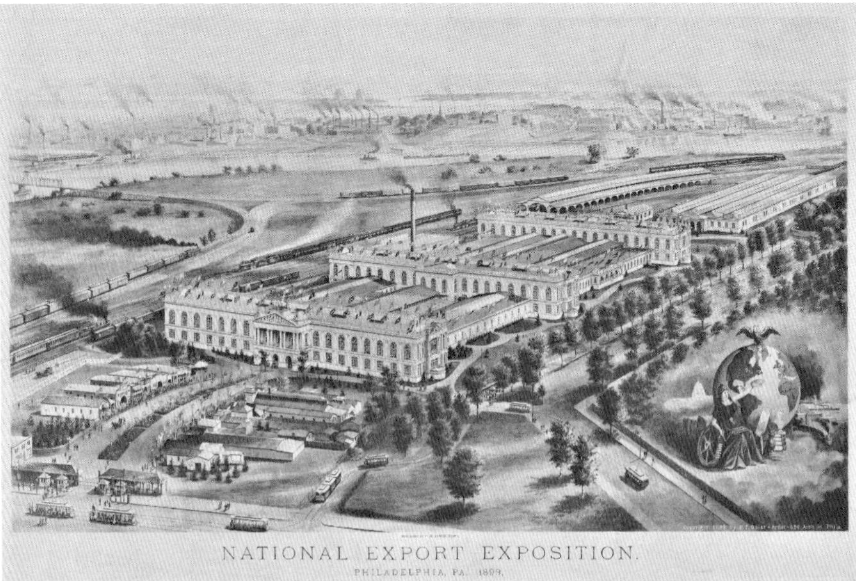

(6.16) The buildings of the National Export Exposition in Philadelphia, built in 1898. *Library of Congress.*

> *British government, and the Delaware River Bridge of the Pennsylvania Railroad Company near Philadelphia, descriptions and blueprints of which were submitted by the company, and are on file with this report.*[318]

After the turn of the century and as part of the American Bridge Company, Pencoyd was involved with two other famous buildings. It provided the structural steel for Ellis Island Immigration Station in 1898–99[319] and for the dome and the various wings of the Pennsylvania Capitol in Harrisburg in 1905–6.[320] This building officially opened in 1906, and Theodore Roosevelt attended the dedication.

MISCELLANEOUS BUILDINGS AND STRUCTURAL ELEMENTS IN BUILDINGS

Pencoyd provided structural steel for a number of other notable buildings and structures, including the U.S. Navy Yard Shop (in 1887 and 1899),[321] the General Electric Machine Shop (1905), Marion Power Station, New Jersey

(1905)[322] and structural elements of the New York City Polo Grounds stadium after the fire of 1911.[323] The widespread recognition of Pencoyd is evident in 1898 from records in Providence, Rhode Island. The Beaman-Smith Mill Building—of historical significance to the state of Rhode Island—had some Pencoyd structural beams incorporated into its design.[324] The use of Pencoyd beams in construction was undoubtedly due to Pencoyd's ability to produce large beams in its rolling mills. Pencoyd produced simple structures such as pavilions and sheds from 1890 onward.[325] Its corrugated floors became widely used and popular and appear in a number of publications for civil engineers.[326] In 1923, the engineer in charge, Francis L. Castleman, patented improved column designs for buildings using the H-shaped compound column construction; standard use of the H-shaped columns had the spacing between girders change at different floors or levels of the building.[327] Castleman's improvement called for standard spacing of the girders from level to level, but altered the column thickness and design on lower floors. Castleman had also patented a rail fastening hardware design in 1918, a demonstration of the powerful combination of designers and structural element fabrication that was possible at Pencoyd.[328]

MARINE

The final few examples are a departure from building construction but nonetheless structural steel applications. The Northern Steamship company built two lake steamers around the time of the 1893 World's Fair in Chicago. These steamers, called *North West* and *North Land* (Figures 6.17 and 6.18) were state of the art with two overhead-cylinder, vertical, quadruple-expansion engines that could develop at least 7,000 horsepower. A vertical air pump, two single-acting cylinders (36″ diameter by 16″ stroke), and twin screws of 13′ diameter by 18′ mean pitch were the major components of the propulsion system. The steam was furnished by 28 Belleville boilers operating at 195 pounds pressure. The engines were so massive that the bed plates weighed 34 tons each. The low-pressure cylinders each weighed 24,000 pounds and were of cast steel. The structural beams in these ships were made by Pencoyd Iron works, and most of the other machinery and components were made by Cleveland companies: Otis Steel Company (plates), Cleveland Rolling Mill Company (angles) and the Globe Iron Works (machinery). The vessels were of a type entirely new to the lakes, patterned after the design of oceangoing

Left: (6.17) The passenger steamship *North West*, built in 1893–94, under construction in Cleveland with deck beams clearly visible. *From Alpena County George N. Fetcher Public Library, Great Lakes Maritime Collection.*

Below: (6.18) *North West* docking on one of its Great Lake cruises. *From Alpena County George N. Fetcher Public Library, Great Lakes Maritime Collection.*

passenger boats and cost $600,000 each. Altogether, they were 360′ on the keel, 380′ overall, with 44′ beams and 34′ deep.[329]

The *North West* and *North Land* were used for seven-day cruises over the five Great Lakes (Ontario, Erie, Huron, Michigan and Superior), and were part of the passenger service between Buffalo and Chicago. The return voyage from Buffalo to Duluth or Chicago took seven days, and one of the most popular stops was at Mackinac Island, where automobiles are still not allowed to this day.[330] In fact, Mark Twain was among the first passengers on the *North Land*. The *North Land* was out of service by 1919, was cut in half for possible transport to Montreal to rebuild and refit for service in World War I, but that never actually happened. It was finally scrapped in 1921.[331] The *North West* had a longer lifetime but a more tragic demise. *North West* was operational until February 1941, when it was sunk by a German U-boat, *U-107*, in the Irish Sea—all 37 crew members were lost.[332]

In addition to the work on the steamers, Pencoyd made over 2000 pounds of steel angles and shapes for the construction of the U.S. torpedo boats USS *Nicholson* (TB-29) and USS *O'Brien* (TB-30).[333] These Blakely-class torpedo boats were constructed at the Crescent Shipyard in Elizabeth, New Jersey, in 1898–99 and launched in 1901.[334] They served for about 10 years until they were decommissioned in 1909 and subsequently used as targets for training. Pencoyd also produced the steel structural elements for a yacht for wealthy Manhattan businessman John Rogers Maxwell built in Wilmington in 1901. This yacht was later entered into the service for the U.S. Navy for World War I as the USS *Sachem* and World War II as the USS *Phenakite*.[335]

Construction, including railway sheds and stations, skyscrapers and industrial buildings, was clearly a strength of the Pencoyd Iron Works. It produced many important (at the time of building though now of course superseded) structures and established a solid reputation in that field well into the twentieth century, as shown by advertisements in real estate and builder journals.[336] Amazingly, construction would be a small part of the ironworks' reputation and expertise. The company would also become known worldwide for bridge making, and much larger projects would ultimately come through the mills. Before this could happen, Pencoyd would have to master the transition from wrought iron to steel production (discussed already in chapter 4) and establish specialized machining and testing facilities, as will become clear in the ensuing chapters.

7

Bridge Building

The Engineers and the Products

American bridge building has a long and rich history and was influenced to great extent by European designs and approaches. Pencoyd is widely recognized for bridge design and building, but what does this really mean in detail? To answer this, some historical perspective is useful and necessary. There are many bridge types—girder, truss, suspension, cantilever, steel arch, trestles and viaducts and later concrete and reinforced concrete. The bridge types that were most widely used during the time of Pencoyd's peak activity were girder, truss, cantilever and viaduct (Figure 7.1).[337] There are also movable bridges, and these have many forms such as lift, swing and bascule (see chapter 8).[338] Thus, any focus on the history and production of bridges at Pencoyd should keep this in mind. Pencoyd mainly produced truss and viaduct designs, rarely to never suspension or concrete or reinforced concrete; the latter came later.

The Pencoyd co-founder Percival Roberts and Percival's cousin George B. Roberts both attended Rensselaer Polytechnic Institute (RPI) in the 1840s and 1850s (see chapter 2). This connection with RPI would continue, as they collaborated with John Murphy, who also graduated from RPI, and Squire Whipple, who was from the Schenectady area. These early connections led to Pencoyd purchasing the patent to the Whipple truss design[339] and production of the many wrought-iron Whipple truss bridges described in chapter 2. Percival Roberts and American bridge engineer Theodore Cooper exchanged correspondence in 1888 regarding Pencoyd's experience

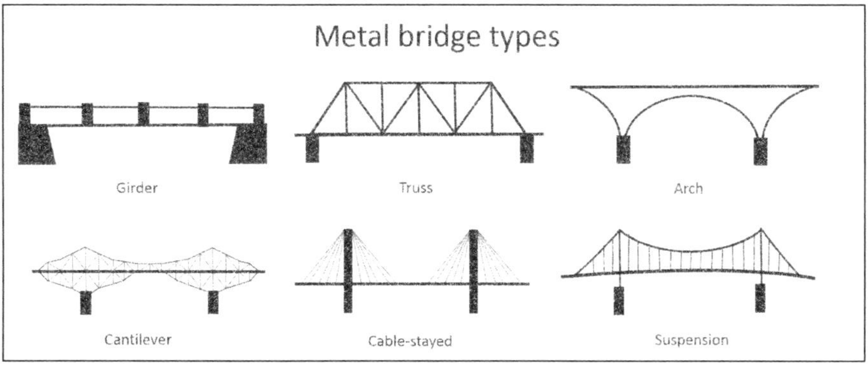

(7.1) Illustration of various bridge types. *H. Petroski,* Engineers of Dreams, *Vintage Books, New York, 1996, redrawn by author.*

with wrought-iron bridgework from 1858 to 1863, again perhaps due to their acquaintance at RPI.[340] The engineering connections would turn out to be critical to the bridge making era that Pencoyd was about to enter.

The great expansion of railroads across the United States and the growth of railroad industry led to the need for waterway crossings, including the Delaware, Susquehanna, Ohio, Mississippi and Missouri Rivers. As this growth occurred in the mid-1800s, bridge design became important, and there were a number of large bridge collapse disasters highlighting this issue. As a harbinger, a Town lattice bridge over Catskill Creek in New York collapsed in 1840 with a locomotive crossing.[341] In 1855, a wooden trestle across the Gasconade River in Missouri collapsed as a train carrying nearly 600 people on its inaugural day collapsed, resulting in the death of 31 people.[342] A third example is a railroad bridge collapse in Bangor, Maine, in August 1871 that killed 1 and injured 30.[343] Finally, in December 1876, a railroad bridge in Ashtabula, Ohio, collapsed, killing 92 and injuring 64 when the train plunged into the river after a section of the bridge failed.[344] Each of these failures was ultimately caused by a design flaw, clearly indicating the need for a sustained effort in bridge design and engineering. Despite these horrible examples, there were bright spots—while disasters like Ashtabula were occurring (1876), Kentucky High Bridge cantilever design was being built successfully (Figures 2.9, 2.10). Highly trained and experienced engineers would be key to successful bridges.

Pencoyd invested in a bridge shop in 1886 and started to focus on bridge building more than ever before. It was this year that it also hired Charles Conrad Schneider as chief engineer (Figure 7.2). One of the

(7.2) C.C. Schneider. *From* Engineering News, *January 13, 1916, 90–91.*

most preeminent engineers of his time, C.C. Schneider was the chief engineer at Pencoyd from 1886 until 1900, when Pencoyd merged with other companies into the American Bridge Company.[345] Schneider ultimately won two Norman Medals from ASCE in 1905 and 1908 for his papers on movable bridges and steel in construction.[346] He also won the Rowlands Prize from ASCE in 1886 for his paper on the Niagara cantilever bridge. His contributions ranged from architectural to bridge designs, with involvement in the Statue of Liberty, Niagara Cantilever bridge and Quebec bridge failure evaluation, among many others.[347] His story is an important one in the history of the Pencoyd Iron Works.

CHARLES CONRAD SCHNEIDER

C.C. Schneider was born at Apolda, in the Duchy of Saxony, Germany, in 1843. After an apprenticeship at a machine shop, he graduated in 1864 from the Royal School of Technology in Chemnitz and came to the United States in 1867. He spent three years as designer for the Roger Locomotive Works in Paterson, New Jersey, but then decided to focus on structural engineering. He spent three years with the Michigan Bridge and Construction Company of Detroit and then moved to New York City in 1873 to take the position of engineer-in-charge of the engineers' office of the Erie Railroad Company, whose chief engineer was Octave Chanute.[348] While there, Schneider checked strain sheets and plans submitted by bridge companies and instructed inspectors. Neither of these duties were general practice at the time, as railroads relied on bridge companies for correct designs, and experienced inspectors were generally scarce. In 1873, systematic bridge inspection was initiated, as it was concluded that uniformity in bridges could be achieved if the plans were prepared by the engineers of the railroad, and Schneider was assigned that role.[349]

In 1877, Schneider opened a New York office as a consulting engineer, and for several years, he was engaged in structures in the western United States.

He was involved with George S. Morison and the Plattsmouth, Bismarck, Blair and Rulo bridges across the Missouri River and the Snake River bridge at Ainsworth, Washington. Schneider's name is associated with the development of the cantilever structure: in 1882 and 1883, he designed the cantilever bridge over the Fraser River for the Canadian Pacific Railway and the Niagara River cantilever for the Michigan Central Railroad.[350] Other design work out west included the extensive wooden viaduct at Marent Gulch on Northern Pacific and the Stony Creek viaduct on the Canadian Pacific Railways. He also designed the anchorage for the Statue of Liberty in New York Harbor.[351]

It was in this backdrop that Schneider was hired at Pencoyd. In 1886, Pencoyd added a bridge and construction department to its iron manufacturing plant, and Schneider became chief engineer.[352] The works developed rapidly. and productivity jumped from 600 tons per month in 1887 to nearly 8,000 tons per month in 1898.[353] This output exceeded the output of bridge shops anywere else, as is discussed in detail in chapter 9.

Schneider was also engaged in designs for bridges over the East River, connecting Long Island with New York City, both in the 1870s and later in 1893–95. The latter project progressed well, with Pencoyd providing the design and steel superstructures and approaches, but the death of the president of the Long Island Railroad Company, Austin Corbin, stalled the project and delayed completion of the bridge.[354]

From 1900 to 1904, Schneider was vice-president in charge of engineering for the American Bridge Company, after which he was retained by the company as consulting engineer, devoting a portion of his time to private practice. When the Quebec Bridge collapsed in 1907, he was enlisted by the Canadian government to be on the investigative board, which resulted in an extensive report in 1908. This influential report had a major impact on subsequent bridge designs around the world, and in 1911, he was appointed by the Canadian government a member of the board of engineers for the building of the new Quebec Bridge.[355]

Schneider was well known for his dedication to high standards in bridge and structural work. He was also known to assist young engineers and was responsible for training large numbers of engineers.[356] Pencoyd enjoyed one of the most exciting, busy and rewarding periods of its history under the guidance of Schneider as chief engineer, with the impressive number of bridges and building construction projects described here and in chapter 6.

PAUL WOLFEL AND FREDERICK KUNZ

Paul Wolfel (Figure 7.3) succeeded Schneider as chief engineer, with an equally distinguished set of accomplishments by 1900. Wolfel had been recommended by Schneider's professor in Saxony, Frankel. Frankel's recommendation of Wolfel, who had passed every branch of his studies with an average grade of excellent—which had not occurred for ten years—led to Wolfel coming to Pencoyd as assistant to Schneider in 1888. Wolfel subsequently contributed to such projects as the Delair Bridge and the Atbara Bridge in Sudan.[357] Wolfel was born in Dresden, Saxony, in 1862. He graduated with a degree in civil engineering from the Royal Polytechnikum of Dresden, in October 1885. After that, he was assistant to Professor Steiner and Privatdozent at the Polytechnikum in Prague, Austria, until 1888.[358] It was during this time that he prepared designs and estimates for bridges for the Prager Machinenbau Actien Gesellschaft. In June 1888, Wolfel came to the United States and Pencoyd Iron Works. Within a short time, he had demonstrated his technical abilities and, by 1890, became assistant chief engineer—a position he held until the merger of the Pencoyd Iron Works with the American Bridge Company in 1900.[359]

Wolfel, like Schneider, actively supported and encouraged apprenticeships, and the Pencoyd drafting room produced many engineers who credited their success to Wolfel's early guidance. He was widely recognized to have a generous and unselfish attitude toward the welfare of his colleagues, partly through his involvement in the Pencoyd Club.[360] Marshall Williams, assistant to the president of the American Bridge Company, wrote of Wolfel, "Mr. Wolfel's active connection with the Pencoyd Iron Works and the American Bridge Company, was ever signalized by a high type of intelligent administration. He was thorough in research, careful in analysis, honest in execution, fair-minded toward his colleagues, and evinced a brotherly interest in the men who served under him."[361]

(7.3) Paul Wolfel. *From* History of Pittsburgh and Environs *(New York, American Historical Society, 1922), 1922.*

During this period, Wolfel was engaged in two large bridge projects: the PRR Delair Bridge and the Atbara Bridge in Sudan. When the American Bridge Company formed in 1900, Wolfel became chief engineer, and Schneider became vice-president in charge of construction. The Thebes Bridge across the Mississippi was constructed during Wolfel's tenure as chief engineer, and he aided in the reconstruction of San Francisco after the great earthquake.[362] In 1908, Wolfel moved to Pittsburgh to assume the duties of chief engineer of the McClintic-Marshall Company. Wolfel became chief engineer of the McClintic-Marshall Company at the time of the construction of the Ohio River bridge at Beaver, Pennsylvania, which was the first large cantilever to be built after the disaster to the first Quebec Bridge.[363] Wolfel gave great care to its design, fabrication and erection, and as a result, the construction of the Beaver bridge overcame many challenging problems.

While at the McClintic-Marshall Company, Wolfel oversaw many major engineering projects, including lock gates for the Panama Canal, viaducts and crossings of the New York Connecting railroad (Hell Gate line) on Long Island and in the Bronx and the Sciotoville bridge of the Chesapeake & Ohio Northern Railway over the Ohio. In addition, he was consulted on the design of the second Quebec bridge over the St. Lawrence River.[364] Wolfel was a leading member of the American Society of Civil Engineers, the Engineers Society of Western Pennsylvania, the Western Society of Engineers, the Franklin Institute, the American Society for Testing Materials and an associate of the American Railway Engineering Association, as well as a member of the Engineers' Club of New York and Philadelphia and the Duquesne Club of Pittsburgh. Wolfel died in Philadelphia on December 28, 1920, at the high point of his career.[365]

Frederick Kunz was another influential Pencoyd engineer. He was from Austria and attended polytechnic school in Prague before coming to Philadelphia in 1891 to work for Pencoyd.[366] While with Pencoyd, Kunz was involved with the erection plans for the Niagara and Clifton steel arch bridges, as well as the Delair bridge. From 1900 to 1903, he served as assistant to the vice-president of engineering for the company, C.C. Schneider. Kunz was appointed to work with Lindenthal and planned for the Manhattan and Queensboro bridges in 1903–4 but then moved to become chief engineer of the bridge department at the Pennsylvania Steel Company in Steelton. While there, he helped construct the Queensboro bridge and later wrote an extensive report on its safety aspects in 1908. Afterward, he became an independent consulting engineer and wrote a classic book on bridges called *Design of Steel Bridges*. Kunz was a close personal friend of C.C. Schneider, and the men remained so throughout their lives, even after they worked together at Pencoyd.[367]

JOHN A.L. WADDELL AND LEFFERT L. BUCK

While Schneider and Wolfel were heading up Pencoyd's bridge and construction department, another great bridge designer, John A.L. Waddell (Figure 7.4) designed and patented the unique A truss design that came to be called the Waddell A truss.[368] Although patented in 1894, actual construction of an A truss came later, and one of them was built by Pencoyd in 1898.[369] Waddell, like the Roberts cousins and John Murphy, graduated from RPI and later returned to teach engineering from 1878 to 1881.[370] The connection with Waddell is another example of how Pencoyd was involved with preeminent bridge designers such as Whipple, Murphy, Schneider and Wolfel.

John Alexander Low Waddell was born in Ontario, Canada, in 1854 and graduated from Rensselaer Polytechnic Institute in 1875. For the next three years, he worked for the Marine Department of Ottawa, did surveying on the Canadian Pacific Railroad and then returned to RPI to teach mechanics from 1878 to 1881. He was professor of engineering at the Imperial University of Tokyo from 1882 to 1886.[371] At Rensselaer, Waddell had taught the first two Japanese students to attend an American engineering school, and they most likely recommended him for the Imperial University post. After Tokyo, he worked as an engineering and design consultant in the United States and abroad, building bridges in Canada, Mexico, Russia, China, Japan and New Zealand.[372]

(7.4) John Waddell. *From* Bridge Engineering, *2 vols. (New York: John Wiley and Sons, 1916), frontispiece.*

When he returned to the United States in 1886, he worked for the Phoenix Bridge Company and designed several major bridges, including the Red Rock Cantilever Bridge over the Colorado River, which was the longest single-span cantilever in the country at that time. In late 1891, he began engineering consulting in Kansas City, Missouri, and began a long career as a designer of bridges.[373] His vertical lift bridge designs were initially met with resistance in 1891 and 1892, but he patented his design for a Chicago lift bridge in late 1893 (No. 506,571), the first of his many lift bridge patents. His lift bridge designs became more widely used between 1907 and 1917, when nearly 40 were built.[374] Waddell also designed many fixed bridges, including cantilevers such as the Goethals Bridge (1928), the Outerbridge Crossing from New Jersey to Staten Island, New York (1928), and across the Mississippi River at Cairo, Illinois (1929); swing bridges at Omaha (1893) and Jefferson City, Missouri (1896); and concrete with the Twelfth Street Bridge in Kansas City, Missouri (1915), the Arroyo Seco Bridge in Pasadena, California (1913) and the Detroit-Superior Bridge in Cleveland, Ohio (1917)—a 3,500′ long double-deck concrete bridge with a 591′ arch of nickel steel.[375]

Well known for numerous innovations in bridge engineering such as the vertical-lift bridge, development of materials suitable for large-span bridges and the use of Ni-bearing steel in girders, Waddell was also an advocate for quality training for engineers and engineers' professional status.[376] He wrote several useful and widely acclaimed books on bridges and bridge engineering, with his main work being *Bridge Engineering* in two volumes, published in 1916.[377] These aspects of his career led to his being awarded honorary degrees from various U.S. and Canadian universities. Over his career, Waddell claimed to have designed over 1,000 bridges in the United States, Japan, Russia, Cuba, Mexico and New Zealand. From 1887 to his death in 1938, he was associated with the following firms: J.A.L. Waddell (1887–1899), Waddell and Herrick (1899–1907), Waddell and Harrington (1908–1915), Waddell and Son (1915–1920), J.A.L. Waddell (1921–1926) and Waddell and Hardesty (1927–1938). He won the prestigious Norman Medal from the ASCE in 1909, 1916 and 1920 in addition to international awards.[378]

(7.5) Leffert Lefferts Buck. *From the* Journal of Bridge Engineering *5, no. 4 (November 2000).*

Leffert Lefferts Buck (Figure 7.5) was born in northern New York, and after several years at the Canton Academy, he pursued his interest in machining and served an apprenticeship as a skilled machinist.[379] After this experience, he enrolled in the first class at St. Lawrence University and likely pursued civil engineering. However, after only two years, the Civil War broke out and Buck left college to enlist in the 60th New York Infantry in October 1861. The 60th New York had an extensive history of action during the Civil War, including participation in the Battle of Antietam (where Buck was wounded in both legs by a Rebel ball).

Buck saw action in Chancellorsville, Gettysburg (where the 60th fought for three difficult days); the siege at Chattanooga, Tennessee; as part of General William T. Sherman's army that marched to the gates of Atlanta; and then Sherman's March to the Sea and Savannah, Georgia, in 1864. The 60th was mustered out of service on July 17, 1865. Buck then studied engineering at Rensselaer Polytechnic Institute—yet another connection between RPI and Pencoyd—as a sophomore in the class of 1868. Although small by modern standards, Rensselaer was the largest engineering school in the country. Buck went on to be chief engineer for many important bridges, including work on Roebling's bridge (cable, anchorage, deck and tower rehabilitation); Upper Falls Suspension Bridge, Niagara (longest span bridge over Niagara, 1889–98); Upper Falls Arch Bridge, Niagara (longest arch bridge in the world, 1898–1938); Driving Park Avenue, Rochester, New York; Platt Street Bridge (Genesee River Crossing), Rochester; Verrugas Viaduct, Peru (highest bridge in the world when built, 1873–89); Verrugas Cantilever, Peru (first cantilever

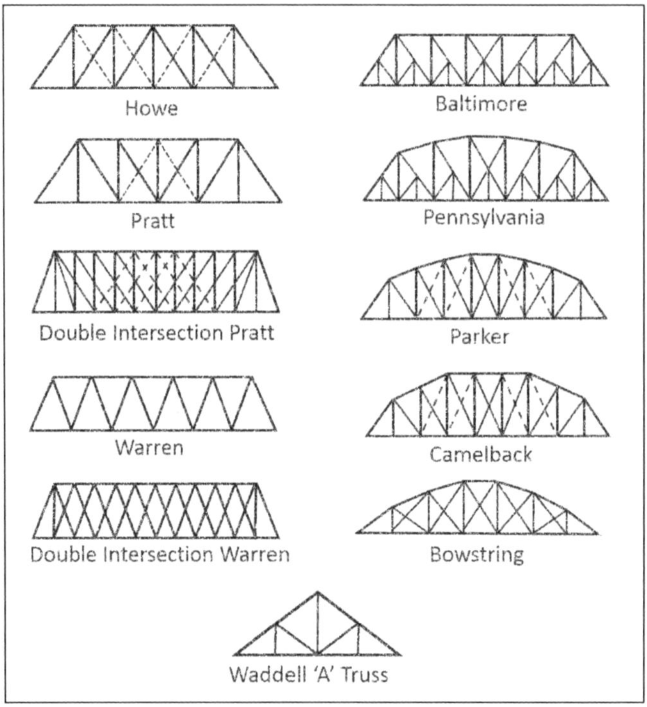

(7.6) Truss bridge designs used in Pencoyd bridge projects. Note also: illustrates the difference between a standard Pratt truss and a Whipple-Murphy (double intersection Pratt) truss (see chapter 2). *After HAER Bridge Truss Type Poster, 1976, redrawn by author.*

in South America, 1890–1938); and the Williamsburg Bridge, East River, New York (longest suspension bridge in the world, 1903–24). Buck worked with Pencoyd on the Platt Street (Genesee River Crossing) and the Upper Steel Arch Bridge (Niagara River) bridges in 1891 and 1897–98, respectively.

By 1886, Pencoyd had opened a new bridge and construction shop, thus expanding its expertise into bridge building. In addition, it had established a bridge and construction office with ample space for designers and template work.[380] Here are descriptions of fourteen of the most important and interesting bridges from this period, crossing some of America's largest and critical waterways (Delaware, Monongahela, Susquehanna, Potomac, James, New, Genesee, Niagara, Missouri and Mississippi): Selinsgrove (1888), Smithfield Street (1890), Genesee River (1891), Mule Bridge (1891), Bellefontaine (1892), Harpers Ferry (1894), Niagara Steel Arch (1897), Waddell A Truss (1898), Mahoning Creek Trestle (1899), Prince Railroad New River (1899), Joshua Falls (1899), 52nd Street, Philadelphia (1902), Rondout Creek viaduct, New York (1905) and the bridge across the Mississippi at Thebes (1905). The various bridges incorporated different through truss designs, including Pratt, Parker, Warren, Pennsylvania trusses and several viaducts or trestles, as will be seen (Figure 7.6). Pencoyd published a book on structural aspects of bridges, one of several influential and heavily utilized texts in the engineering world.[381]

SELINSGROVE (1888–1892)

The Susquehanna River crossing in Selinsgrove was made as early as 1871 by the Sunbury & Lewistown Railroad, then by the Pennsylvania Railroad via the Schuylkill and Juniata Railroad and then finally in 1902 by the Pennsylvania Railroad. The Selinsgrove Bridge is a single-track structure that utilizes Cherry Island to make the river crossing two shorter spans—east and west. The spans are wrought-iron Pratt trusses of two different designs, made by two different companies. The east channel piers were built in 1888, and an 1892 contract with A.&P. Roberts (agents for Pencoyd Bridge & Construction Company) stipulates the removal of "four Howe trusses" but does not indicate the material of those spans.[382] Pencoyd erected four wrought-iron, pin-connected Pratt through trusses (28′-0″ deep, placed 16′-0″ on center), each 173′-0″ long, with a 12′-6″ skew (Figure 7.7). The portals have a distinctive Greek Revival pediment. Most of the panels are

(7.7) Selinsgrove Bridge over Susquehanna. *HAER PA-554, Pennsylvania Railroad, Selinsgrove Bridge, Spanning Susquehanna River, south of Cherry Island, Selinsgrove, Snyder County, Pennsylvania.*

21′-7½″ long, and the aforementioned skew is created with a 16′-4½″ end panel opposite a 27′-10½″ half-hip end panel at both ends. It is thought that some Pennsylvania Railroad maintenance work in 1930 may have been carried out to distribute loads among the eye-bar members and to strengthen stringers and floor beams. The 12 west channel spans were constructed by the Keystone Bridge Company and have unusual subdivided end panels, in which an extra diagonal delivers part of the first-floor beam's load to the midpoint of the end post. The first two spans from the east are 175′-0″ long; the remainder are 10 172′-0″ spans, and all 12 spans were built during 1888 and 1889.[383]

GENESEE RIVER CROSSING (1891)

The Platt Street Bridge, or Genesee River Crossing (Figure 7.8), is a 858′ long truss bridge that connected the east and west sides of Rochester when it was built in 1891.[384] The bridge also allowed a panoramic view of Rochester that was lost when the Falls Field was converted into industrial space in the 1880s. The bridge closed permanently in 1977, as the City of Rochester decided to convert it into a landscaped pedestrian walkway lined with benches.[385] When it was completed in 1982, the bridge was renamed the Pont de Rennes in honor of Rochester's sister city in France. This bridge was designed by Leffert L. Buck, who also designed the Driving Park bridge in Rochester, which was replaced in 1988.[386]

(7.8) Genesee River Crossing (or Platt Street Bridge) in Rochester. *From the Albert R. Stone Negative Collection, Rochester Museum and Science Center, Rochester, New York.*

MULE BRIDGE MANAYUNK (1889)

The Philadelphia & Reading Railroad's Mule Bridge was built in 1889 and takes its name from an 1818 wooden structure that it replaced.[387] The first Mule Bridge was for the Schuylkill Navigation Company's canal towpath, while its successor was for the PRRR's Venice Branch freight railroad. The single-track bridge connects lower Manayunk to the PRRR main line on the west bank of the Schuylkill River (Figure 7.9). The bridge is 623′ long, with an S-curve alignment. It begins on the south end with 93′ and 55′ half-through plate girders, followed by a deck plate girder, then two 93′, one 92′ and two 78' spans, all riveted wrought-iron lattice deck girders on stone piers. The bridge curves northwest and comes ashore on the north side just behind the Manayunk Brewing Company.

(7.9) The Mule Bridge connecting Lower Merion and Manayunk, for the P&R Railroad. *HAER PA-552, Philadelphia and Reading Railroad Mule Bridge, 2000.*

SMITHFIELD STREET BRIDGE, ADDITION OF THIRD LENTICULAR TRUSS (1890)

Smithfield Street bridge over the Monongahela River in Pittsburgh was designed by Gustav Lindenthal and utilized a double-truss lenticular design.[388] This unusual design was originally one lane, but expansion to a second lane (and third truss) was part of the original plan. The original structure was built in 1883; the third truss was added in 1891.[389] Pencoyd designed, fabricated and erected the third truss, which allowed street trolley access across the bridge as well.[390] The two lanes were different widths, and the bridge had an asymmetry in the distances between the three trusses (Figure 7.10). In 1911, the third truss was moved upstream several feet so that the lanes would be of equal length, and that is the current configuration of the bridge.[391]

BELLEFONTAINE (1892)

Designed by George Morison and built over the Missouri River near the Bellefontaine Bluffs (Figure 7.11), the steel superstructure consisted of four Baltimore through trusses with pin-connected detailing.[392] Each span was 440′ long and 55′ tall, subdivided into 16 panels, 27′6″ long. The truss width for the double-track structure was 30′ between centers of the

Top: (7.10) Smithfield Street bridge in 1900, with third truss on left side; third truss made by Pencoyd Bridge and Construction Company. *HAER PA-2, Smithfield Street Bridge, 1974.*

Bottom: (7.11) Bellefontaine Bridge over the Missouri River near St. Louis. *HAER MO-26, Bellefontaine Bridge, 1985.*

webs. Morison specified open-hearth steel exclusively for the Bellefontaine Bridge. This material was rolled by several eastern mills: the Carbon Steel Company, Carnegie Steel Company, Midvale Steel Company, Pencoyd Iron Works, Pennsylvania Steel Company and the Standard Steel Casting Company. The Union and Keystone Bridge companies produced the eyebars, and the New Jersey Steel and Iron Works fabricated all the bridge components. With each of the four spans weighing 2.8 million pounds, the total superstructural weight of the Bellefontaine Bridge exceeded 11.2 million pounds.

Harpers Ferry (1894)

The original bridge at Harpers Ferry was designed by Latrobe in the 1830s, and in 1892–94 the bridge and train station were redesigned and rebuilt. The new train station was designed by architect E. Francis Baldwin and is notable for its long service to the region. The new double-track bridge across the Potomac River was completed in 1894 and located just upstream from the old Bollman bridge (Figure 7.12).[393] The new bridge was stronger and much needed to handle the larger and heavier engines and trainloads using the B&O line. To build the substructure, cables stretched from the West Virginia to the Maryland banks, allowing construction crews to lower the Gettysburg Granite stones that would make up the new bridge's eight masonry piers set on solid bedrock. The bridge's steel superstructure was fabricated by Pencoyd and consisted of a combination of six deck plate girder spans and three Pratt through trusses. The stronger bridge could accommodate the heavier loads but was also 8′ to 11′ higher than the previous bridge, making it less vulnerable under flood conditions. Finally, the trestle work—for which 500,000 linear feet of lumber was required—was completed by contractor James McLean. The significance of this bridge is summed up by the Historic American Engineering Record (HAER) document describing its history and construction: "Though not particularly long or massive, the new bridge represented state-of-the-art engineering in the 1890s. Still in use today, the bridge has been called an excellent representative of steel, pin-connected trusses and standardized bridge design of the period."

(7.12) Harpers Ferry bridge with three Pratt through trusses on the right. *HAER MD-16, Baltimore & Ohio Railroad, Harpers Ferry Bridge Piers, Junction of Potomac & Shenandoah Rivers, Sharpsburg, Washington County, Maryland.*

Niagara Steel Arch (1897–98)

(7.13) Upper Steel Arch Bridge from Canadian side of Niagara Falls. *Niagara Falls (Ontario) Public Library.*

The Upper Steel Arch Bridge over the Niagara River was built in 1897–98 by Pencoyd, under the direction of engineers L.L. and R.S. Buck, and replaced an earlier suspension bridge.[394] This bridge was situated north of the American falls and was the fourth bridge built at this site. When built, it was the greatest steel arch bridge in the world, spanning 840′ with trusses connecting the main span to the top of each shoreline (Figure 7.13).[395] The bridge had a double track for electric car service but was wide enough to also allow carriages and pedestrians.

High winds caused the bridge to sway, as they also did for suspension bridges. There were multiple incidents of pedestrians and vehicles nearly being blown off the bridge. An additional issue was the slippery wooden floor, which enabled a motorist to skid off the bridge into the gorge.[396] But the factor that led to the ultimate demise of the bridge was not rain or wind but ice. One year after the Upper Steel Arch bridge was completed (1899), spectacular ice bridges formed below the falls, and ice collected around the bridge abutments to a height of 80′. The force of the ice against the bridge cause some of the steel piers to bend—this led to construction of protective walls around abutments the following summer. From 1899 until 1938, there were no problems, but on January 23, 1938, a large amount of ice from Lake Erie again went over the falls, jamming up the river gorge, and pushed against the abutments and hinge supports of the bridge, causing severe structural damage.[397] The bridge remained intact for a few days, but it was clearly going to fail and thus attracted great crowds of spectators. At 4:20 p.m. on January 27, 1938, the ice pushed the bridge from its abutment on the American side, pulling the bridge off its abutment on the Canadian side, and the structure fell into the river in one piece. Salvage operations began on February 2 and led to breaking the span into two pieces using dynamite. As the ice subsided, portions of the bridge broke away and either sank to the bottom of the gorge or floated on large chunks of ice until finally slipping off in the deepest portions of the river gorge and valley to ultimately disappear beneath the surface as well.[398]

WADDELL A TRUSS (1898)

The Waddell A truss bridge over Linn Branch Creek near Trimble, Missouri, is, as of June 1980, one of only two surviving examples of this truss type (Figure 7.14).[399] In 1898, the Linn Branch Creek Bridge was built as part of the Quincy, Omaha and Kansas City Railway connecting Kansas City with Pattonsburg, Missouri. The line was primarily used for agricultural service and transportation of farming products to the end users. After a 1939 merger into the Chicago, Burlington and Quincy Railroad system, the line between Kansas City and Pattonsburg was abandoned, and the Waddell A truss bridge over Linn Branch Creek remained unused for over a decade. In 1953, it was converted into a highway bridge as part of Missouri Highway State Route 4. Nearly 25 years later, construction of the Smithville Dam by the U.S. Army Corps of Engineers required its removal, and HAER assisted in documenting and archiving the bridge and this important type of structure. It was moved to its site in English Park along the Missouri River.

The A truss is a significant type of a late nineteenth-century short-span railroad bridge that used pin connections to join its major structural members and was designed and patented by J.A.L. Waddell.[400] When Waddell returned to America (from Japan) in 1886, he was interested in developing an effective short span bridge. He was dissatisfied with the design of railroad bridges for short spans between that of plate-girder and a length of about 150′; pin-connected ordinary trusses were too light, and riveted structures were not yet reliable, with field riveting of uncertain and inconsistent quality. He had an opportunity to design some short span bridges for the Kansas City, Pittsburg and Gulf Railroad Company in 1893, which subsequently built four approximately 100′ span bridges. Waddell received a patent for this bridge on November 13, 1894 (Patent No. 529,220). The bridges exhibited excellent rigidity under traffic, were economical (less metal and high interchord bracing) and practical (pins not rivets) and were used on the St. Louis Southwestern Railway and by the Nippon Railway Company of Japan. The A truss thus became Waddell's ideal solution to the problem he originally

(7.14) Waddell A Truss in its original location in Missouri. *HAER MO-8 Waddell "A" Truss Bridge, 1981.*

confronted when criticizing the British-designed Japanese railroad bridges of the early 1880s (see chapter 9). In Waddell's patent, he acknowledged that the A truss configuration had been commonly used for roof trusses, and he specifically confined his patent to railroad bridge structures, where the trusses are connected by lateral bracing.

Eventually, with the advent of more reliable and efficient pneumatic field riveting equipment, the need for rigid short span, pin-connected bridges dwindled. The A truss bridge design and specifically the Linn Branch Creek Bridge represents the period when American bridge designers and civil engineers began challenging European approaches internationally.[401] The Linn Branch Creek Bridge is thus a rare and distinctive structure of national significance.

Mahoning Creek Trestle, Pennsylvania (1899)

The 1,000′ single-track trestle carries the CSXT Railroad over Mahoning Creek in northwest West Mahoning Township, Pennsylvania (Figure 7.15). Built in 1899, the trestle consists of nine spans, with the main center span Warren deck truss measuring 120′ and all other spans deck girder sections. The steel latticework rests on reinforced concrete piers, and stone abutments at the sides anchor the trestle to each bank. The trestle was built for the Buffalo, Rochester & Pittsburgh (BR&P) Railway and is significant in the county's transportation history; it carries part of a BR&P line connecting Punxsutawney and Dayton that was constructed in 1899.[402]

(7.15) Mahoning Creek Trestle built in 1899. *HAER PA-266 Mahoning Creek Trestle, 1987.*

PRINCE RAILROAD BRIDGE, NEW RIVER, WEST VIRGINIA (1899)

(7.16) The Prince railroad bridge across the New River at flood stage. *From West Virginia and Regional History Center, WVU Libraries.*

The town of Prince was established in 1870 and became a ferry location and store. As coal mining operations grew in the area and across the river in Royal, the town fluorished. The Chesapeake and Ohio Railroad built a depot and bridge in Prince in 1899.[403] The three spans connected Prince and Royal. The bridge is still in use and has survived some impressive river levels (Figure 7.16).

JOSHUA FALLS BRIDGE, JAMES RIVER (1901)

In 1901, the Chesapeake and Ohio Railroad built four steel bridges in Virginia and West Virginia: one near Joshua Falls, Virginia, over the James River (771′ long); one near Snowden, Virginia (714′ long), over the James River; one near Longdale, Virginia, over the Cow Pasture River (298′ long); and the fourth near Lowell, West Virginia, over the Greenbrier River (560′ long). The bridges were all built on old masonry except at Third Greenbrier, where four piers were making a total of eight piers.[404]

The Joshua Falls Bridge is associated with a nationally significant transportation corridor, the James River of Virginia, and constituted the only crossing of the James River by rail between the cities of Richmond and Lynchburg (Virginia), several miles downstream from the city of Lynchburg.[405] This crossing was in the same location as two earlier transportation systems—the James River and Kanawha Canal and the Richmond & Alleghany Railroad. The bridge was constructed in 1901 by Pencoyd for the Chesapeake and Ohio Railway. It was a five-span Pratt through pin truss structure supported by stone abutments and piers that were constructed in 1881 for an earlier railroad bridge; the trusses are identifiable as Pratt trusses for their distinctive arrangement of vertical compression members and diagonal tension members.[406] The bridge is significant, as the bridge's five spans are about 153′ to 154′ long, which is unusually long for historic Pratt trusses; the total length of the bridge was 781′–3½″, with trusses measuring 28′-6″ in height from the centers of the top and bottom chords. The end posts are encased in exterior cover plates with interior lattice reinforcing. The sides of the trusses are formed by vertical latticed posts (or struts) and diagonal eye-bars that link the top and bottom chords.

52ND STREET BRIDGE, PHILADELPHIA (1902)

In the late nineteenth century, many large American cities required railroads to remove their tracks above city streets. The 52nd Street Station complex was a transformation of the tracks in grade-separation efforts in Philadelphia, which resulted in an elevated embankment carrying the main line of the Pennsylvania Railroad (PRR) parallel to Lancaster Avenue.[407] The problem was that the railroad's Schuylkill Division diverged from the main line west of 52nd Street, turning sharply northward on its way to Reading. In the opposite direction, Schuylkill Division trains had to cross over outbound main-line tracks on their way into Philadelphia. To eliminate this conflict, PRR engineers designed a three-level solution in 1901, separating not only inbound and outbound trains but also freight and passenger traffic. The 52nd Street bridge is a single-track fly-over bridge built to carry outbound passenger trains over the freight yard. This bridge is significant in that it is an exceptionally long pin-connected Parker through truss, crossing the freight tracks at an obtuse angle.[408] The bridge is 45′-0″ deep at midspan and measures 387′-10″ from center to center of its endmost pins, which exceeds the commonly accepted practical limit of 300′-0″ for the Parker type.[409] Although the bridge span was significant, the eastern approach to the Parker truss is also notable and consists of 48 deck girder and truss spans.[410]

THEBES BRIDGE (1905)

The double-track bridge across the Mississippi River at Thebes, Illinois, is 36 miles north of the confluence with the Ohio River. It was completed by the Southern Illinois & Missouri Bridge Company to connect the Illinois Central, the Chicago & Eastern Illinois and the St. Louis Southwestern Railroads on the Illinois bank with the Frisco System, the Iron Mountain and the St. Louis Southern Railroads on the Missouri bank of the river; its construction was authorized by an act of Congress on January 26, 1901.[411]

At this point, the river is about 2,700′ wide between high-water banks and about 50′ deep. Between the viaducts, the steel superstructure has a length of 2,750′ 4″ (Figure 7.17). The bridge was one of the largest across the Mississippi River or elsewhere in this country in regard to the number of long, heavy spans, and has a long 671′ center channel cantilevered span. About half of its $2.8 million cost was for the 26,880,000-pound steel superstructure, which was made with five spans of continuous pin-connected trusses supported on six piers of ashlar masonry with foundations in solid rock, with pneumatic caisson footings. The superstructure is symmetrical about its center with a 521′ intermediate span and a 518′ shore span on each side.[412]

Several designs were considered, and details of those are worth mentioning. One design called for five free spans of about the same total weight; erection of such spans on high falsework in deep water could not have been accomplished in one season. Although the free spans would have been more rigid and perhaps more aesthetically pleasing than the cantilever chosen, they would have required wider piers and been more costly. A second design with a center cantilever span, two anchor spans and two free short shore spans was considered but would have involved a much larger number of different truss members, thus adding cost as well. The design chosen had the greatest number of duplicate members, and omission of towers allowed the use of an overhead traveler for the erection of the channel span, thus ensuring a more regular outline for the bridge.[413]

How was this bridge constructed? Most truss members are pin connected, but some are also riveted. All of the superstructure except the 671′ center span was erected on pile falsework by an ordinary three-bent wooden gantry traveler. All steel and timber were loaded and unloaded by four self-propelling wooden derrick cars of 20-ton capacity. Carloads of material were delivered to the bridge mainly by locomotives, except for a few central spans for which the material was drawn by locomotives from the yard to an incline, where it was transferred to barges and towed to one of the piers. A 50-horsepower hoisting engine and a steel derrick on the pier top then hoisted materials up from the barges, where they were loaded on push cars and sent to their destination.

Erection was commenced simultaneously on both sides of the river in the middle of the intermediate spans and progressed on false work both ways to the river piers and to the abutments, after which it was continued between the center piers by the cantilever method.[414]

The gantry travelers were built of pine and fir, mounted on four four-wheel trucks on standard-gauge tracks, and were rigged with manila rope main tackles, rope runners and small tackles, all operated by one six-spool and one eight-spool hoisting engine, carried on cars on standard-gauge tracks directly behind the travelers. The travelers were secured by four guy lines from the top of each to the falsework, by chocks under the wheels and by clamps operated by steamboat ratchets.[415]

The 671′ center span was erected simultaneously from the two piers by a pair of overhead simple cantilever travelers (Figure 7.18), each about 128′

Top: (7.17) Completed Thebes bridge in 1905. *From the* Engineering Record, *July 22, 1905, 98.*

Bottom: (7.18) Thebes cantilever bridge with travelers in place to finish connection. *From the* Engineering Record, *September 16, 1905, 330.*

long and 57′ high. Besides travelers, the erection machinery included a locomotive, a tug, a steamboat, two car transfer barges, two air-compressor plants, a 10-ton steel derrick and a four-spool hoisting engine. Alfred Noble and Ralph Modjeski were the engineers of the bridge, and the American Bridge Company of New Jersey—Paul L. Wolfel, chief engineer—was the contractor for the superstructure, which was built at the Pencoyd and Lassig plants. The American Bridge Company of New York—S.P. Mitchell, chief engineer—was the contractor for the erection, which was executed on a subcontract let to the Kelly-Atkinson Construction Company of Chicago, F.C. Fisher, engineer in charge.[416] As with many of the bridges described in this chapter, the Thebes bridge remains in use today, over 110 years later.

RONDOUT VIADUCT, NEW YORK (1905)

The West Shore Railroad crossed the Rondout Creek about one mile from Kingston, New York, on Bridge No. 141, the longest structure on the line, being 1,228′ between abutments and having a height of 154′ from high water to base of rail. The bridge was designed for 82-ton locomotives and 30-ton cars operated at comparatively low speeds. Improvements intended to make this road take the fast and heavy freight and traffic called for a heavier structure.[417] It was required to replace the old structure by the new without interrupting the train service. This requirement together with the height of the track above water level, the poor quality of the bottom, the depth of the water and the necessity of preserving a wide opening for navigation, made the erection of the bridge exceptionally difficult and expensive. The steel for the superstructure was delivered by cars to a storage yard on top of the bank about 500′ south of the bridge. It was unloaded by two standard American Bridge Company steel derricks with 40′ masts and 65′ booms and was classified and stored in piles until delivered for erection on small cars pushed by hand to the bridge site.

The floor system for the channel span was first assembled, after which the trusses were erected and the pins driven from the outsides of the trusses with a 400-pound battering ram made from a section of steel rail. Field rivets were driven by pneumatic hammers and bucked up by hand. The superstructure weighed about 3,000 tons and was erected by an average force of 50 men in about six months. It is notable that notwithstanding the great height of the structure and the difficult character of operations, the work was completed without any fatalities. The 270′ span weighed 798-tons and excepting the eye-bars, which were made at Athens, was built at Edge Moor. The whole of the superstructure was built at the Edge Moor, Athens and Pencoyd plants of the American Bridge Company of New Jersey, Paul L. Wolfel, chief engineer. The bridge was erected by the American Bridge Company of New York under S.P. Mitchell, chief engineer, and H.F. Lofland, manager of the eastern division.

The bridges covered in this chapter are just several examples of the types and sizes of structures known to have been designed and fabricated by Pencoyd. A more complete list of those of known location in the United States (120) is given in Table 7.1 and Figure 7.19. In many cases, Pencoyd may have provided the superstructure for a contractor who received credit for the work/project or the project may have been built by the American Bridge Company—but the Pencoyd plant contributions are not easily identified especially after (circa) 1905. Certainly, many projects of the American Bridge Company from 1905 onward used materials and components from their various plants for any given bridges, and since Pencoyd was for many years the largest producer, Pencoyd products were certainly used in numerous bridges that are not listed here because they have not been easily identified as such. Therefore, the number of bridges listed in Table 7.1 is a minimum; the true number is much higher. Additionally, some of the bridges have been removed or destroyed and their exact location unknown, so they do not appear in Figure 7.19. For example, the locations of the early wrought-iron bridges designed by John W. Murphy and called Beale's bridges are not easily found or known but are included as a single entry in Table 7.1. On the other hand, other bridges that may have been destroyed but their location is known do appear in Figure 7.19.

TABLE 7.1

Bridges in the United States with Full or Partial Pencoyd Role

*indicates featured in this chapter; @ indicates moveable bridge featured in chapter 8

1) Saucon Creek, NPRR | 1856
2) Easton/Phillipsburg, Morris Canal (165′ span) | 1859
3) Frankford Creek, Bridesburg (65′ span, with draw) | 1859
4) Foglesville Railroad (50′ span) | 1859

5) Illinois Central Railroad, under General McClellan; Ullin, Illinois Cache River (160′ span) | 1859
6) Jordan Creek at Allentown, Lehigh Valley Railroad (2 x 125′ spans) | 1859–60
7) A. Campbell & Co., canal at Manayunk (50′ span) | 1859–60
8) Poteau River Iron Bridge, Fort Smith, Oklahoma (example of one of Beale's Bridges erected for the U.S. hovernment; seven Whipple-Murphy bridges for Beale's Wagon Route on the Plains, 4′ x 100′ and 3′ x 50′ spans, on the Whipple plan, with cast-iron arches) | 1860
9) Mauch Chunk, Lehigh Valley Railroad |1863
10) Kentucky High Bridge (first) | 1875–77
11) C&BL/Little Conemaugh River, Pennsylvania | 1886
12) Blackstone River Bridge, Milbury, Massachusetts | 1889
13) Blackstone River Bridge, Uxbridge, Massachusetts | 1889
14) Fishing Creek Bridge, Reading, Pennsylvania | 1889
15) Frisco Bridge, Memphis, Tennessee/Mississippi River | 1889–92
16) Walnut Street bridge, PA1781 HAER | 1889–93
17) Broad Street Bridge, Providence, Rhode Island | 1890
18) Smithfield Street third truss, Pittsburgh, Pennsylvania | 1890–91 *
19) Seaford Railroad station swing bridge, Delaware | 1890 @
20) Riverton Bridge, West Mifflin, Pennsylvania | 1891
21) Clarksville/Cumberland River Swing, Tennessee | 1891 @
22) Genesee River Crossing and viaduct, Rochester, New York | 1891 *
23) Mule bridge, Manayunk, Pennsylvania | 1891 *
24) Layton Bridge, Youghigheny River, Pennsylvania | 1892
25) LIRR, Beach Channel Drawbridge, New York | 1892
26) Michael Haverty Bridge, Kansas City, Missouri | 1892
27) Wabash River Bridge, Attica, Indiana | 1892
28) Susquehanna River Island Bridge, Selinsgrove, Pennsylvania | 1892 *
29) Mahaffey Railroad Bridge | 1892
30) Bellefontaine Bridge, Missouri River | 1892 *
31) Dutch Kills Creek Swing Bridge, New York | 1893 @
32) Harpers Ferry/Potomac River, West Virginia | 1894 *
33) Levisa Branch Bridge, Kentucky | 1894
34) Old Katy Bridge, Lyon Creek, Kansas | 1895
35) Katy Trail, Rivaux Creek, Missouri | 1896
36) Clark Fork River Bridge No. 2, Missoula, Montana | 1896
37) Bitterroot River Bridge, Missoula, Montana | 1896
38) Delair Bridge, Pennsylvania–New Jersey | 1896 @

39) Newaukum River, Washington | 1896
40) NPRR, Wilkeson Creek Bridge, Washington | 1896
41) Willapa River (2nd crossing), Washington | 1896
42) Snoqualmie, Washington (now gone) | 1896 (moved in 1916)
43) Fitchburg Line Overpass, Massachusetts | 1896
44) Henry's Fork Snake River Eastern Idaho Railroad | 1896 (relocated 1914)
45) Susquehanna Railroad Bridge Wrightsville, Colombia (PRR) | 1897 (removed 1964)
46) Honeymoon Bridge, Niagara Falls | 1897 (collapsed 1938) *
47) Spreckels Sugar factory, near Salinas, California | 1897 (Spreckels, Conway Thesis, 1999)
48) Katy Trail, Loutre River, Missouri | 1897
49) Katy Trail, Bonne Femme Creek, Missouri | 1897
50) Moniteau Creek | 1897 (destroyed 1942)
51) Joplin Branch Spring River Bridge | 1897
52) Pryor Creek, Oklahoma (near Tulsa) | 1898
53) Passumpsic River, Vermont | 1898
54) Snohomish Whitehorse Trail, Oso, Washington | 1898
55) New Bedford–Fairhaven Middle Bridge, Massachusetts | 1898–99 @
56) Katy Trail, Little Bonne Femme Creek, at Missouri River, Missouri | 1898
57) Waddell A Truss, English Landing Park, Missouri | 1898 *
58) Danville Riverwalk Bridge, Dan River, Virginia | 1898
59) Maiden Lane Bridge, Albany New York | 1899 @
60) Sumantown Road Bridge, Maryland | 1899
61) Rock Island Arkansas River Bridge | 1899
62) Mahoning Creek Trestle, Pennsylvania | 1899 *
63) Pine Creek Kittaning, PA (3) | 1899
64) Katy Trail, Hart Creek, Missouri | 1899
65) Katy Trail, Hillers Creek, Missouri | 1899
66) Katy Trail, Logan Creek, Missouri | 1899
67) Katy Trail, Massie Creek Loutre Slough, Missouri | 1899
68) Mount Vernon Dry Creek Bridge, Mount Vernon, Ohio | 1899
69) Kokosing River Bridge, Mount Vernon, OH | 1899
70) Prince Railroad Bridge, West Virginia, New River | 1899 *
71) Kiskiminetas River corssing near Freeport, Pennsylvania | 1899
72) Clarion River Crossing near Ridgeway, Pennsylvania | 1899
73) Fort Point Channel Bridge, Summer Street, Boston, Massachusetts | 1899
74) Broadway/Colonie Street Overpass, Albany | 1900
75) PRR Allegheny River Bridge, Pennsylvania | 1900

76) Pencoyd Bridge, Pencoyd, Pennsylvania | 1900
77) Mustang Creek Pony Truss (near Sadler, Texas) | 1900
78) Red River Bridge, Ogden, Arkansas | 1900 @
79) Bay Saint Louis, Mississippi | 1900 @
80) Tensaw River, Alabama | 1900
81) Mobile River, Alabama | 1900
82) Streams north of Mobile, Alabama | 1900
83) Bellaire Bridge, Benwood, West Virginia (approach) | 1900
84) Chase Creek Railroad Bridge, Arizona | 1901
85) Chicago Sanitary and Ship Canal, Eight Track Bridge Cook County, Illinois | 1901
86) LV–Delaware River Bridge, Phillipsburg, Pennsylvania | 1901
87) Joshua Falls CSX, Virginia | 1901 *
88) Second James River, near Snowden, Virginia | 1901
89) Cow Pasture River, near Longdale, Virginia | 1901
90) Greenbriar River, near Lowell, West Virginia | 1901
91) Craig Creek, north of Roanoke Virginia near Surber | 1901 (single span)
92) Craig Creek, north of Roanoke Virginia near Surber | 1901 (double span)
93) 52nd Street Bridge, Philadelphia, Pennsylvania | 1902
94) Gray's Ferry swing bridge, Philadelphia, Pennsylvania | 1902 @
95) Des Moines River Viaduct, Fort Dodge, Iowa | 1902–3 (Pencoyd eye-bars)
96) Port Perry Bridge, Pittsburgh, Pennsylvania | 1903–4
97) Thebes Bridge | 1905 *
98) Rondout viaduct, New York | 1905 *
99) Walnut Street viaduct, Pennsylvania | 1905
100) Susquehanna River Bridge, Perryville, Maryland | 1905
101) Chew Avenue girder, Germantown, Pennsylvania | 1905
102) Point No Point swing bridge, Newark, New Jersey | 1905? @
103) Swing bridges for ML&T (Opelousas Bay, Bayous Teche, De Glaise and Grosse Tete) | 1905–6
104) Harlem Ship Canal Swing Bridge, New York | 1906 @
105) Warehouse Point Bridge, Connecticut River, Connecticut | 1907
106) George's Creek, near Greenville, South Carolina | 1907
107) Seabrook, Texas swing bridge | 1907
108) Dickinson, Texas swing bridge | 1907
109) Bayou Boeuf, Louisiana swing bridge | 1907
110) Mermentau, Louisiana swing bridge | 1907
111) Blackwell's Island Bridge (Queensboro or 59th Street), Queens approach viaduct | 1908

112) Lewes Creek Swing Bridge, Lewes, Delaware | 1915
113) Mystic River swing bridge, Mystic, Connecticut | 1919
114) Anna Marsh Hunt Bridge, Brattleboro, Vermont | 1920
115) Charles Dana Bridge, Brattleboro, Vermont | 1920
116) Lake Champlain Bridge, New York–Vermont | 1927–29
117) Kerhonkson bridge, Wawarsing, New York | 1930
118) Trinity River Bridge, California (CA-1365 HAER) | 1930
119) Winding Stairs Bridge, Nantahala, North Carolina | 1935
120) Davidson River Campground Bridge, Pisgah, North Carolina | 1935

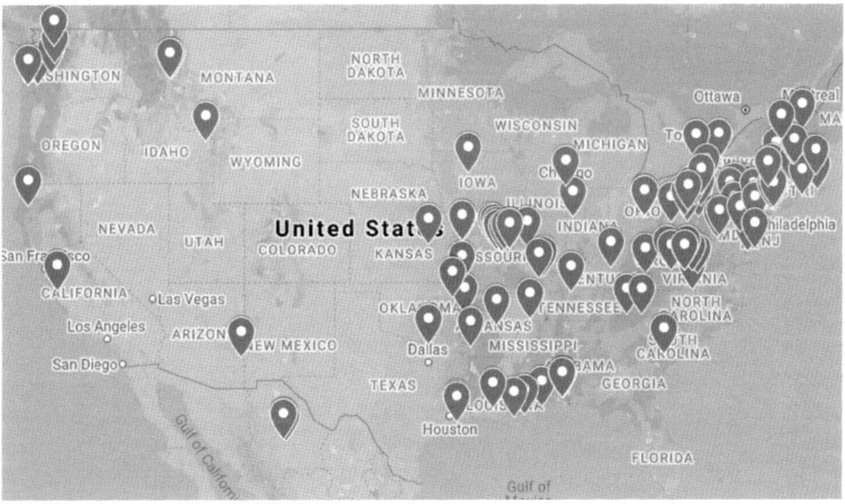

(7.19) Bridges built by Pencoyd Iron Works in the United States. This is not an exhaustive list of Pencoyd bridges, but rather those that can be identified and documented; there are likely many more that have simply not been documented to allow identification (see also Table 7.1). *Map prepared by author.*

8

Moveable Structures

Moveable bridges were a specific strength of Pencoyd Iron Works, primarily due to the influence of C.C. Schneider. Schneider designed center-bearing swing bridges for many railroads from 1880 into the twentieth century. In addition to the numerous swing bridges, Pencoyd built many railroad turntables that operated on similar principles. Its shops built and sold railroad turntables all over the world and put Pencoyd at the forefront of this high-demand technology.

Moveable bridges have various designs, including swing, bascule, retractable, lift or transporter.[418] As we will see, Pencoyd was involved with swing and bascule bridges (Figure 8.1).

The bascule bridge was made famous by the Scherzer Rolling Lift Bridge Company of Chicago, and the vertical lift bridge was made famous by J.A.L. Waddell.[419] Schneider's influential role in swing bridges and in the design of moveable bridges in general was evident with the publication of his paper "Moveable Bridges" in 1907 for the *Transactions of the American Society of Civil Engineering*.[420] This paper won him the Norman Medal of the ASCE in 1908, an honor he had previously received in 1905 for his paper "The Structural Design of Buildings."[421] In "Moveable Bridges," Schneider laid out the specifications for moveable bridge design, including bridge types, power, motors and materials.

Swing bridges were a specialty of Schneider's, and his experience and designs led to many swing bridges, including 19 for the Pennsylvania Railroad alone and 75 center-bearing swing bridges built by Pencoyd or

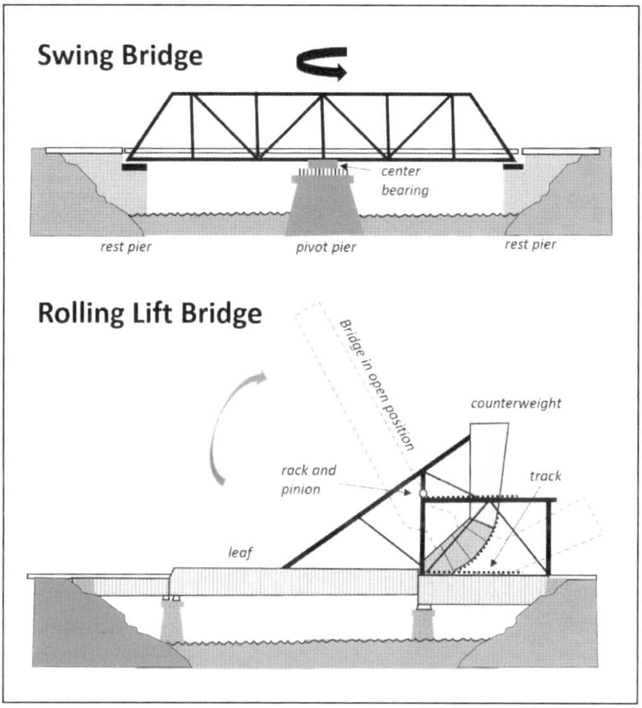

(8.1) Illustrations of two types of moveable bridges: swing and rolling lift (or bascule). *After Delaware moveable bridge report, 86–113, and redrawn by author.*

American Bridge up to 1907.[422] In a paper for the *Journal of the Western Society of Engineers*, Schneider credits his brother Ernest Schneider, a draftsman and engineer in the template shop at Pencoyd, with developing improvements in the swing bridge designs.[423]

Many of these swing spans are still working, and a few are even more than 125 years old. In this chapter, several of these bridges are described, including those still in operation at Seaford, Delaware; Cumberland, Tennessee; Dutch Kills, New York; Perryville, Maryland; New Bedford and Fairhaven, Massachusetts; and Delair, New Jersey.

A few others may have been replaced in part or in whole due to hurricane damage (Bay St. Louis, Mississippi) or wear or just in need of replacement due to their location in a rapidly changing world, such as in Chicago and Albany and Harlem, New York. In these examples will be illustrated the rim-bearing design (New Bedford, Fairhaven) or the center pivot design (Newark, New Jersey), the merits of which were discussed by Schneider.[424] Ultimately, the center-pivot design would be most widely applied.

Seaford Swing Bridge, Delaware, 1890

The first railroad bridge across the Nanticoke River in Delaware was built in 1839—a drawbridge that allowed access to several industries located upstream from Seaford. In 1856, the Delaware Railroad began service, and the end of the line was at Seaford on the Nanticoke River. As service expanded and industry grew along the Nanticoke, service was extended south, eventually requiring a more robust bridge at Seaford. In 1890, the Pencoyd Iron Works built a swing span bridge at Seaford (Figure 8.2).[425] The Nanticoke River moveable railroad bridge is an iron through-truss structure carrying a single track. Remaining in operation today, the swing span is part of a National Historical Site that includes the Seaford Railroad Station, Seaford Freight Station, the Nanticoke River moveable railroad bridge and mainline railroad tracks.[426] The moveable span adjoins the north shore. From the moveable span to the south bank, the railroad crosses a timber trestle and a causeway. The span pivots on a large iron turntable at its center. A control house over the pivot still contains manual controls, but the bridge may be operated electrically from the station.

(8.2) Seaford Swing Bridge at Seaford, Delaware. *https://blades.delaware.gov/2014/09/09/railroad-bridge-on-the-nanticoke-river*.

Cumberland (1891)

A beautiful example of an existing swing bridge is the Cumberland bridge in Clarksville, Tennessee.[427] Originally built for the Louisville & Nashville Railroad (L&N) and the New York, Chicago, & St. Louis Railroad (NKP), it is now associated with the R.J. Corman Railroad (RJCR). The swing is a pin-connected through truss, with the approach spans composed of a pair of pin-connected, eight-panel camelback through trusses.

Dutch Kills Swing Bridge (1893)

In 1880, Schneider designed a double-track swing bridge over the Dutch Kills on the Long Island Railroad (LIRR). At that time, the Dutch Kills was not navigable, but the law required a swing bridge. Schneider decided that the bridge should sit on substantial supports—as a fixed span—but could nonetheless be opened when necessary. Here he designed what may have been the first use of wedges as supports at the center of the bridge; the arrangements for operating the wedges were crude.[428] When the channel was made navigable in 1893, the 1880 bridge was replaced by a three-track structure with a center-bearing turntable of a more improved design meeting the requirements of navigation and the increased traffic of the railroad.[429] The plans included widening of the channel between the draws from 32′ to 50′ and use of electric motors to operate the draws. This was one of the westernmost extents of the LIRR.

Delair Bridge (1896)

The Delair Bridge was built in 1896 and was the first Delaware River crossing at Philadelphia, replacing a ferry crossing for passengers and freight bound for southern New Jersey.[430] From 1896 to the 1930s (when Ben Franklin Bridge opened for automobile traffic), the Delair bridge was the only crossing of the Delaware River downstream from Trenton. The bridge crosses the lower Delaware River where its extreme width, tidal currents and soft bottom made foundation work difficult and thus has several extremely long and heavy spans. Foundation work required efforts of the Philadelphia contractors Drake & Stratton Company and P. McManus Company to carry out the timber caisson foundation work beginning January 15, 1895, and the masonry piers were completed by November 1 of that year. The piers were composed of concrete cores sheathed with large granite blocks, some of which weighed more than 20 tons.[431]

Delair Bridge construction in 1895 and 1896 was of worldwide interest due to its unusual length and weight.[432] When completed, the bridge was 4,396′ long, with three 533′ Petit through-truss spans, one 323′ swing span, and 2,453′ of riveted deck approach trestles (Figure 8.3). Pencoyd Iron Works used a traveling gantry crane to erect the fixed spans, each weighing 2,091 tons, on temporary wooden falsework. The swing span (931 tons including machinery) was erected in the open position, using the fender pier as a working platform.

A lengthy trestle on the Philadelphia side elevated the tracks over city streets and climbed a slight grade up to the grade of the truss spans over the river, whereas the New Jersey approach was shorter and mostly earthen embankment. The girder spans were mostly 40′-0″, with one that was 77′-6″ on the Philadelphia side.[433]

Heavy traffic on the lower Delaware necessitated a high or movable bridge; engineers compromised by building the bridge 50′ above the river level, while also providing a swing span for the tallest vessels.[434] The swing span was the world's heaviest center-bearing swing span when built and has several innovative features, probably devised by Pencoyd's chief engineer C.C. Schneider:

> *At midspan, two heavy floor beams deliver the truss's weight to the center bearing, an unprecedentedly large steel casting with a phosphor bronze bearing surface 27″ in diameter. Another novel feature was the counterweighted latching mechanism, which failed to engage if the operator closed the bridge too quickly. To Schneider's innovations, PRR signal engineers added a control system interlocked with the railroad's signal system, to prevent trains from approaching the swing span when open. The swing span was driven by a steam engine located above the clearance envelope at mid-span, designed and built by Cyrus Currier & Sons of Newark, New Jersey.*[435]

Pencoyd's erection of the superstructure took only four additional months, as PRR officials and guests rode a ceremonial train across the nearly finished structure on March 9, 1896; regular service began on April 19.

(8.3) View along the length of the Delair Bridge. *From the* Engineering Record, *November 25, 1899, 594–97.*

The swing span is still in place, but it was replaced by a double-track vertical-lift span in 1959. The American Bridge Company added the vertical lift span by making alterations to two of the fixed spans and replacing the fixed truss west of the swing span with a 542′ long riveted Warren through truss between the lift towers. The Delair Bridge remains in active service today, carrying Atlantic City–bound passenger and freight trains.

NEW BEDFORD FAIRHAVEN BRIDGE (1899)

The rise of the whaling industry in the 1700s and thus the growth of the towns of New Bedford and Fairhaven led to the need for a bridge to Fish and Popes Islands from New Bedford and Fairhaven, respectively.[436] In 1800, wooden spans were built—only to be destroyed by hurricane in 1815. Its replacement completed in 1819 had a relatively uneventful life until it, too, was destroyed by a September storm in 1869. A new narrow wooden and stone bridge was built, replete with swing spans, and by 1876, a line of tracks was installed across the bridge. Horse-drawn cars began carrying passengers across the river, and by 1893, the railway had started using electric streetcars. Because all this heavy traffic had degraded the bridge, government officials called for a replacement. After several years of debate over issues such as collection of tolls, location of the draw portion and the point of entry and grade crossings in New Bedford, the bridge inched closer to reality when William Fish Williams and George Swain were hired for its design. The contract was initially awarded to Edge Moor Iron Works of Delaware but got delayed when the costs of the bridge nearly tripled. The county intervened, terminated the award to Edge Moor and awarded it instead to Pencoyd in 1897; by June 1898, portions of the bridge were completed and shipped to Massachusetts.[437]

In 1897, the New Bedford newspaper proudly proclaimed, "The draw span of the New Bedford and Fairhaven bridge will be one of the longest and finest in New England, and one of the greatest draw bridges of the country. Nothing this side of New York will equal it, and in some respects it will be the only one of its kind." The resulting bridge system, consisting of two highway sections on harbor islands and three bridge sections between the islands and the mainland, have lasted to this day, serving these harbor towns well—but not without rocky times.[438]

The West Bridge between New Bedford and Fish Island has ten plate girder spans (from 33′ to 71′ long), the Middle Bridge between Fish and Popes Island has a 288′ swing span and five plate girder spans (from 73′ to 82′ long), and the East Bridge spans the channel between Popes Island and Fairhaven and has nine plate girder spans (~73′ long). The total length, including the three bridge sections and portions of highway on Fish and Popes Islands, is around 4,000′. The entire crossing is known collectively as the New Bedford–Fairhaven Bridge. The Middle Bridge's swing span is of historical significance given its size and age and remains the only portion of the bridge that has not been significantly altered. The Middle Bridge is around 675′ in length and consists of a swing span and five plate girder spans, one to the west and four to the east of the swing span (Figure 8.4). The swing span measures 54′ in width between the trusses and 70′ to the edges of the sidewalks. The bridge structure is made of various plates, angle irons, lattice bars, channels, eye-bars and pins, all made from Pencoyd's open-hearth steel.[439] In June 1898, Williams visited Pencoyd to check on construction and reported that the turntable was complete and that it would soon be shipped and put together about half of a mile from the bridge for inspection before its final placement on the center pier. On June 27, 1898, the erector's outfit, derricks and engines left Philadelphia. On July 20, the laying of the steel girders for the Middle Bridge commenced with the crew laying girder spans on either side of the draw span first. They then commenced to set the carriage and drum in place on the central pier. The crew erected the tower over the drum and began to work toward either end of the draw using false work to support the steel beams. The swing span was built in the open position, and on October 30, 1898, the bridge swung into place with a perfect fit. On March 12, 1899, engineer Williams certified the Middle Bridge complete in all its details.[440]

The details of the swing span design deserve some mention:

> *The operator's house, a 10′ x 12′ wood-frame structure, contained the controls for operating the hydraulic jacks and for engaging the swing mechanism. When open, the whole draw span rests on two box girders, 54′ on a side, and joined at the top by a 4″ thick steel plate. These two girders, in turn, rest upon a system of four girders that, in turn, rest upon the circular steel drum upon which the bridge turns. The four girders (3′x13′) provide stability and distribute the weight of the swing span evenly upon the drum, which is 50″ deep, ~36′ in diameter and made of ½″ thick riveted steel plates. The drum turns on sixty-nine steel rollers, 18″ in diameter* [Figure 8.5]. *The axles of the rollers are attached to a spider frame running to the central pin of the turntable. Two electric motors, housed inside the drum, supply the power to turn the bridge. When engaged each motor turns a separate system of beveled gears that transfer the power to two vertical shafts on the drum's exterior. In turn, these shafts operate a pinion gear moving along a rack on the circumference of the drum* [Figure 8.5]. *The gears and shafts operate in opposition to each other, 180 degrees apart on the drum's circumference.*[441]

By 1899, the bridge had cost well over $1 million, and locals began calling it the "Million Dollar Bridge." The general assembly grew tired

(8.4) Photo of the middle bridge of the New Bedford Fairhaven Bridge. *HAER MA-101 Bedford-Fairhaven swing bridge, 1990.*

(8.5) Detailed images of the drum and bearings of the Bedford Fairhaven swing bridge during construction. *Courtesy of the Trustees of the New Bedford Free Public Library, NBFPL-0127.*

of passing new appropriations bills and decided to investigate the rising costs. The county let the contract for the last Western Bridge section to the American Bridge Company, and it was completed in 1903. The New Bedford–Fairhaven Bridge had taken ten years to build at a cost of $1,387,261.21. Although the state has at a few points considered replacing the bridge, either due to funding or economic problems, in 1987, the state decided to instead rebuild the bridge's mechanical and electrical systems.[442]

MAIDEN LANE, ALBANY (1899)

A double track bridge for passenger trains over the Hudson River at Albany was erected in 1872 and consisted of 12 pin-connected spans and a plate girder viaduct on columns and one draw span, for a total length of 1,800′.[443] However, increasingly heavier locomotives and cars required replacement of the older structure with a modern bridge. The city underwent a major renovation by building a new railroad bridge, passenger station and elevated tracks to keep the street level free of railroad traffic. Pencoyd designed the superstructure of the Hudson River Bridge (5,300 tons of steel); the Union Bridge Company designed the superstructure of the passenger and baggage subways and street crossings, Dwyer & Huntington of Buffalo the masonry (22,000 cubic yards) and Norcross Brothers of Worcester, Massachusetts, the passenger station.[444]

The new bridge (Figure 8.6) consisted of four fixed spans of riveted through truss of Petit design (each 181′6″ long) and one draw span (269′1″ long), seven through plate girder spans (70′3″) over the Albany Basin and one through plate girder (113′6″) over Quay Street and the Delaware & Hudson Canal Company's Railroad and a solid floor deck plate girder

(8.6) View of the Maiden Lane Bridge, Albany, under construction. *From "New York Central Improvements at Albany,"* Railway Age *28, no. 17 (October 1899): 804.*

viaduct on columns over Maiden Lane. The entire structure weighed approximately 3,700 tons.[445]

The first work done was the erection of false work under the fixed spans of the bridge. A special pile driver was built by the contractors (A.&P. Roberts Company) low enough to float under the bridge. The tracks were raised from their original level to the new grade between July and September; all the work of raising the tracks at the station and on the bridge was done without interruption of traffic or use of temporary tracks and without accident or delays. The draw portion of the bridge was completed last, designed by C.C. Schneider, consisted of radial girders on a central pivot pier and moved with electric motors.[446]

The bridge lasted until the 1960s, when an Amtrak station was built in the city of Rensselaer on the east side of the river; Interstate 787 was built along the west side of the river. These new transportation options soon made the bridge obsolete, and it was demolished in 1968.[447]

CHICAGO EIGHT-TRACK BASCULE (1900)

The crossing of the Chicago Drainage Canal, near Campbell Avenue, by eight parallel tracks of the Pittsburgh, Cincinnati, Chicago & St. Louis

Railroad, the Chicago Terminal Transfer Railroad and the Chicago Junction Railroad was a major advance in moveable bridges—before it was built, the largest movable bridges carried only four tracks. These roads operate eight tracks, there being four for the Pittsburgh, Cincinnati, Chicago & St. Louis and two for each of the other railroads. During the early work on the canal, fixed plate girder spans were used to carry the tracks over the narrow channel then required for the passage of tugs and scows.[448]

Swing designs were considered for this span, but the swing was not ideal due to concerns about the swing span remaining open in case of repairs and cutting navigation entirely whether by rail or water. An additional concern was that the center pier would be so large that it would require very narrow channels and thus restrict water passage when the span was open, thus prolonging the duration of open time and delaying the rail traffic. After deciding to abandon the swing design approach, the Sanitary District called for designs and bids for a more appropriate moveable bridge. They received plans from six companies, with the contract being awarded to the Scherzer Rolling Lift Bridge Company. A fixed bridge would be built and then transformed into a moveable bridge when the parts for the latter were ready. Bridge engineer Ralph Modjeski acted as consulting engineer for this project.[449]

The bridge crosses the channel at an angle of about 68 degrees and allows 120′ between the piers at right angles to the center line of the canal. On each side of the waterway provided for navigation is placed a main supporting pier. The McArthur Brothers Company of Chicago built the substructure and made the excavation for the full width of the channel at the site of the bridge, with work starting in May 1899. The substructure work was carried on around the clock and was completed by January 1900. The superstructure of the fixed bridge was built by the A.&P. Roberts Company (Pencoyd) and consisted of four independent double-track Scherzer rolling lift bridges, placed side by side. The spans were operated by two operators, one on each side of the canal. The movable spans were designed as three hinged arches and were to remain in this condition until such time as the canal might be opened for navigation. When the bridge was to be made movable, the track girders, rolling segments, operating struts, machinery supports, machinery and electrical equipment would be added (Figure 8.7). To open the bridge, the center pins would be unlocked by means of electrical devices and the spans rolled upward and backward on the track girders. The movable spans were counterweighted so as to be at rest at an angle of about 40 degrees When finished, the bridge could be opened or closed in 30 seconds by four

(8.7) Eight-track bascule bridge across main channel for Chicago Sanitary District, 1900. *From the* Journal of the Western Society of Engineers *15, no. 4 (August 1910): 513–28.*

40-horsepower electric motors on each side of the channel. The electric motors on each side were governed by a controller placed in the operator's house, one of which was on each side of the channel.[450]

The plans to make this a moveable bridge were changed in 1908, when the Sanitary District realized it would be essentially the same cost to convert the bridge to single-leaf bascule, as it would to transform the fixed bridge to a moveable double-leaf bascule as originally planned. Therefore, the Chicago Bridge & Iron Works was awarded a contract to erect new single-leaf spans using the existing approach spans and piers; the use of a single leaf reduced future operations and maintenance costs.[451]

Louisville and Nashville Swing Bridges (1900)

In 1900, the Louisville & Nashville (L&N) Railroad added bridges and swing spans to numerous locations in Alabama and Mississippi.[452] The Tensas River bridge, which is 2,050′ long and situated near Mobile, Alabama, was rebuilt—the grade of the crossing was raised 6′ without interruption to traffic or navigation. The 1870 bridge superstructure was replaced by 20 spans of steel deck plate girders, 75′ long each, two through Pratt truss spans of steel 150′, 6″, and a through drawbridge (swing) 258′ Pratt truss with inclined top chords. The material for these structures was furnished by Pencoyd (A.&P. Roberts) as well as the Louisville Bridge & Iron Company of Louisville, Kentucky. In addition, an 1870 iron Whipple truss draw 254′ span over the Mobile River near Mobile was replaced with a 257′ steel Pratt truss swing drawbridge, similar to the bridge at Tensas. L&N also contracted with the Louisville Bridge & Iron Company for three drawbridges, each 139′ long and one 190′ long, all with steel plate girders, steel floor beams and track stringers and erected across streams just north of Mobile. And finally, a steel drawbridge was erected at Bay Saint Louis, consisting of 11 Pratt trusses with parallel chords, steel floor beams and track stringers, with all material furnished by A.&P. Roberts. All these drawbridges were center bearing. Some of these may still be in use, but at least the Bay St. Louis Bridge is likely to have been replaced either in part or in whole from normal wear and corrosion coupled with the various hurricanes affecting the Gulf Coast since 1900.

POINT NO POINT SWING BRIDGE, PASSAIC RIVER, NEWARK (1905?)

The Point No Point swing bridge across the Passaic River was built around 1905 by the American Bridge Company. It is a center pivot swing bridge with hydraulic wedges at the ends of the span that were used to lift the ends of the bridge while swinging. This bridge was featured in a 1907 booklet on bridges of the American Bridge Company and nicely illustrates the design of the wedges used on many of the swing spans (Figures 8.8 and 8.9).[453]

(8.8) Wedge design and movement of hydraulic wedge arm—real example from the Mystic Swing Bridge, Connecticut (*right*). *HAER CT-26, Mystic River Bridge.*

(8.9) Point No Point Bridge (*top*) with focus of wedge detail (*below*). *From American Bridge Company, 1908, pamphlet.*

PERRYVILLE HAVRE DE GRACE SUSQUEHANNA RIVER BRIDGE (1905)

As the Susquehanna River reaches the Chesapeake Bay, it widens considerably starting near Perryville, Maryland. In 1905, the Philadelphia Baltimore & Washington division of the Pennsylvania Railroad erected a double track bridge from Havre de Grace to Perryville. New York–Washington trains would achieve higher speeds than previous runs, while also running 27′ higher than the previous bridge, which was about 150′ south of and parallel to the new location. With a total length of 4,154′, the bridge is divided into 18 openings of four different spans: two 197′ end spans, seven 200′ spans at the southern end, one 280′ draw span and eight 260′ spans at the northern part of the river. These relatively straightforward spans make an imposing structure, and the swing span is still in operation.[454]

Each of the three types of spans consists of a pin-connected Pratt type deck truss. This bridge was built by two companies: the Pennsylvania Steel Company manufactured and erected the 200′ spans and the shore span on the south end, whereas the Pencoyd Works of the American Bridge

Company manufactured and erected the draw span and all spans north of it. The division of the bridge superstructure between two different companies is unusual, but it was adopted in this case due to the great length and in the expectation that a considerable amount of time would be saved by following this plan. Recall that Pencoyd worked with Edge Moor Iron works to construct another Susquehanna River Bridge in 1892 (see chapter 7), so such an arrangement was not unknown to Pencoyd, albeit 12 years earlier. Wm. H. Brown was chief engineer of this work—he was frequently involved in bridge work with Pencoyd.[455]

HARLEM SHIPPING CANAL (1906)

Near the turn of the nineteenth century, rapid transit service was extended to the Harlem Ship Canal and crossing over to Van Cortlandt Park needed a more robust bridge than the existing one at Broadway and 221st (Kings Bridge), which was built in 1896 to carry a highway and two sidewalks.[456] It was decided to build a new bridge capable of expanding the service to Van Cortlandt Park and move the existing swing bridge farther down the canal to near 207th Street, where it would be used for a crossing there. The existing structure contained a pin-connected swing span about 45′ deep mounted on a rim-bearing turntable and operated by steam power, which opened it in about 15 minutes. The replacement structure would be a double-deck structure designed to carry three railroad tracks, two electric car tracks, the highway and two 10′ cantilevered sidewalks.

It was required that the replacement of the bridge be carried out without serious interruption to vehicular traffic and with minimum obstruction to navigation, so it was therefore determined to erect the new spans at positions nearby and then float them to their final positions while also floating the old spans to their new substructure at 207th Street. The superstructure was fabricated by the American Bridge Company, built mainly at the Pencoyd plant. The new span was built nearby to the old span, and once complete, the old bridge was floated downriver. Using barges and a combination of water ballast, rising tides and jacking capabilities, the old bridge was lifted off its supports and replaced by the new one within a half hour and with a crew of 30 men. The older span was left for several months in a temporary position until it was convenient to reload it on barges and move it about a mile down the canal to its new site. It was ultimately set in place at 207th

Street using a similar process but in reverse, seating the ends of the swing space using barges, cribbing and tides.

All the members for the pivot-bearing girders and the center panels and center posts of the pivot-bearing draw span were assembled and match-marked at the bridge shop at Pencoyd; later on, they were erected with minimal difficulty on pile falsework in the ship canal parallel to the bridge axis and about half a mile distant from it, the bottom of the canal near the bridge not being suitable for the erection of falsework there. The shop fitting and trial operation of all of the operating mechanism and the center panels of the span ensured accurate fitting and greatly facilitated the erection—in which no expense was involved for fitting or altering the structure. The erection was done by the Terry & Tench Construction Company, which also operated the bridge for 30 days after the draw span was put in service. The bridge was successful: the wedges could be pulled and the latch drawn in 30 seconds, the total interruption of traffic necessary to swing the span being only 4 minutes. The bridge was only out of service about 56 hours during the replacement of the draw span.

RAILROAD TURNTABLES

Because some of the design and engineering details were similar to swing spans, Pencoyd also engaged in production of railroad turntables. Production of turntables also coincides with the hiring of C.C. Schneider, undoubtedly reflecting his influence on the company's ability to expand into this market. Information on the turntables is not easy to find, but we have pieces of information that taken together weave an interesting story.

As early as 1886, a Pencoyd turntable was installed at the Little Falls, New Jersey station of the Lake Erie Railroad. Tracking back to Little Falls is difficult. There may have been turntables at Little Falls and Great Notch, but it is unclear which location this one may have come from. However, it was apparently only in service until 1917, when it was moved to Port Jervis. After being in storage until 1923, it was made part of the Shin Hollow Road Bridge, near Port Jervis.[457] Coincidentally, nearby is the Erie Turntable National Historic marker, which features a turntable exhibit.[458]

In 1890, the Virginia and Truckee Railroad installed a Pencoyd turntable in Virginia City, Nevada (Figure 8.10).[459] This 60′ turntable replaced a wooden structure and remained in service until 1941. A Cuban iron ore

(8.10) Virginia and Truckee crews jacking and cribbing a Pencoyd turntable in front of the Virginia City Roundhouse in 1890. *From S.E. Drew,* Nevada's Virginia & Truckee Railroad, *2014, 60.*

company built a railroad at the mining operation near Sigua, Cuba (south coast), in 1892, including Pencoyd turntables at each end of the nine-mile-long railroad.[460] This operation had a short lifetime, as it was later destroyed during a battle between Cuba and Spain sometime before 1898.[461] There was also a Pencoyd turntable installed at the B&O Southwest railroad shop in Chillicothe, Ohio, in 1899. This turntable was operated by an electric motor and turned by use of a trailing rail car wheel at one end that runs in the circular track.[462]

In 1900, Pencoyd produced and shipped (from New York) a turntable to the Imperial Railways of North China.[463] And in the same period, Pencoyd had an exhibit at the Pan American Exposition in Buffalo, New York. Outside the railroad exhibit and building there was a 70′ turntable installed for exhibit, and on display was a Brooks Locomotive.[464] Like the bridges and buildings, the spread of these turntables around the world further established the international reputation of Pencoyd and gave it a unique foothold in the burgeoning railroad industry.

9

Steel Bridge Building

DEVELOPMENT OF SPECIALIZED EQUIPMENT THAT STREAMLINED PRODUCTION

The fantastic design and construction of bridges initiated in the 1880s, some of which are described in detail in the previous chapters, were enabled by the development of new technical capabilities. Several of these were developed in house by Henrik Loss and James Christie and others by Philadelphian engineers such as William Sellers. The high productivity of the Pencoyd Bridge and Construction Company in the late 1890s is a result of several innovative pieces of equipment that were part of the production process. Processes developed there led ultimately to the design of the Ambridge, Pennsylvania plant of American Bridge Company (circa 1905), combining all the best practices of the 24 companies that were part of the merger, drawing heavily on Pencoyd.

Although Pencoyd built bridges in the 1850s and 1860s using wrought iron, in 1886, it built a dedicated shop with the necessary machinery and tools for the manufacture of railroad bridges and viaducts, first out of wrought iron and then eventually out of steel. The initial output that year was 300 tons per month.[465] In 1888 and 1890, the bridge shop was extended and production boosted to 600 and 2,000 tons per month.[466] By 1894, the shop was remodeled again and doubled in size, making it a building 448′ by 200′ wide.[467] The efficiency of the shop was increased by the installation of advanced modern methods. Old machinery was rearranged, and new and specially designed machines were installed. Power use shifted from steam to electricity, and machines could be operated independently of others, as opposed to many run from a centralized engine. Electrical power hoists

(9.1) Pencoyd panorama from around 1898. *From* Steel in Construction, *1898.*

and reamers and pneumatic riveters and tools were used extensively in all plant operations.[468] For fabrication efficiency, material was taken into the shop at one end and moved along an assembly line toward the other end, where it was taken out finished, loaded onto railroad cars by two 30-ton overhead cranes and shipped away. By 1901, the Pencoyd Iron Works had expanded to a length of over 3,000′ along the Schuylkill River (Figure 9.1), and production in the bridge and construction department had increased to 7,000–8,000 tons of finished product per month.[469]

SPECIALIZED EQUIPMENT

Bridge and viaduct design in the late 1800s moved toward more riveted structures. With that, bridge building needed a riveting approach that could be used both in the shop and at the construction site. In addition, beams, girders, eye-bars, chords and other bridge components had to be produced in high quantities and of high quality. This means taking the raw materials from the blooming mill and transforming them into usable bridge parts. As a result, much specialized equipment was designed to roll, punch, drill, cut, shear, anneal, rivet, forge and assemble various bridge components. Here we focus on the developments in hydraulics that allowed riveting to be performed at an all-time-high level of efficiency and the pressing, drilling and annealing of steel bars to make eye-bars. We also focus on several other pieces of specialized equipment developed by William Sellers.

Hydraulics

Innovation for aspects of the process involving hydraulics was provided by a Norwegian engineer named Henrik V. Loss. Hydraulic power was needed for eye-bar forging and riveting, and Loss, who worked at Pencoyd, made several innovations that led to improved techniques.

The first and most generalized invention involved an improved hydraulic packing design.[470] Loss's design combined a hemp packing material with a U-shaped ring on both the piston shaft and the piston head. This combination utilized the best qualities of each material; normally, either one or the other was used but not both.[471] Hydraulic packing of this design was used on a 21″ diameter ram at the Pencoyd Iron Works with pressure ranging from 1,300 to 8,000 pounds per square inch, depending on the work done. A bloom shear of the same diameter ran with water generally hot to the touch and with pressures ranging all the way up to 2,500 pounds.[472] A 10″ diameter hydraulic bridge riveter, averaging 3,000 to 4,000 rivets per day, had packing lifetime of six to eight months under pressures from 1,600 to 2,100 pounds per square inch. These enhanced performances allowed many aspects of the bridge part fabrication to be more reliable and consistent and also extended the useful lifetime of the hydraulic

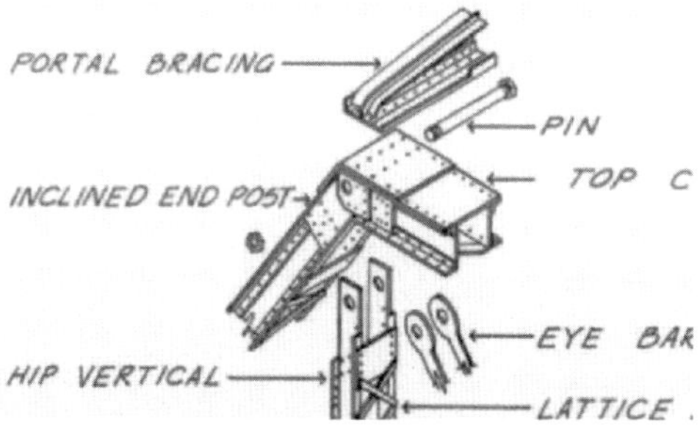

Top: (9.2) Details of pin-connected truss for steel bridges. Wrought-iron pin connections started as early as 1859 in Pencoyd designs and were common for the company; wrought iron would be replaced by steel in the 1890s. *HAER Bridge Truss Type Poster, 1976.*

Bottom: (9.3) View of eye-bar shop in the bridge and construction department, in 1895–1905 timeframe. *From* Dinglers Polytechnisches Journal *87, no. 5 (1906): 67.*

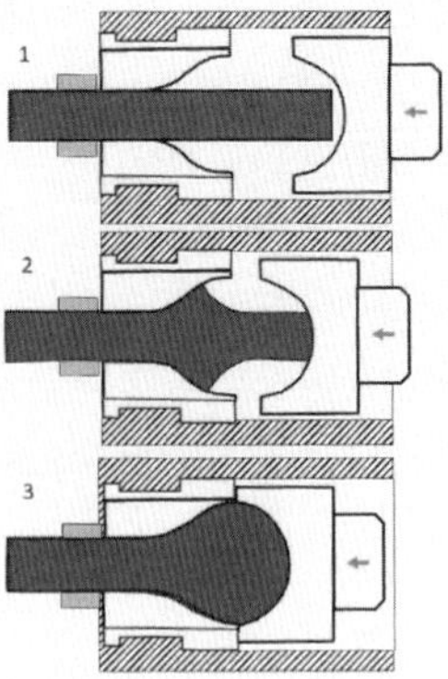

(9.4) Dies designed by Henrik Loss used to form eye-bars in the hydraulic eye-bar forge at Pencoyd. *From the* Railroad Gazette, *January 19, 1894, 43–45, and redrawn by the author.*

equipment, reducing maintenance time and cost.[473]

Loss's hydraulic system was also used in the making of eye-bars for bridges, where a multistage process had been developed at Pencoyd. Eye-bars were part of the pin-connected truss design and were the diagonal pieces connecting the upper and lower chords of a bridge (Figure 9.2).[474]

The eye-bar shop contained hydraulic machinery, embracing pumps, accumulators, upsetting machines, shearing, punching, rolling, straightening and boring tools and all the necessary heating and annealing furnaces (Figures 9.3 to 9.5).[475] Equipment developed to make eye-bars had to upset (or flatten) wrought-iron or steel bars, drill holes in the flattened portion and then anneal, re-press and straighten the length of the eye-bar for final use.[476] The eye-bar shop was designed for the manufacture of eye-bars up to 8″ wide with heads 18″ in diameter (Figure 9.3). In January 1891, 242 heads or 121 eye-bars were produced. By August 1901, after installation of a hydraulic testing machine with a pulling capacity of 600 tons operating on bars of 40′ long, 1,732 heads or 866 eye-bars were made.[477] Several of the steps in the process involved hydraulic rams, and Loss's contributions were well documented.[478]

The dies used to produce an eye-bar from an iron or steel rod were designed by Loss and utilized three different hydraulic systems operating in x, y and z directions. Loss's experiments with metal deformation in molds led to an optimum design.[479] When the rod bars are squeezed into the die, the geometry of the eye is produced as the rod is pressed into the mold (Figure 9.4).

The dies were loaded into large hydraulic presses (Figure 9.5).[480] The two large cylinders compressed the bar in the x and y planes, whereas the smaller cylinder pressed in the z plane, the latter essentially holding the rod in place while the two cylinders acted to upset the metal rod into the die. After upsetting, a hole was punched in the flattened head, and then the entire bar was rolled through the rolling machine (Figure 9.6) to remove any deformation or cutting fins from the previous steps.[481] Finally, the bars could be heated in specially designed furnaces in order to make the metal more workable, for example, in forging or rolling.[482] In this way, Pencoyd made hundreds of eye-bars annually, supporting an enormous number of bridge projects. After the merger with American Bridge Company, an eye-bar plant was designed for the new Ambridge, Pennsylvania location, and much of the design innovations developed by Loss for Pencoyd were incorporated into the new plant.[483] Ultimately, within years (1906–7), Pencoyd ceased making eye-bars and the eyebar forge was closed.[484]

Henrik Loss was born in 1861 in the port city of Christiansand, Norway, where his father was a merchant. After spending one year in a machine shop, he attended Horten's Technical School and graduated in 1878 at the age of eighteen. For five years, he held various jobs in Norway, including with the state railroad service, but in 1883, he went to America looking for broader experience.[485] He started as a mechanic in Philadelphia and then worked as a draftsman for the Baldwin Locomotive Works, but his connections to Carl Barth, his instructor at Horten, landed him a job with William Sellers as an

Top: (9.5) Upsetting machine for eye-bars. *From the* Engineering News Record, *September 29, 1898, 194–97.*

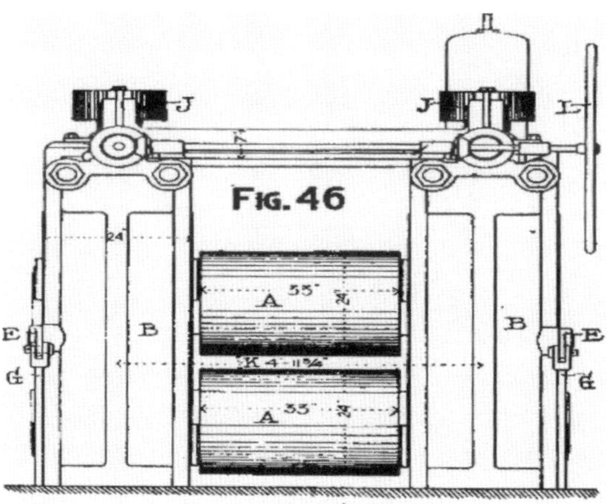

Bottom: (9.6) Eye-bar rolling machine for use after eye-bars are upset, punched and trimmed (view 46). Two chilled-steel rollers AA are adjustably set in cast steel housings BB. The lower roller is fixed, bearing in a stationary journal box, while the upper roller is adjustable. The hydraulic cylinders were of 9″ bore and 30″ stroke and supplied with a hydraulic pressure of 1,500 pounds per square inch through pipes. *From the* Engineering Record, *April 8, 1893, 377.*

engineer at the Edge Moor Iron Works, where he worked for four years. Sellers, who is discussed later in this chapter, would carry out experiments that led to the development of the rotary puddler, special gas ovens, hydraulic machinery and various additional innovations in the rolling mills.[486] Edge Moor was an inspiring and influential place for the bright mind of Loss, and he obviously broadened his experience with hydraulic machinery considerably while there. Loss next moved to the Keystone Bridge Company, one of Andrew Carnegie's firms, in Pittsburgh, where he was chief engineer.[487] Soon thereafter, he went to the Pencoyd Iron Works, where his first inventions were patented, and he helped design and build a $500,000 plant for producing eye-bars.[488] Although 1893 saw Loss open a consulting company in Philadelphia and establish a number of patents involving hydraulic technology, his business was unsuccessful.[489] By 1895, he was inspector for the construction and operation of passenger and freight elevators in Philadelphia, where he worked out elevator regulations for the city and state that were later adopted by New York and Chicago and ultimately became an international standard. Loss rounded out his career by working as consulting engineer at the Pressed Steel Car Company and then the Schoen Steel Wheel Company at Pittsburgh, where he developed hydraulic machinery needed for the construction of solid steel wheels for railroad cars.[490]

While at Pencoyd, Loss developed a riveter that overcame the tendency toward loss of energy in ordinary riveters.[491] He also carried out experiments on the pressing of steel and, in general, the flow of metal, the results of which were described in two speeches (and papers) given for the Franklin Institute.[492] He also demonstrated that the power needed to punch metals was less than that required for shearing, an outcome that was initially questioned by many.[493] But experiments made previously were power punches, possessing great speed of penetration, whereas the experiments conducted by Loss were all confined to hydraulic machines, where the velocity of the flow of metal during the process was under the control of the operator. The speed during the actual punching was from three to six times as great on a power machine as on one driven by water pressure, and Loss demonstrated this effectively and convinced the remaining doubters of his assertions.[494] His work at Schoen led to an improved design for steel wheels in the all steel railroad cars. Cast-iron wheels had been breaking, and Loss demonstrated that steel wheels actually weighed less, provided greater mileage and thus offered a large financial advantage. In 1899, his boss C.T. Schoen negotiated with German engineers for a mill to roll wheel centers. Loss developed innovations to this design that led to a combination of rolling and pressing of the steel car wheels, which ultimately allowed the production of wheels with rims and centers of equal quality.[495]

It is clear that Loss not only had a significant influence on the Pencoyd Iron Works but also contributed many additional important inventions, especially the design of steel railroad car axles and wheels. He was one of the most important Philadelphia engineers at the turn of the century.

RIVETS AND HYDRAULIC RIVETING

Riveting became important in both the shop and field for assembling large structures for bridges. Rivets were an integral and essential part of the business, and Pencoyd even took a leadership role in the use of rivet symbols and rivet indicators on drawings.[496] Loss influenced this field as well, developing the theory of riveting pressure as he outlined in a paper for the Franklin Institute and the Engineers Club of Philadelphia.[497] In 1889, rivets and bolts were first manufactured at Pencoyd, and the output of three rivet machines and one bolt machine in August 1890 was 160,237 pounds of rivets and 5,268 pounds of bolts. Improvements to the bolt and rivet operations, such as the heating and annealing process, led to a huge

(9.7) Hydraulic riveter with travelling gantry at Pencoyd's bridge shop. *From the* Engineer, *March 6, 1903, 238.*

(9.8) Riveting of a 35-ton chord for the Thebes bridge. *From the* Engineering Record, *April 8, 1893, 376.*

increase in output in the ensuing decade, with production for August 1901 being 852,440 pounds of rivets and 216,949 pounds of bolts.[498] Loss also contributed to the development of the traveling riveter in the bridge shop at Pencoyd (Figure 9.7)[499] as well as portable hydraulic riveters that could be used in the shop (Figure 9.8) or in the field.[500] By 1899, pneumatic riveting hand hammers, such as the Boyer rivet hammers, were also being used and were making field and portable riveting even easier.[501]

MULTIPLE DRILLING GANTRY

One particularly interesting invention was a multiple drill machine (Figure 9.9) designed by William Sellers & Company, a Philadelphia firm renowned for developing and designing specialty tools and equipment for industrial processes.[502] William Sellers & Company developed a wide variety of machine tools, including drilling and boring machines, shears, planers, slotters, gear cutters, straightening machines, punching, surfacing, steam hammers and riveters, and lathes.[503] Pencoyd undoubtedly had many machines fabricated by William Sellers & Company, but the eight-drill gantry drilling machine was probably the largest and most widely acclaimed and reported at the time, being featured in popular and engineering journals alike.[504]

William Sellers was born on September 19, 1824, in Upper Darby, Delaware County, Pennsylvania.[505] Sellers's first ancestor in this country was Samuel Sellers, who came from Bristol, England, in 1682 and settled on a tract of land in Upper Darby under Penn's patent. In this sense, there is some parallel between the Sellers and Roberts families, as they were both originally farmers in the era of William Penn. William Sellers's mother was Elizabeth Poole of Wilmington, Delaware, whose grandfather William Poole was sent to this country by the Royal Geographical Society of England to observe a transit of Venus and decided to remain here. Sellers's paternal great-grandfather, John Sellers, was appointed by the American Philosophical Society (APS) and was a founding member of the APS. Thus, Sellers's ancestors on both sides had significant connection with science.[506] He received his early education at a private school (at the time of his education there were 34 students) built and conducted by his relatives. At the age of 14, he started working as an apprentice at the Brandywine machine shop of his uncle J. Morton Poole. He then moved to the Providence, Rhode Island shops of Fairbanks, Bancroft & Company and Bancroft, Nightingale & Company, manufacturers of steam engines and mill gearing. Two years later, Sellers came back to West Philadelphia and began manufacturing on his own.[507] Machinists moved frequently in this period, and receiving training in multiple and successive shops was typical. In fact, while at Bancroft, Nightingale & Company, William met George Corliss, the inventor of the Corliss steam engine.[508] Shortly thereafter, in 1848, Sellers partnered with his former employer Edward Bancroft to form Bancroft & Sellers to manufacture machine tools and mill gearing. Intermarriage between

Delaware and Rhode Island machinist families was quite extensive in this period; Edward Bancroft married William Sellers's sister Mary.[509] By 1855, however, Edward Bancroft had passed away. John Sellers Jr. joined the company, and the firm name became William Sellers & Company. William's brother John Jr. and his cousins Coleman, Escol and Charles had been involved in developing machinery and industrial supplies in the mid-1800s in Philadelphia and other cities in the East and Midwest, and their experiences shaped the career path and decisions that led to William's success.[510] In 1868, William established the Edge Moor Iron Company in Delaware and, in 1873, became president of the Midvale Steel Company at Nicetown.[511] Edge Moor Iron Company made much of the iron for the Centennial Exhibition of 1876 and the Brooklyn Bridge. While president of the Franklin Institute in 1864, he delivered a paper on "Screw Threads and Nuts" that subsequently became the standard for the form of thread in the United States and Europe. The valuable work of Wilfred Lewis on belting and the strength of gear teeth and more was carried out under the auspices of William Sellers & Company.[512] Sellers was vice-president of the 1876 centennial board of finance, director of the Reading Railway and of the Philadelphia, Wilmington and Baltimore Railroad, a trustee of the University of Pennsylvania (1868), a member of the National Academy of Sciences (1873) and a corresponding member of the Paris Société d'Encouragement pour I'Industrie Nationale (1874).

(9.9) Multiple drilling gantry designed by William Sellers and Company. *From* Dinglers Polytechnisches Journal *86, no. 46 (1905): 726–31.*

At the Paris Exposition of 1899, the highest award, the Grand Prix, was given to William Sellers & Co. Inc., together with several medals. At the close of the exposition, Sellers received an individual diploma and was also made a chevalier of the Legion of Honor.[513] Some of Sellers's and his firm's highest honors were won at the Paris Exposition of 1867 and the Vienna World's Fair of 1873.[514] His activity in the Franklin Institute, American Philosophical Society and the Engineering Club of Philadelphia exemplify the extent of his leadership in Philadelphia and the world.

OTHER SPECIALIZED EQUIPMENT

The production line aspects of Pencoyd's bridge shop were likely arranged by James Christie and included a number of machines specially developed for making or shaping bridge components. Christie undoubtedly worked with other machinery companies to develop the equipment needed for various products, such as the rotary planar, the spacing and multiple beam punches and the angle and plate shears (Figure 9.10).[515]

(9.10) Automatic spacing punch was designed especially for punching plates and angles, punching up to 10 holes at a stroke and automatically spacing by sixteenths of an inch up to eight inches. *From* Dinglers Polytechnisches Journal *86, no. 46 (1905): 726–31.*

TRANSPORT INNOVATIONS

Various kinds of material transport innovations dramatically changed the workflow at Pencoyd. In 1891, a 20-ton overhead electric traveling crane was placed in the blooming mill. This was the first crane of this type used at Pencoyd. It was used to move work pieces and change out rolls in the rolling mills.[516] Overhead cranes became common in many parts of the plant. In 1892, a 6-ton overhead traveling crane was installed to cover the space between the 12″ and 20″ mill building and the machine shop and was used to load material on railcars for shipment (Figure 9.11).[517] Locomotive cranes were used in the shipping yard to move large items and completed work onto trains for shipping.[518] The shipping yard (Figure 9.12) utilized an overhead crane (30 tons) to move completed girders and beams and load them onto railroad cars.[519] Use of overhead cranes in the rolling mills (to change out rolls) and the shipping department was noted in 1901 as a unique characteristic of the Pencoyd operation.[520]

Ingenious devices were invented to help efficiently move heavy items as well. In his 1902 examination of the productivity and efficiency of American workshops, Molesworth noted, among many other gadgets, clip hooks and electromagnets that were used to pick up and move angle bars and the clip hooks that were used to pick up and move large joists (Figure 9.13).

Pencoyd could prepare immense orders of bridge parts and ready them for shipping, as exemplified in a news item from 1900: "A 240-car train loaded with materials for bridges in the Pacific Northwest was preparing for the trip west."[521] At any time, there might be multiple jobs and work—an example from 1899 documents the diversity of work: "Three 400-ft spans for the Arkansas River Bridge on the Kansas City, Fort Scott, and Memphis Railroad; three 240′ spans for the Allegheny Valley Railway, nine 150′ spans for the Philadelphia and Reading Railway; a viaduct for the Chihuahua and Pacific Railroad; a bridge at Albany, NY; the structural work for the Immigrant Station at Ellis Island; and two large Philadelphia Buildings, and considerable amount of small work."[522] The trade journal *Real Estate Record and Builders Guide* noted, "The Pencoyd plant of the American Bridge Co. shipped during March (1901) 7339 tons. We believe this is the largest shipment ever made by any bridge shop in the world."[523]

In 1899, James Christie, Alfred Major, Charles Major, Frederick B. Johnson and Charles C. Price, all affiliated with the Pencoyd Iron Works, incorporated the Wissahickon Bridge Company and planned

(9.11) View of a six-ton electric traveling crane from near the office building looking in the up river direction toward bridge and construction shop (between Hammer Shop and Rolling Mill on left and Machine Shop on the right). In the distance, one can see the four-story Bridge and Construction Office Department and the end of the Fitting Up Shop and the Bridge Shop, the latter directly behind the crane pulley. *From Brownhoist Crane Inc. Cleveland, Ohio catalogue, 1901, 58.*

(9.12) View of the shipping yard at Pencoyd with beams and girders ready for shipping. *From* Scientific American, *December 12, 1903, 432–33.*

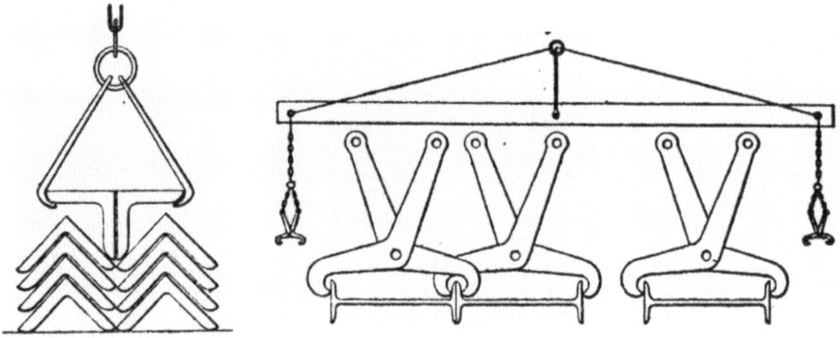

(9.13) Pairs of angles (*left*) and single beams or pairs of beams could be picked up with specially designed clamps that were controlled from above by overhead cranes. *From* Minutes of the Proceedings of the Institute of Civil Engineers *148 (1902): 58–74.*

the construction of a steel bridge across the Schuylkill River.[524] The Wissahickon Bridge Company had acquired land on the north side of the Schuylkill that would be developed to support the bridge and construction industry. In 1903, Pencoyd and Wissahickon built new foundry and machine shops across the river that were state of the art and had several unique design features. Pencoyd installed turntable jib cranes that allowed easy movement and alignment of large pieces of work in the machine shops.[525] Pencoyd had designed and installed special two-ton turntable jib cranes hung from the ceilings. The traveling trolley from which the crane was suspended was supported on rails suspended from the overhead girders by brackets. The wheels were driven by a belted motor. The turntables were carried on balls and rollers, and radial arms suspended motor-driven hoisting hooks in multiple galley bays. A foundry was located parallel with the machine shop. An overhead traveling crane ran in front of and connected the ends of the two buildings and thus could deliver heavy castings to cars on the tracks on the projecting platforms. Railroad tracks also ran into the buildings under this crane, and heavy forgings were delivered to the gallery in the same way. Carrying work to and from the upper gallery elevators also depended on the overhead traveling crane. These turntable jib cranes thus created an efficient and flexible environment for fabrication and loading.

Birth of the American Bridge Company

All of these innovations in design and technology resulted in a large increase in production in the bridge department as well as the finishing mill (Figure 9.14), with both seeing great changes from 1887 to 1900.[526] The first half of 1901 saw a gross output of nearly 40,000 tons at Pencoyd.[527] In 1901, 28 companies from Wisconsin to New Jersey—including Berlin Iron Bridge Company (Connecticut), Edge Moor Bridge Works (Delaware), American Bridge Works and Lassig Bridge and Iron Works (Illinois), Lafayette Bridge Company (Indiana), Gilette-Herzog Manufacturing Company (Minnesota), Trenton Iron Works (New Jersey), Buffalo Bridge and Iron Works, Elmira Bridge Company, Groton Bridge and Manufacturing, Hilton Bridge Construction, Horseheads Bridge Company, Post and McCord, Rochester Bridge and Ironworks and Shepard Bridge Works (all in New York), New Columbus Bridge Company, Wrought Iron Bridge Company, Youngstown Bridge Company (all in Ohio), Keystone Bridge Company, Pencoyd Iron Works, Pittsburgh Bridge Company, Schultz Bridge Company, Shiffler Bridge Company and Union Bridge Company (all in Pennsylvania) and Milwaukee Bridge and Iron Works (Wisconsin)—merged into a single company called the American Bridge Company.[528] Pencoyd was the most productive of all the companies at the time and continued to be after the merger as well, as production jumped from 40 to 84 kilotons between 1894 to 1903.[529] In fact, Pencoyd's capacity was between 11 to 17 percent of the entire amalgamated companies in American Bridge. Even the highly productive Keystone and Edge Moor plants represented less than 10 percent of the production capacity during this time frame. Pencoyd's personnel also had a significant presence in the management of the new company, with Percival Roberts Jr. being the president, soon replaced by Alfred J. Major. Others included Vice-President (for engineering) Charles C. Schneider, chief engineer Paul L. Wolfel and mechanical engineer James Christie, all of whom were also on the board of directors. The combined tonnage of the plants of the new American Bridge Company was 50,000 tons per month, or at the rate of 600,000 tons per annum, "by far the largest production of railway and highway bridges and steel structures of any company on the face of the earth."[530] In 1901, the American Bridge Company had general offices in the American Surety Building, 100 Broadway, New York; was also organized under the laws of the State of New Jersey; and had branch offices in Boston, Philadelphia, Pittsburgh, Chicago, Cleveland, Baltimore,

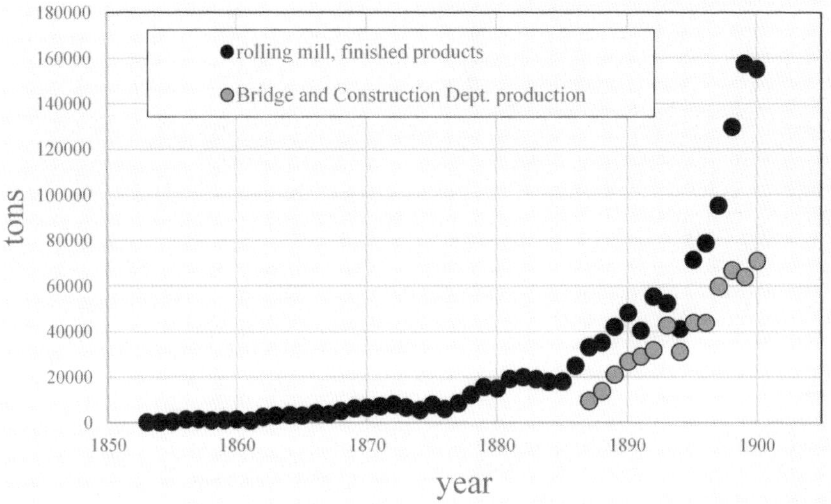

(9.14) Production from the rolling mill, finished products, 1852–1900 (*solid circles*), and from the bridge and construction company 1887–1900 (*gray circle*). *Redrawn by author using data from the* Iron Age, *January 30, 1902, 10–12.*

Minneapolis and New Orleans.[531] By 1902, the American Bridge Company was merged into U.S. Steel, along with eight other companies. Together, the company comprised 90 percent of the manufacturing capacity in railroad and highway bridges and structural work of the United States.[532] Pencoyd's role, being the most productive of the companies, was tasked with building up stocks of raw materials. Pencoyd was one of the most improved rolling mills in the world and was run almost exclusively to supply raw material for the various plants of the company. At nearly all of the plants, large stocks of raw material were also carried, its aggregate amounting to hundreds of thousands of tons, so that the company was able to furnish on very short time any ordinary bridge or building.[533]

It was this backdrop, then that moved Pencoyd into the twentieth century as a leader in bridge building and structural steel work and poised to expand nationally and internationally. Pencoyd had established a production line of specialized machinery that allowed it to be cutting-edge in technology while also among the top producers of construction and bridge work. The sounds of the mill must have dominated the surrounding communities on each side of the Schuylkill River. It is no wonder that the great historian of Pennsylvania, Cornelius Weygandt, wrote in 1942:

The rumors of Pencoyd, the drum and peal of its rollers, the crash and pound of its hammers, the smoke of its chimneys, and the defacement of the river bank by its dumping grounds and coal storage have for years made us all in Germantown continuously aware of its presence and condemnatory of it, but when it fell silent, we would have had it, for all its disagreeable features, busy again if we could. Its products are great utilities, and, what matters as much, symbols of a world at work.[534]

10

Bridge Building Goes International

The amazing array of domestic projects Pencoyd had engaged in by the end of the nineteenth century and the steady increase of production led to expansion into international markets. Although Pencoyd's construction of a bridge in Africa in 1899 received a lot of attention, much of which implied this was its first project abroad, Pencoyd's first international bridge activity was actually in Japan and continued in Africa, Asia, Australia and Mexico.

In 1897, Pencoyd bid on a railroad bridge across the Yssel (Ijssel) River in Arnhem near Westervoort, Netherlands. Its lowest bid ($474,000) caught the attention of worldwide construction experts,[535] and even though many assumed the contract would be offered, it was instead offered to a Dutch company whose bid was $13,000 higher than Pencoyd's.[536] Perhaps this was the harbinger of things to come, because bridge contracts in Japan and Africa were to follow quickly thereafter.

Japan

Bridge engineers J.A.L. Waddell and T. Cooper, both of whom attended RPI and likely had known Percival and George B. Roberts, spent time in Tokyo teaching civil engineering between 1882 and 1886.[537] As discussed in chapter 7, Waddell possessed great interest in engineering education, and in the early 1880s, he served as visiting professor of civil engineering at Tokyo University. It was at this time that Waddell became embroiled in the controversy that ultimately led to his development of the A truss for railroad use. During his stay in Japan between 1882 and 1886, Waddell took careful notice of the bridges then in use on Japanese railroads. They were almost all designed by British engineers and, except for one, all were 100′ or less in length. For a variety of reasons, Waddell considered them to be inferior to American truss bridges of the time, and he prepared a study published by Tokyo University titled "A System of Iron Railroad Bridges for Japan" that strongly criticized the British truss bridge designs used in most Japanese railroad bridges.[538] British engineers were naturally offended by Waddell's criticisms and initiated a series of criticisms and responses between British engineers, Japanese engineers and Waddell (in an American trade journal called the *Japan Mail*), weighing the pros and cons of American and British bridges.[539] When Waddell had returned to America in 1886, he had clearly influenced Japanese engineers and government officials; the emperor bestowed upon him the rank of knight commander in the Order of the Rising Sun for his services.[540]

His influence led to two major outcomes. First, Waddell, realized that British truss bridges (1) were pony trusses and not deep enough for lateral bracing between top chords, and (2) used riveted connections that had not yet been perfected in field use. Waddell thought use of pin connections was more reliable, and together with the bracing issues, this led him to design the A truss.[541] Second, Japanese officials took his criticisms to heart and began a renewed infrastructure campaign to replace or expand railroad bridges. Railway bridges in Japan had up until that time been dominated by British engineers and designs, and the Japanese government railways had been overseen by C.A.W. Pownall from 1882 to 1896. The influence of Waddell and Cooper in Japan was enhanced when in 1893 the director of the Japan railways changed from Masaru Inoue, who had studied in England, to Soichiro Matsumoto, who had studied in the United States. Under Matsumoto, design gradually changed from British to American style.[542] Cooper and C.C. Schneider were commissioned to design truss girders to handle the loads of the newer heavier trains; 100′, 150′ and 200′ span deck and through trusses, double track 100′ and 200′ trusses and up to 300′ through trusses were being used in designs according to Cooper's specifications.[543] In the late 1890s, there was also a movement from pin trusses to riveted structures, such as the Yodogawa bridge in Osaka (1899), which may be one of the earliest and largest of the riveted structures. Much to the surprise of this author and his wife, we realized she rode across this bridge as a child numerous times. The other development in Japan was that by 1911–12, many bridges were designed and built by Japanese engineers and companies rather than American or British.[544]

(10.1) Amarube viaduct on the north coast of Honshu. *From* Japan Railway & Transport Review *no. 62 (2013): 38.*

One of the most notable projects in Japan was the Amarube Viaduct on the north coast of Honshu. Built in 1912, the viaduct was 40 meters high and 310 meters long and bridged a river valley between two tunnels (Figure 10.1).[545] Steel for the structure (652.5 tons of trestle legs and 12.5 tons of anchor bolts) was made at Pencoyd and shipped to Kyushu and then transferred to a landing barge for delivery to the bridge site. The bridge is close to the coast (Sea of Japan), and thus there is potential for sea salt corrosion, but it was kept covered in bright vermilion paint—giving it a striking appearance and making it a favorite of train aficionados and local residents—while also giving it an extended lifetime. This viaduct remained in use until 2010, when it was replaced with a newer structure. The replacement was prompted by an unfortunate accident—high winds in 1986 caused an out-of-service train to be blown off the bridge, killing six people. Although standards for train operation on the bridge were revised so that trains would not be allowed on the bridge for greater than 15 meters/second winds, local residents and engineers decided in 2002 to build a new bridge that would ensure train operation at up to 30 meters/second winds.[546]

The Tarumi railway built a multiple span through truss bridge across the Ibu River in Gifu in 1900. It is still in use and well maintained over 100 years later.[547] Many other Pencoyd bridges were built in Japan—a good portion of them after the incorporation of Pencoyd into the American Bridge Company. In 1904, Pencoyd was awarded a contract from the imperial government of Japan for 7,000 tons of work that comprised about 100 small spans.[548] A full list of nearly 40 bridges is detailed in the appendix and shows the bridges were built all across Japan from the northeast near Sapporo to the southwest near Kyushu.

Sudan

Events of 1898 put Pencoyd into the international spotlight again. The British government needed to have a bridge over the Atbara River near the Nile in Sudan, in support of military actions. In order to continue his campaign against the Dervishes, General Kitchener required extension of the railway line as far south as Khartoum.[549] The timing of this bridge was critical, and when the government first put bids out for the bridge in early October 1898, the British and European companies submitting bids could not provide the bridge fast enough or for a reasonable price. A promise of one year for shop work and one year for erection was the best offer. The reason given by the British manufacturers for this slow work was the overcrowded conditions of their shops.[550]

Second bids were subsequently requested of two American and five British firms, with rapid completion being the main consideration. These bids (and associated plans) reached Egypt in late December 1898.[551] It was then found that, because the bidders proposed the use of false work for bridge construction in their designs, the work could not be carried out until after the summer flood season. During part of the year, the riverbed was entirely dry and used for camping grounds by the wandering tribes; but during the summer months, the 1,100′ wide Atbara River bed saw full and vigorous activity. Therefore, bridge erection with false work could not be completed until the following winter or spring, which would mean the loss of a year to General Kitchener.[552]

Accordingly, new bids based on cantilever erection or launching were requested. New bids were received, with the Patent Shaft and Axle Company being the only British firm responding to the final call. Pencoyd's bid (2.5 cents per pound; 42 days in New York) was significantly lower than the competing bidders both in price and time frame (up to 3.37 cents/pound and up to 4 months in New York), and the British government selected Pencoyd much to the dismay of British competitors.[553] Pencoyd not only fabricated the steelwork early but also proceeded to build the bridge on time to the great satisfaction of the customer. The situation drew much international interest and made Pencoyd famous overnight.[554] Although the bridge was rather ordinary in size and design, the most unusual aspects of the project were its international crew (American foremen and native workmen) and its erection without false work.[555]

The structure is a single-track narrow-gauge railway bridge with seven Pratt pin-connected through spans each 147′ long. The weight of the bridge superstructure was 268,300 pounds and, including other items such as temporary steel work, traveler, cast-iron pier-caps, duplicates and extras amounted to a total of 1,512,900 pounds.[556] The substructure was built by a Cairo firm, which was the only one with facilities in Egypt for the quick prosecution of that part of the work. The Pencoyd Iron Works designed and furnished for New York delivery the entire superstructure under a lump sum contract, the cast-iron pier caps and the erection plant and tools under a special pound-price contract. It also furnished the expert erection force, composed of a superintendent, two foremen and five men (riveters, riggers and so on). Pencoyd was also held responsible for complete and proper erection.[557] The workmanship was made to conform to standard American practice, subject to the inspection of Messrs. Booth, Garrett and Blair of Philadelphia, who also made the customary tests on the material and all the full-sized eye-bars.[558]

The one feature of the design that required more than the usual amount of attention was the method of erection without false work, which was conceived and carefully worked out in detail under the supervision of Schneider and Wolfel. Printed instructions and detailed plans were issued to the superintendent of erection just prior to the departure of the workforce.[559] One span on shore initially served as an anchor. Then a steel traveling derrick moved from shore toward the first pier. The traveler was made almost entirely of steel and was, of course, made as light as possible. The booms were about 45′ long and composed of two 12″ channels, latticed; the posts were 5″ channels latticed, the struts 6″ channels and the diagonal bracing 1″ square rods. The traveler was carried on cast-iron

(10.2) View of the Atbara River bridge with near shore completed and traveler at far end where work continues to the far shore. *From the* Proceedings of the Engineers Club of Philadelphia *16, no. 6 (1899): 324–45.*

wheels running on rails, which rested on short timber ties bolted to the top chords of the bridge. After the connection over the pier had been made, the erection proceeded in the customary manner for cantilever bridges (Figure 10.2). As soon as the span was completed far enough to enable the booms to reach the next pier, the cast-iron pier caps were set. The span was then completed and thus ready to be self-sustaining. When the cantilevered span was completed, the far end of it was raised by means of jacks, and the temporary connection between the two spans was removed using the rear boom of the traveler. After the far end of the span was lowered to the pier, the anchor span was then taken down and the erection of the next span carried out the same way.[560]

The crabs, operated by a few men and shown in position on the traveler, furnished the power used for hoisting. The maximum load lifted by each boom was between 8,000 and 9,000 pounds.[561]

Since the timing of bridge construction was one of the important aspects of this project, here is a brief timeline:[562]

January 7	The first inquiry is received; no mention, however, is made of cantilever erection.
January 13	The cantilever erection is specified.
January 16	The loading is received.
January 20	The quotation is sent to England based on this loading and cantilever erection.
January 24	The specifications and order are received for the bridge.
January 26	Two days later, the change of span length is ordered.
January 27	The stress sheet is finished.
January 31	The shop drawings are started, just one week from date of order, two or three days of which were wasted on account of wrong data. Within 10 days, the shop drawings are finished and all material ordered.
February 6	Work is started in the template and the bridge shops.
March 7	Just a month later, the entire structure is shipped from Pencoyd, although seven days were lost on account of a blizzard, when the shop was closed. The entire time from receipt of final data to date of shipment was close to six weeks.
April 26	Order is received to replace one chord section, 25′ long, weighing 3,200 pounds, which had been lost overboard during transshipment in England; 18 hours after receipt of order the chord section is shipped from Pencoyd.

April 22 Erection crew of eight men leaves New York and, from that time until their return in October, are in the employ of the British government.

The bridge is shipped to Alexandria, Egypt, by way of Liverpool, requiring one transshipment at the latter place, and reached there early in May. In Alexandria, it is transferred to the Egyptian Railroad and reached the bridge site early in June, requiring three transshipments—one from broad to narrow gauge at Luxor, from railway to steamer at Assuan and vice versa at Wady Haifa.

June 16 The entire erection crew arrives at the Atbara

August 19 A little over two months later, the bridge is completely finished (cover image)—in other words, less than seven months from the date of the placing of the contract. This included the erection and removal of the anchor span and actually represented the erection of eight spans and the removal of one. This would be equivalent to erecting say nine spans in 63 days, or an average of one span in 7 days. The shortest time on any one span was 4 days. The entire erection was carried out precisely as planned, without the loss of life either from accident or sickness. The ordinary labor employed was composed of Sudanese and Egyptian convicts and soldiers—about 200 men in all. An interpreter was needed to translate the orders of our foremen and men.

The British were critical of the U.S. success in the case of the Atbara Bridge and offered several reasons why it worked so well: (1) there were parts in stock, (2) British designs were more customized and thus took longer, and (3) the British shops were full of out-of-date machinery and thus less efficient.[563] Pencoyd likely did not have parts in stock because the capacity of the Pencoyd bridge shops ranged from 5,000 to 15,000 net tons per month. On the basis of 5,000 tons per month, the 750 tons comprising the Atbara contract represent only about four days' work for the shop. Pencoyd Iron Works did not need to have the Atbara Bridge "in stock," as so many British papers asserted. One explanation of the difference of construction time specified by the British compared to Pencoyd lies in the standardizing of structural shapes and in the improved machinery in use at Pencoyd. Additionally, American bridge designers aimed to duplicate parts in designs to reduce template work and to make the shop work as uniform as possible with standard shapes. On the other hand, British designers were known for the value of originality and consequently no uniformity in shop work. Special shapes were used, and thus new rolls had to be made for nearly every contract.[564]

General Kitchener's address at the formal opening of the bridge is an indication of how well received the work was by the British customers:

> *The opening of this bridge today is due to their (i.e., American) energy and ability, and the power they possess in so marked a degree of turning out work of this magnitude in less time than can be done by anyone else, I congratulate the American foremen and workmen on the excellent success which has crowned their efforts in the erection of this bridge in the heart of Africa, far from their homes, during the hottest months of the year, and depending solely upon the labor of men speaking a foreign tongue. They have shown by the work the real grit they are made of.*[565]

To show his gratitude, Kitchener made and presented plaques to the bridge foreman crew members Wennas, Melton, McQuarrie, Siegfried, Aspenliter, Olsen, Schaffner and Murray, with the engraving "I congratulate the American foremen and workmen on the excellent success which has crowned their efforts in the erection of this bridge in the heart of Africa."[566] In addition, when the crew arrived back in Philadelphia, Superintendent Wennas and the seven skilled structural iron workers each received a gold watch from Percival Roberts Jr.[567]

MEXICO

The rugged Sierra Madre Occidental mountains of western Mexico offered another international challenge to bridge makers. Pencoyd was involved in the construction of bridges and viaducts for the Chihuahua & Pacific Railroad between Santa Isabel and westward into San Andres and Anahuac, to the beginning of what eventually became known as the copper canyon near Creel.[568] Pencoyd provided 550,000′ of steel in 1898 for the construction of these bridges and viaducts.[569]

The Chihuahua & Pacific Railroad is a standard-gauge line. The first 200 kilometers from Chihuahua to Minaca was built in 1898–89 by the Mexican government, to more easily connect the western coast with this region on the east side of the Sierra Madre, with elevation changes of nearly 1000 meters along this stretch. An 88-kilometer extension from La Junta to Temosachie was built in 1905–6 to reach timber lands, and then an additional 53 kilometers were built by the Greene Consolidated Mining Company to San Pedro. Prior to the construction of the CPRR, access to these regions was limited: supplies were freighted by wagon to Guerrero and then packed on mules and burros into the mountains.[570]

All the bridges were designed and built by Pencoyd under the general inspection of Messrs. Hidreth & Company of New York. The steel bridges consisted of I-beams (less than 4 meters) and plate girders (up to 25-meter opening). Two trusses were built, one at Santa Isabel over the Santa Isabel River and the other at El Carpio over the Guerrero River. Besides these there were four viaducts in the Aldana Canyon (Figure 10.3), the dimensions of which were 414′, 430′, 506′ and 299′, 12–13 degree tangents and grades from 1.44 to 2 percent.[571] The capstones for the pedestals supporting the bents of these viaducts were of the hard volcanic fine-grained gray porphyry, which was also used in the cathedral and other buildings in Chihuahua and set in Portland cement.[572]

The bridges were erected by men furnished by Pencoyd, working under the direction of the chief engineer and employed directly by the railroad company. Local labor was used almost entirely in building the masonry

(10.3) Viaduct No. 2 along Chihuahua & Pacific Railroad (CPRR) in 1899. *From the* Engineering Record, *March 2, 1907, 241–43.*

and was found to be entirely satisfactory. An attempt was made to bring in masons from the United States, but the results attained did not warrant the higher wages the American masons were paid over those paid to local masons.[573] Surveys started in December 1897 and construction the following spring, the work being practically completed rand eady for traffic by the spring of 1900. The whole project was under the direction of Ed. S. Safford, chief engineer, and supervision of F. Lavis for location and construction.[574]

UGANDA RAILWAY

By 1901, Pencoyd was again making steel bridge parts for an African location—a series of bridges and viaducts for the Uganda Railway, which is a single-track line 584 miles long, running from Mombassa on the Indian Ocean to Port Florence on Lake Victoria.[575] In efforts to construct a railway from Mombassa to Lake Victoria, rail lines were extended through the region between Mount Kenya and Mount Kilimanjaro near the border between Kenya and Tanzania.[576] These viaducts were under the auspices of the American Bridge Company, but the steel was made at Pencoyd. As with the Atbara case, Pencoyd's bid was £18 per ton (erected), which was significantly lower than the British and American competitors.[577] The portion of the railway between Koru and Njoro, or more broadly between Port Florence (now Kisumu) and Lake Nakuru, covered terrain requiring many viaducts, and the work carried out by Pencoyd (American Bridge) included 27 viaducts.[578] The 27 simple plate-girder viaducts with alternating 20′ and 40′ spans varied from 160′ to 880′ in length and from about 40′ to 112′ in height, for a combined length of 3,000′ and weight of 8,000 tons (Figure 10.4). After being manufactured at Pencoyd, the steel bridge parts were shipped on railroad cars to New York, where they were sent by three separate shipments direct to Mombassa—the first left New York during the summer of 1901, the second in September 1901 and the third in January 1902. A.B. Lueder was sent in advance by the company to receive, unload and forward the material and to make preparations for the erection party, which consisted of superintendent N.P. Jarrett, seventeen skilled bridge erectors and a cook.[579]

The erection party set sail on October 26, 1901, from New York to Rotterdam and from there to Mombassa via the Suez Canal. They arrived at Mombassa, 31 days after leaving Rotterdam and 46 days after leaving New

(10.4) A curved viaduct along the Uganda Railway. *From the* Engineering Record, *September 10, 1904, 310–12.*

York, at the railway terminus at Port Kilindini, about 70 miles northeast of Zanzibar, where a train was waiting and immediately transported them by rail to the site of the first of their six camps. This first camp was designated Mile 468, which was the distance in miles from the adjacent first viaduct to the coast; all other camps were named in the same manner, with the last camp designated Mile 541.[580]

The bridge parts were color coded (for each viaduct and part) and stored until ready for distribution to the bridge sites. Although every piece for each of the 27 viaducts was marked and billed for its exact position, the upper stories of the towers and many of the girders, beams and other members were interchangeable, and much time and labor was eventually saved by using some of the regular pieces indiscriminately. Because of interest in keeping space and loading requirements to a minimum, many bridge pieces that would ordinarily be shop-riveted were shipped loose. This ultimately required an unusual and undesirable amount of field-riveting. All small pieces were packed in wooden boxes made of 1¼″ boards bound with steel hoops, many of which burst in transit.[581] One bridge man and 25 Africans were always sent ahead to unload the material at each site in advance of the erection party. The erectors worked at a radius of 5 miles from camp, going and returning on a construction train when the distance was too long to walk; they were followed by the riveters and finally the carpenters. The working outfit, taken from the Pencoyd shops, included a 40,000-pound steel traveler and four American Bridge Company standard steel guyed derricks used for unloading material from the cars at the storage yards. Seven of the smaller viaducts were erected by derricks and gin-poles and the other 20 using the steel traveler, which was a rectangular riveted tower, 9′ wide, 38′ long and 31′ high. The travelers had four vertical posts with a single double-flange wheel under the foot of each, and the wheels moved on a 9′ gauge track laid on the permanent steel transverse beams of the deck. A Mundy hoisting engine, a wood-burning furnace boiler and four capstan-head horse-power windlasses were used to operate the unloading derricks and were manned by about 15 local workmen pushing on long horizontal levers. Extra pieces of the engine and derrick fittings, as well as a large quantity of tackle, hydraulic jacks, jack screws, hand tools, many steel bars, shapes and a stock of rivets and bolts were valuable in enabling the crew to build several new bridge members to replace some that were lost.[582] After the work was finished, the traveler and derrick and the hoisting engine and small tools were sold at a fair price, and none of the plant was brought back to the United States.[583]

After the formation of the American Bridge Company and the merger into U.S. Steel, there was enhanced international activity under the auspices of U.S. Steel Products Export Company. Formosa was under the influence of Japan, and erection of bridges in that island country by the Japanese government led to the Taiwan iron bridge.[584] By 1902, Pencoyd had also built a bridge in Australia—a two-span through truss at the north edge of Goulburn, New South Wales.[585]

International work was not limited to bridges. Pencoyd, under the auspices of U.S. Steel Exports, continued to make structural steel for buildings all over the world, including some notable buildings in Brazil, Argentina, Mexico City and Australia.[586] The Kalgoorlie carbarn in western Australia housed a fleet of streetcars—the steel structure formed the skeleton over which the barn roof and walls were constructed (Figure 10.5). The Plaza Hotel in Buenos Aires was also a steel cage structure building with multiple stories and is today in use at park's edge in the heart of Buenos Aires (Figure 10.6). The five-story Mutual Life Insurance Company in Mexico City was also built in this time frame and today is a bank building.

Left: (10.5) The Kalgoorlie (Australia) car barn under construction. *From* Far East Review, *July 1911, 52.*

Below: (10.6) Plaza Hotel in Buenos Aires, Argentina, built in 1910. *Public domain, Wikipedia commons.*

Once Pencoyd was merged into the American Bridge Company, international work was more common, but attribution of any American Bridge Company structures to Pencoyd became difficult, since any particular project may have used the combined resources and specialties of the numerous plants in the company. We cover these examples from Japan, Australia, Africa, Mexico, and Taiwan because the steel and bridge parts were produced exclusively at Pencoyd; these examples demonstrate how this modestly sized company could establish an international reputation.

11

Diversity and Challenges of the Pencoyd Workers

Pencoyd grew from a dozen or so employees from its beginning in 1852 to nearly 6,000 employees at its peak around the beginning of the twentieth century.[587] The combination of steel plant and bridge company and all the supporting power and motive requirements created a huge diversity of technical expertise. From steam boilers, coal handling, hydraulics, electrical, machine shop, water pumping, steel plant charging, ingot pouring and stripping, beam and rod rolling, to steel cutting specialists and then in the bridge department there were shearing, cutting, planing, straightening, drilling, riveting and eye-bar upsetting, pressing, drilling, annealing specialists. In the designing departments there were template makers, draftsmen and building and bridge engineers. All of these shops and departments had large teams and groups of workers. Many group photos exist of Pencoyd employees over the decades of the mill's operations. Some include men who may have been managers or draftsmen wearing jackets and ties and posing in front of the mill office building (Figure 11.1), while other photos include men who may have been associated with a specialty such as boilerhouse or machine shop (Figure 11.2). Such photos can also be found in regional histories of the Schuylkill River or Roxborough.[588]

The Industrial Revolution in America drew thousands of people to the Philadelphia area, not only from within the United States but also from abroad. The workers at Pencoyd were a mix of new immigrants and descendants of families who had lived in the Philadelphia or eastern Pennsylvania region for many generations. Many of the engineers and

(11.1) Photo of a group of Pencoyd machine shop employees, circa 1915. Front row, third from left is Madison Smith (foreman), fourth from left is Charles Major and fifth from left is Walter Righter. This photo was taken at the entrance to the Pencoyd office building. *From the collection of R.B. Righter.*

(11.2) Photo of a group of Pencoyd machine shop (night force) employees, circa 1915. Front row, fourth from right is Charles Major, third from right is Walter Righter, second from right is Charles Haberlein and at right end is William Grennor. *From the collection of R.B. Righter.*

draftsman had been educated at universities such as Rensselaer Polytechnic Institute, Lehigh University and other eastern colleges and universities with engineering departments. Some of the new immigrants came from technical backgrounds such as Schneider, Wolfel, Kunz and Loss (Germany, Austria and Norway) while others came as either skilled or unskilled laborers from

England, Ireland, Scotland, Wales, Germany, Italy, Albania, Hungary, Russia and Poland. Many families lived in West Manayunk in Lower Merion, but most lived in Philadelphia's Manayunk and Roxborough and could walk across the Pencoyd bridge to the plant grounds. These communities were full of cotton and wool mill workers and their families, as the Schuylkill River area was the heart of the flourishing textile industry.

DANGEROUS WORKPLACE

All the specialized equipment developed to increase efficiency and boost production propelled Pencoyd to the top of its field, but with the advances came some dangerous and, in some cases, deadly conditions. The technical advances and new machinery installed at the mill were perhaps unparalleled in the United States, but the change led to some stressful situations at the mill and some dangerous working conditions. In fact, in the early twentieth century, Pencoyd's social club, the Pencoyd Club, had a publication called the *Pencoyder*. It highlighted workers' safety in a time when 50 percent of hospitalizations at the nearby St. Timothy's Hospital were industrial accident related.[589]

Much of the operations relied on railroad car access and railways. Many accidents occurred in connection with the railroad, sometimes involving brakemen but also commonly involving those unconnected with the plant. In January 1890, an "unknown man" was found dead along the railroad near Pencoyd Station. He was "ordinarily dressed and bore the appearance of having worked in an iron works or on a railroad," and the coroner judged it an "accidental death."[590]

In October 1891, Thomas Dugan (aged 21 years and a resident of Falls of Schuylkill), a brakeman on the Reading Railroad, was run over by an engine and killed near Pencoyd Station. He was coupling cars when he lost his footing, and the engine, which was backing, knocked him down. The wheels passed over his left forearm, crushing it badly, and although he was taken to the Episcopal Hospital, he did not recover from the shock of the accident.[591] Nearly a decade later, in February 1901, George E. Donnelly, a brakeman on the night shift at Pencoyd, was found dead with both legs crushed and his head gashed. Found at 1:00 a.m. in the Pencoyd yards, he was apparently run over and killed by one of the two trains that passed the point at 12:15 p.m. that night.[592]

A major railway accident in October 1892 was apparently caused by a Pencoyd Station operator who mistakenly allowed a train of empty coal cars to proceed northward while a southbound passenger train proceeded along the same track. Four passengers, two trainmen and a newsboy died, and nearly 35 persons were injured in the wreck of the Shamokin express at 9:20 a.m. on the main line of the Philadelphia and Reading Railroad at Flat Rock dam. The Manayunk fire department extinguished the fire caused by the wreck, and the injured were taken to St. Timothy's Hospital, Roxborough.[593]

Railroad cars famously catch the attention of homeless or vagrant people, and in 1907, there was an incident leading to a loss of over $350,000 for Pencoyd. "The fire is supposed to have been started by tramps, who were smoking in one of the cars, and who had found lodging there for the night, it was from the blazing car that the building was ignited."[594] The fire started shortly before two o'clock in the morning and spread to the carpenter shop (on the northern end of the plant grounds) and a number of freight cars on sidings; valuable patterns were destroyed. "As soon as the night watchman discovered the blaze he sounded the siren whistle, which aroused hundreds of the employees of the company, and brought to the scene the fire brigade belonging to the plant. It was unable to cope with the spreading flames, and in response to an appeal for aid made to the Philadelphia department, engines were sent from Manayunk, Falls of Schuylkill and Roxborough." They were not able to save the shop, and many of the workman residing close to the plant (of whom many were foreigners) were in a state of panic. Much of the monetary loss was in the destroyed patterns, in process of shipping to Peru, Indiana, where a Pencoyd project was underway.[595]

The mill environment also led to injuries and deaths from either inhalation, fire, falls, floods or machinery. In January 1902, while cleaning out one of the stacks connected with the gas manufacturing retorts, Charles Riebow (of Manayunk) was overcome by fumes, fell to the bottom and was killed. Three weeks earlier, John Bohn (also of Manayunk) fell from the stack and was not found until the next day.[596] A third such death occurred in February when Antonio Gezmeir was suffocated at the Pencoyd Iron Works by gas in a smokestack. In this last case, a jury rendered a verdict of accidental death and recommended that the A.&P. Roberts Company erect safeguards in the smokestacks. Around the same time, Luigi Coffui, a 35-year-old Manayunk resident, died from a fall from a 50′ scaffold at Pencoyd when he lost his footing and landed on his stomach.[597]

The amazing hydraulic shears (Figure 4.15) commanded respect in day-to-day operation as discovered by Jacob A. Phiercosposkl, 32-year-old

Manayunk resident, and Laurence Kelsel, 25-year-old Manayunk resident. Phiercosposki worked on one of the shearing machines, used in cutting plate iron, and somehow his left arm got under the blade and was cut off at the elbow. Almost simultaneously, Kelsel fell against a revolving circular saw, terribly lacerating his left shoulder. Both were taken to St. Timothy's Hospital in Roxborough.[598]

Electrical developments also exposed workers to new technology and new instrumentation, such as the dynamo and arc lamp installation in the 1890s. While revolutionizing the capabilities at the plant, the breakthroughs were not without danger. On November 22, 1900, while working on an arc lamp at Pencoyd, 20-year-old Samuel W. Levins died by electrocution.[599]

Some dangers were of natural causes, and the most concerning of these was flooding of the Schuylkill River. A regional summer storm caused major flooding in 1889 from Philadelphia to New Jersey to Virginia:

> *Floods in all directions have recently interfered with manufacturing operations, and in some instances have caused a temporary suspension of work. The Pencoyd Iron Works, in Philadelphia, were flooded. The De Witt Wire Works, in Belleville, N.J., could be approached only by boats and rafts. All the factories on the Raritan River, in New Brunswick, were shut down. At Danville, Va., all the foundries and machine-shops were submerged, and considerable losses have been sustained in damaged machinery and stock.*[600]

In 1908, a winter storm caused a rise of the Schuylkill River such that Matson's Mill Dam was breached, and River Road (from Spring Mill to Flat Rock dam, on the west side of the river) was covered with two feet of water at ten o'clock in the evening. All the manufacturing plants at Manayunk had their basements flooded as the gradual filling in of the river on both sides by the Pencoyd Iron Works and other establishments caused a rise of nearly fifteen feet. Mill owners had removed all perishable goods to the upper stories. Occupants of the houses along the river road at West Manayunk were compelled to move to the second stories of their houses. At Spring Mill, as a precautionary measure, the Reading Railway station, which was surrounded by the high water, was secured with ropes. Large quantities of lumber with two outhouses, a pig pen and a number of barrels came down the river shortly before nine o'clock Wednesday night.[601]

PAY/STRIKES/UNIONS

Labor conditions at Pencoyd were largely amicable. The owners and workers could usually agree to terms without strikes or belabored negotiations. However, one early exception was in 1891, which was in general a time of labor unrest and union activity was rising all around the East Coast. Pencoyd's troubles in 1891 preceded the Homestead riots of 1892, which, of course, attained international renown and deserve some description here.

The Amalgamated Association of Iron and Steel Workers (AAISW) organized many of the workers in Andrew Carnegie's Homestead Mills. The AAISW originated in 1876 with the merger of three existing unions: The United Sons of Vulcan (iron puddlers); the Associated Brotherhood of Iron and Steel Heaters, Rollers and Roughers; and the Iron and Steel Roll Hands of the United States. In 1876, AAISW had 3,775 members, but by 1891, it had grown to 25,000 members, with 290 lodges, making them one of the most powerful unions in the country.

Andrew Carnegie and his business partner, Henry Clay Frick, wanted to eliminate unions in all their steel plants, and although Carnegie had allowed the union at Homestead for many years, he decided that Frick could lock out union workers on June 29, 1892, a day before the union contract expired. The heart of the issue was wages (workers were paid by the ton)—Frick wanted the price to be set at $22/ton, and the union wanted $25/ton. In addition, the company claimed that workers earned as much as $12 to $14 a day, but they actually made closer to $1.40–$2.50/day. Afraid that the workers might take the plant over, Frick erected a three-mile-long wooden fence with barbed wire around the plant, stationed sharpshooters at sentry towers and called in 300 private guards from the Pinkerton Detective Agency in Chicago.[602]

The Pinkertons, armed with Winchester rifles, were transported by rail to McKees Rocks on the Ohio River just below Pittsburgh, and then on July 5, they floated up the river on two steel barges to the Monongahela River and then on to Homestead. Knowing of their arrival, a crowd of about 5,000, including John McLuckie, the mayor of Homestead, took over the plant and then tried to stop the barges from coming ashore. The battle that took place that July 6 took 13 lives. The Pinkertons finally surrendered their weapons for safe passage, but on their way up from the river shore to the railroad station, they had to walk through a gauntlet of townspeople (including woman and children) armed with sticks, umbrellas, and rocks.[603]

The workers then controlled both the plant and the town. Six days later, the governor of Pennsylvania (convinced by Frick) declared martial law and sent in the state militia. Scab workers were hired; the plant reopened with military protection. By the end of 1892, about 2,000 scabs had been hired, the union had been destroyed and only 800 of the original 3,800 employees were rehired. The Homestead Strike ended steel unions until Roosevelt's New Deal in the 1930s and the passage of the Wagner Act (enacted in 1935, it guaranteed workers the right to organize into unions and practice collective bargaining)—it was then that steel mill workers would organize under the Congress of Industrial Organizations (CIO).[604]

The labor troubles at Pencoyd started in April 1891. For years, it had been the custom on April 1 for a committee of the puddling employees and the representatives of A.&P. Roberts Company to agree on a scale of wages for one year without attaching their names to any contract. In 1891, the puddlers organized a branch of the Amalgamated Association of Iron and Steel Workers, and under the regulations of the organization, they were prohibited from working for any firm or company unless a specific contract was formed and signed by both parties. At the expiration of the mutual agreement on April 1, the employees presented an Amalgamated Association scale of wages. The company refused to sign it but expressed a willingness to the workmen's committee to follow the custom and also pay wages equivalent in each department to that desired by the proposed written contract. In response, about 400 men went on strike.[605]

To add fuel to the fire, James Taggert, an employee of the works, was assaulted by a crowd of locked-out puddlers, and in self-defense, he shot and seriously wounded one of his assailants.[606] By May 15, a portion of the mill affected by the strike was being run on a single shift by some of the bosses and non-union men from the other departments, but no attempts had been made to restart the puddling and finishing departments. Both parties remained determined to stick to their demands; in the meantime, some locked-out workers got jobs elsewhere, some of them well out of the city.[607] At this point, the firm addressed a circular to its employees in which the terms on which work could be resumed were plainly stated. The statement was also regarded as an ultimatum.[608] By May 21, the strike was ending with the striking workers losing out; gradually, operations in all departments would return to normal.[609] By the end of July, one after another of the departments started up until the entire works, with perhaps the exception of one mill, were back in operation.[610]

In 1891, the Amalgamated Association lost strikes at iron and steel mills across the eastern region. Outside Pennsylvania, the union was defeated at the Elmira Iron and Steel Company of Elmira, New York, and the Riverside Iron

Company of New Castle, Delaware. In eastern Pennsylvania, Amalgamated lost disputes at the Norristown Iron Works, the Lochiel Iron Company of Harrisburg, the Lebanon Iron Company, the Lebanon Rolling Mill, the East Lebanon Iron Company, the Hamburg Rolling Mill Company, the Pottsville Iron and Steel Company, the Gibraltar Iron Works in Bucks County, the Taggart and Howells Rolling Mill in Northumberland, the Pencoyd Iron and Steel Company and the Catasauqua Rolling Mill. The Pennsylvania Steel Company won a two-week strike by 2,000 workers at Steelton, Pennsylvania, and declared its new mill at Sparrow's Point, Maryland, an open shop at the same time. This dispute is particularly noteworthy because management there hired Pinkerton guards to protect their mills and several hundred black replacement workers to defeat the strikers. Over the next year, these eastern mills exploited their lower labor costs to penetrate markets in western Pennsylvania that had been dominated by Pittsburgh firms. This only increased the pressure on western Pennsylvania manufacturers to jettison the union."[611]

The events of 1891 to 1892 passed with no radical change at Pencoyd. In fact, by 1902, under the new management of the American Bridge Company, workmen employed by Pencoyd received a 25 percent increase in pay beginning in May (from 40 to 50 cents/hour), along with an enforced 8-hour day. This agreement was reached between Joshua Hatfield, president of the American Bridge Company, and D.F. McIntyre, secretary of the International Association of Bridge and Structural Iron Workers, after a negotiation period of over a month.[612]

Worldwide Economic Influences

Economic conditions were as important as labor negotiations, and the economy has strong and weak periods that are influenced by world events. There was a world economic recession in 1873–78 that affected many industries and financial institutions across the world.[613] It is perhaps fortunate that Philadelphia was focused on the Centennial Exhibition these years. Because Pencoyd was involved in the centennial building construction, perhaps this provided much-needed work in a period where work would otherwise have been slow. The year 1904 was another such period of economic uncertainty, and this time it directly affected Pencoyd. Fewer orders in April were making plant management worried about a recession or even a depression. Portions of the plant had to close due to a slowdown in work orders. New orders were being received, but the lead time was so long (for example, castings for the Pennsylvania tunnel in New York City) that the activity would not pick up for two or three months at the earliest and possibly six months or a year.[614] By the end of April, however, Pencoyd's bridge works started up again, and

> *over 1000 employees went to work at the call of "Big Ben," the mill whistle. Four of the six steel furnaces were put in full operation and the other two will be charged as soon as repairs can be made. The blooming mill is rolling out steel ingots that were piled up in the yard since October last. The 28-inch mill is turning out structural steel as fast as two sets of hands can handle the material with the help of the automatic machinery, and orders have been received to get the 20-inch mill ready as soon as possible. In addition to the departments that were started up yesterday the steel and iron foundries and the bridge shop are running on hurry-up orders. Several hundred employees who were given employment at Ambridge and other establishments near Pittsburgh have returned to their old places.*[615]

There were undoubtedly many examples of economic pressure causing temporary plant closures and layoffs. But the specialized nature of the Pencoyd products, coupled with their widespread need and use, meant that suspension of any plant operations would only be temporary.

REPUTATION AMONG NATIONAL AND INTERNATIONAL ORGANIZATIONS

Pencoyd's reputation in the engineering world is described in chapter 6, as many of the chief engineers had key roles in obtaining and designing work for the company. Another way Pencoyd shined was by playing a leading role in the national and international engineering community.

Pencoyd and Percival Roberts Jr. opened their doors to groups of engineers and visitors associated with national meetings of the American Institute of Mining Engineers in 1881, offering tours of Pencoyd on February 16.[616] At this point, Pencoyd specialized in wrought-iron structural shapes and railroad car axles, so the visitors saw the puddling and rolling mills, the forges, the boiler houses and pumphouses, the machine shop and the newly installed Houston-Thomsen arc lamp system.[617]

In 1889, a large delegation of American engineers visited Germany hosted by numerous German technical works. There was a Pencoyd delegation that specifically visited the Rheinishe Stahlwerke (along with delegates from Bethlehem, Standard, Homestead, Linden and Joliet), where they made both Bessemer and open-hearth acid and basic steel, rolling shapes, bars, sleepers and rails. The German hosts gave tours of the coal plant at Bulmke, the steel works at Oberhausen, the blast furnaces of the Shalker Gruben and Huetten Verein, all of which were working at impressive levels of output. The German hosts, and in particular, a Herr Schroeder, spoke on the importance of gatherings of engineers in bringing into closer relationship countries so widely separated as Germany and America. The Americans even got a visit with Empress Augusta, the widow of Kaiser Wilhelm I, who was fluent in English fluently and spoke of her interest in charity, such as the American Red Cross and providing help to the victims of the (then) recent Johnstown Flood of 1889.[618] The representatives from Pencoyd may have included some of German descent or origin, as we know that Schneider and Wolfel, for example, both came from Germany, and there must have been others.

In 1899, the American Society of Civil Engineers held its annual meeting in Philadelphia, and Percival Roberts Jr., James Christie and C.C. Schneider met a number of delegates at Pencoyd for a tour on Saturday, July 1, after the meeting week. The delegates arrived by special train, and they got to see, among other things, the newly installed electric cranes and the eye-bar forging shop.[619] Pencoyd was then a world leader in engineering and production of structures and was of great interest to the meeting attendees.

BRIDGE CREWS—UNITED STATES AND INTERNATIONAL

One of the more unique capabilities of Pencoyd was constructing bridges or structures in the field and, eventually, even the construction of bridges internationally. Although the projects are described in chapters 7, 8 and 10, this section focuses more on the experiences of the crews both at the plant and at construction sites in the United States and abroad. Most of the projects had Philadelphia-based personnel, whether bridge engineers, erectors or other specialized personnel.

Many construction projects utilized a traveler, which allowed building a span from one pier or from a shore to the first pier. The traveler rolled along the rail lines and had a platform for providing power or steam to operate cranes or riveters or other equipment and thus had a large associated crew. The Newark Viaduct, built in 1905, had a sizable traveler that also served as a great backdrop for a crew photo (Figure 11.3).[620] Similarly, the Thebes Bridge, across the Mississippi, utilized travelers to construct the cantilevered design (see chapter 7); the traveler at this site also was a spectacular location for a crew photo (Figure 11.4) high above the river.[621] A PRR bridge across the Susquehanna River (Wrightsville to Columbia) was built in 1897 by two different companies: Pencoyd Iron Works and Edgemoor Iron Works.[622] The construction crew for this project posed in front of the portal end of the completed through truss bridge (Figure 11.5).[623]

International bridge projects offered another level of challenges above those of a domestic bridge project. One challenge was getting the bridge

(11.3) Crew on the traveler during construction of the Newark Viaduct, 1905. *From* Engineering News, *July 22, 1905, 102–4.*

Left: (11.4) Crew on traveler during Thebes bridge construction. *From the* Engineering Record, *September 16, 1905, 330–35.*

Right: (11.5) Crew of Susquehanna Wrightsville to Columbia bridge completed 27 spans crossing 1 mile. Pencoyd and Edge Moor worked together and completed this bridge in 21 days. *From the collection of the York County History Center, York, Pennsylvania.*

parts ready for transport—whether by railroad (bridge parts for an 1896 bridge project in the state of Washington were delivered by about 250 railroad cars across the middle and western United States or by combination of railroad and steamer (for example a 1930 project in California had the parts shipped by sea via the Panama Canal).[624] And of course, international projects like Atbara or Uganda involved shipping bridge parts by steamer through intermediate points (Liverpool or Rotterdam) and shipping canals (Suez).[625] Getting crews to the construction sites and housing them there for extended periods offered challenges as well. In extreme cases, there were tragedies for crews such as the 1913 Iron Bridge project in Formosa (modern-day Taiwan), where apparently 42 workers died during construction.[626] In other cases, crews had to become accustomed to local cultures and regional climates and living conditions. Some crew experiences from Sudan, Mexico and Uganda, based on detailed accounts from engineering journals, follow.

ATBARA

A glimpse of the work on the highly touted Atbara bridge project in Sudan was provided by one of the foreman, C.J. Wennas, who inserted some modesty into the discussion of the Pencoyd work in Sudan: "Some of our friends are making too much of this hero business. We were picked out to go over there and put up the bridge, and while we naturally did the best we could under the circumstances, I think we did no better than any of the other men could have done." He continued to describe the climatic conditions, which were very hot, with the thermometer reading 120° to 130°F in the shade at 11:00 a.m. The crew ate lots of goat and gazelle meat and plenty of wild game, ducks, rabbits and so on. The water was "just like Philadelphia water—wants filtering." He described the crews (numbering as many as 250) as the finest specimens physically that he ever saw, but also "the laziest." "They could only do one thing in one day. The man who hooked a chain on a car would not shove that car. He would call on twenty or more of his friends. It was necessary to have seven or eight different squads for each kind of work." Communications were difficult and involved interpreters, since some were Sudanese and some were Egyptians. Despite the communication differences, they were able to teach the native crews how to rivet. The religious disposition of the crews also was noted, as there were frequent prayers, and it made "no difference whether they have a hot rivet in a hole or not." Because of the heat, they went to work at 5:30 a.m. and worked until 8:00 a.m., then from 8:30 a.m. to 11:00 a.m., then from 3:00 p.m. to 6:00 p.m. or later. However, it was impossible to work between 11:00 a.m. and 3:00 p.m.[627]

UGANDA

Available descriptions of the crews of the Ugandan railway viaducts give some insight into the daily life and interactions between different cultures. The bridge erectors taken from Philadelphia were mostly between 25 and 35 years of age, native Americans (born in the United States) and selected from the most competent and reliable men among several hundred employed by the American Bridge Company. Their wages were about twice that for similar work in the United States, and because there was very little opportunity for them to spend their money, most of them returned home with satisfactory sums to their credit—a few even having sufficient funds to purchase comfortable homes upon their return to America. These men did most of the erection proper, handling the steel, assembling it and other skilled work. They were assisted by about 150 Hindus, mostly riveters, carpenters and mechanics, who were each paid 45 rupees per month and their daily rations. There were also 150 native Africans who were employed wholly for crude labor (on the ground as opposed to aloft) and were paid 10 rupees per month and rations.[628] The nine-hour working day was from 7:00 a.m. until 7:00 p.m., without any interval for lunch.

The Pencoyd workers occupied five 12′ by 30′ one-story wooden frame bungalows, sheathed and roofed with corrugated iron. One house was for cooking and dining, one for the superintendent (N.P. Jarrett) and the other three each accommodated six men. A total of 10 bungalows were provided by the railway company—5 of them were erected at Mile 468 in advance of the party's arrival, while the other 5 were installed at the next site so they would be ready when the next bridge segment was to be worked on the line. Then the first set of 5 was moved ahead, and so on, so that accommodations were ready in advance for optimum time efficiency. The bungalows were furnished with cots, mattresses and blankets brought from America; other furniture, including excellent chairs and tables, was made by Hindu carpenters. At the camps, the American workers prepared gardens and sowed many different kinds of vegetable seeds brought from Philadelphia, all of which grew well, except cabbage.[629]

The Hindus employed were described as "quite intelligent and efficient" and were "well trained in riveting."[630] A riveting gang consisted of six men, two men holding the dolly-bar, two to drive, one to blow the forge and one to heat the rivets. Ordinarily, each gang could drive 90 to 100 rivets daily. Of interesting note is that many Hindus signed paperwork with a thumbprint rather than a standard signature. Hindu clothing was very irregular, ranging from little to more standard clothing and some even sporting accessories like watches rather than fancy clothes. Many were also willing and able to work at heights. As with Atbara, some crew members performed only one task: the rivet heater would not blow the forge, and the dolly-bar man would not strike the rivet and so on.[631]

The Africans, who were from the local pastoral or agricultural tribes, lived in crude huts constructed of whatever materials were most convenient, such as old corrugated iron or pieces of discarded canvas, more commonly small round huts of brush and grass plastered for waterproofing. The Africans were divided into three parties of about 50 men each, governed by a head man or overseer who ruled and disciplined them with considerable severity and kept them at work.[632] There were also at times settlements and roving tribes of Maasai who were "more or less war like and armed with spears having very long iron blades, bows and knives."[633] The camps and herds were guarded by native watchmen armed with spears and large shields of thick hide probably sufficient to turn an arrow. One class of the men were trained porters and were used exclusively for transporting materials, which they carried on their heads. Regular loads were 60 pounds, and travel of 18 or 20 miles a day, unprotected from the blazing sun, was typical. According to the accounts of the erecting crews, a constant feud was maintained between the Africans and the Hindus, which sometimes led to severe tension between the crews.

The viaduct construction was at an elevation of 5,000′ to 8,000′ in rolling or mountainous country, with about half of the viaducts being in jungle and the others in the open. One of the camps was established in latitude four degrees south, and the northernmost point reached by the work was 15 miles south of the equator. Torrential downpours accompanied by fierce thunder and lightning were common, usually in the later afternoon into the night. The climate was dry, and daily temperature could swing from 90° F at noon to white frost in the morning. In fact, the intense sun compelled the light-complexioned men to wear pith helmets and heavy khaki coats to avoid sunburn. As in Atbara a few years previously, rain and stream water was always filtered or boiled before drinking.[634]

The country abounded in large game, including almost innumerable quantities of deer and antelope (as well as more tough waterbeste of many kinds. Many antelope were shot in the vicinity, and some other large game was secured by expeditions that went out on hunts of several days' duration, attended by a number of Africans for guides and porters. Even though there was a great abundance of game, live meat was purchased with as many as 25 cattle and 75 sheep available for butchering as required. The construction party also had a large amount of canned meats and vegetables, condensed milk and similar supplies. English physicians also apparently recommended drinking whiskey daily.[635]

There were very few poisonous insects or dangerous animals. One small insect was very troublesome in getting underneath the toe nails, where it caused bad sores, and on this account, it was a rule never to step barefooted on the floor but to keep a pair of slippers by the bedside.[636] One 14′ snake was killed, and one lioness was shot from the locomotive early one morning as she was watching a zebra. This was the only lion shot by the members of this party, but on the section adjacent to them, where the latitude was much lower and the line was through dense forests, 22 men were killed by three lions just before the bridge erectors arrived.[637] There was no fever or other severe sickness in the American camp—the men enjoyed excellent health—but when they returned to the coast and waited 13 days for the steamer, they were all severely attacked by the coast fever. The bubonic plague broke out in the African and Hindu camps about 100 miles from the bridge men's camp, and a number of deaths resulted. The camp was strictly quarantined, and the disease was easily checked after burning the camp and subjecting the natives to a thorough bath.

There was a little leisure time amid the work schedule. The men celebrated July 4 by making an excursion on a special train to the large native trading city at Lake Victoria and, occasionally during the progress of the work and after its completion, made hunting trips for large game. The communication with America was very slow and infrequent, with the average time required to receive a reply to a letter about three months, and the shortest time for a letter between Mombassa and Philadelphia was four weeks.[638] Elephants, rhinoceros, zebras and many small monkeys and baboons were to be found nearby. Two of the latter were kept in the camp as mascots and became great pets.

In general, the men considered the work comparatively easy and the conditions pleasant and would be willing at any time to return on a similar expedition to the highlands but under no consideration would undertake such work near the coast.[639]

MEXICO

The climate of northern Mexico is ideal for outdoor work, and railroad construction can be carried on uninterrupted through the year. Even the summer days were never excessively warm due to the high altitude, and in winter, although the nights were quite cold, there was never any frost in the ground.[640]

Costs of labor and food were documented in the descriptions of the work on the Chihuahua Pacific Railway work and give interesting examples of the relative costs of labor and supplies. The prices of labor were approximately as follows (shown in Mexican currency, which at the time was MXN $2.20 = USD $1.00):

> *Laborers, $1.00 per day; foremen of laborers, $1.50 to $2.00 and board; general foremen, $3.00 to $6.00 and board; American blacksmiths, $3.00 to $4.00 and board; commissary clerks, $3.00 and board; masons and stonecutters, $2.00 to $4.00 and board. A wagon and six mules was worth $6.00 a day, and each additional mule $1.00. Lime delivered on the Work cost $1.00 to $1.25 per 100 1b., and Portland cement at the railhead $11.00 per barrel.*

Standard food supplies cost about as follows in Chihuahua, and it is necessary to add about $0.40 per ton per kilometer for transportation beyond the railhead: beef, native delivered, $0.25 per kilo; corn, maize, $3.25 per hectoliter; hay, $40.00 per ton; flour, $6.00 per 100 pounds; Mexican coffee, $0.50 per kilo; sugar, $0.25 per kilo; beans, $0.07 per kilo.; kerosene, $0.80 per gallon. One drawback was a lack of good drinking water in some parts.[641]

The great success of the Pencoyd in making wrought iron, steel and the many bridges and steel frame structures all over the world could not have been possible without the dedication, hard work, skills and resolution of the many workers contributing at such a wide variety of levels and expertise. Clearly much of the innovation was driven by the engineers placing requirements on structures and utilizing the latest technology in both the mill and in the bridges and structures being designed. The crews generating power, moving raw materials, rolling, cutting or shaping products or building structures must have attained the highest level of perfection in their respective endeavors, or the company would not have achieved the successes it did over many decades. Descendants of the mill workers should be proud of their connection to the mill. (I know I am—Walter Righter must have had his hands full first in the machine shop and later as superintendent of motive power for Pencoyd from 1882 to 1932.) It could be a dangerous and dirty place, but it was also the site of one of America's great success stories.

12

Epilogue and Lasting Tributes to Pencoyd

Incorporation into U.S. Steel and World War I

The merger of 28 companies into the American Bridge Company in 1900 led to Pencoyd being part all of a large operation under the American Bridge umbrella. This continued to an even greater extent when U.S. Steel purchased American Bridge Company in 1902. The activities at Pencoyd documented in annual reports for the company indicate continued upkeep of the facilities and refurbishing aspects of the mill to stay current and competitive with new technologies into the 1920s.[642]

Activity at the plant during World War I included fabrication of plate girders for five U.S. naval railway gun mount cars (and associated 6 locomotives and 72 auxiliary cars) that were ultimately deployed in France.[643] These gun mounts were a joint project with the Eddystone shop of the Baldwin locomotive works in Philadelphia, and the Standard Steel Car Company in Pittsburgh. Plates were rolled in Pittsburgh and then promptly shipped to Pencoyd for fabrication.[644] The girders were ready to ship to Baldwin works ahead of schedule, as were many of the other components. The gun mounts were scheduled to be completed by June 15 but were finished and ready for operation by May 25, 1918.[645]

After some testing operations in the United States, the railway cars were deployed in France. During the period from September 6, 1918, until the signing of the armistice, five U.S. naval batteries, each composed of one 14″ .50-caliber gun carried on a special railway mount attached to ammunition and auxiliary cars, bombarded German bases and positions behind the lines in France with remarkable efficiency and important results.[646] These guns were more powerful than any others in use at the front and played a prominent part in destroying railway and supply bases and generally in hampering concentration behind the German lines, besides lowering the enemy's morale.[647] They thus contributed materially to the victory of the Allied forces.

After World War I, the plant continued operations under U.S. Steel until 1936, when it became part of Carnegie Illinois Steel Company.[648] During that period, it was involved with several notable bridge projects. In 1928–29, Pencoyd produced steel for the Lake Champlain Bridge in Crown Point, New York. This bridge connected New York and Vermont near the southern end of Lake Champlain and lasted for 80 years, until it was destroyed in 2009 to be replaced by a new bridge. In 1930, American Bridge Company completed the Trinity River bridge in California—most of the steel was rolled at Pencoyd, and the bridge was assembled in Elmira, New York, and then shipped by steamer via the Panama Canal to San Francisco.

In 1939, Pencoyd became inactive—it was briefly activated during World War II but then closed for good in 1944.[649] The decline of Pencoyd can be attributed to two main factors: the restrictions of the size and geometry of the land along the Schuylkill River and the subsequent investment in new technology and design by American Bridge and U.S. Steel at their other locations, especially in Pittsburgh (Ambridge). In some ways, Pencoyd was a victim of its own success, as much of the technology and detailed industrial processes developed at Pencoyd were then implemented at the new locations, thus ultimately making Pencoyd obsolete.[650] The site of the mill has been used since for a number of smaller businesses, including Connelly Containers. More recently, Penn Real Estate is housed in the newly refurbished mill office building.[651] There are plans to develop the site, including hotel designs that incorporate some of the old Pencoyd steel structures.[652]

A REVERENCE FOR BRIDGES

I have tried to convey the history of the Pencoyd Iron Works, including the founders, the people who led it to its peak of innovation, the buildings and bridges they produced and the various equipment and processes used to achieve this. Examples of Pencoyd products occur all around the world, and they are moving and lasting tributes to the many people associated with the company and the products. Many bridges and a few buildings are over 120 years old. Although with all this great success and achievement by Pencoyd, upon writing this book, I realized that there are a few examples of Pencoyd structures suffering unfair demise. The Broad Street Station experienced a debilitating fire in 1923;[653] the Wabash River bridge accident affected Attica, Indiana, in 1914;[654] the molasses tank explosion in Boston in 1919 affected several spans of the Boston Elevated railway;[655] and the Big Bayou Canot train derailment accident in Mobile, Alabama, in 1993 was caused by a barge hitting the bridge supports just hours before the accident.[656] In all these cases, Pencoyd structures were involved in but not the cause of a horrific accident. That their structures were involved in such incidents is more attributable to the extent of Pencoyd bridges and structures around the country.

A more positive and lasting tribute to a structure or bridge is one that has been relocated or preserved and utilized in a different area or for a slightly different purpose than its original intent. Bridge relocation and restoration are widespread around the world. I turn to the work of Frank Griggs Jr., who describes restoration of iron bridges in the northeastern United States and in some historical locations such as Troy, New York (Union College).[657] I was also happy to discover many Pencoyd bridges being restored, with examples in Japan, Taiwan, Missouri, Kansas, Arkansas, New York, Texas and even at Pencoyd itself. Below is a brief description of the bridges at some of these sites, now many of which are over 100 years old.

Many bridge restorations have involved repurposing a railroad bridge to a pedestrian bridge, and there are two wonderful examples of this in Nagoya, Japan, and Kansas City, Missouri. The bridge in Kansas City, originally near 2nd Street and Broadway, was built in 1892 and consisted of two truss spans across the Missouri River.[658] In 2006, it was moved downtown near Union Station, where it is now a pedestrian walkway over the city rail lines.[659] It is a striking and unique design that adds a historic element to the city skyline. Similarly, in Aichi-ken in Nagoya, there is a Pencoyd bridge that was originally built over a river in Kyoto.[660] It was moved in 1930 to the new site, where it serves as a pedestrian walkway over numerous rail lines at a railway station.[661]

The Waddell A Truss bridge design described in chapters 7 and 11 was built in many locations all over the world. One of the only surviving examples was built in Trimble County, Kansas, in 1898. In 1960, this bridge was relocated to English Park along the Missouri River, where it is now preserved and used as a pedestrian bridge that connects two parts of the park that are separated by a small creek.[662]

In 1900, Pencoyd Iron Works built a bridge across the Schuylkill River that connected the plant (near the mill office) with Manayunk across the river.[663] It was meant to allow easy pedestrian access to the ironworks for those workers residing on the Manayunk and Roxborough side of the river and also provided rail access between the Pencoyd operations on each side of the river. With the decline and permanent closure of the plant after World War II, the bridge fell into disrepair. More recently, it has been refurbished and reopened as a pedestrian and bike trail—part of the Cynwyd Heritage Trail—in 2016 (Figure 12.1).[664] In addition to the bridge, Pencoyd Landing is a proposed new hotel project on the site of the Pencoyd Iron Works. Some structural elements of the mill are incorporated into the planning for the site, a fitting tribute to the mill and the office building.[665]

The Boston Elevated Railway expanded to 11 stations throughout Boston in 1899, with the bulk of the steel provided by Pencoyd and the Pennsylvania Steel company. When it was dismantled in the 1980s, the Northhampton Station was removed and placed in the Seashore Trolley Museum in Kennebunkport, Maine.[666] The entire station, as well as some underlying steel structure, is preserved there for any elevated railway aficionados to see in person.

The Clinton Presidential Library in Little Rock sits along the Arkansas River and opened in 2011. The design of the new library incorporated the Choctaw-Memphis railway bridge into its design, allowing access to the full bridge and adding a unique touch to the park and library grounds.[667] The bridge, built in 1899, can be accessed from the library and consisted of four through truss spans and one swing span; the original swing span was replaced with a vertical lift span in the 1970s.[668]

The Lake Champlain bridge, built in 1928–29, joined New York and Vermont at Crown Point, New York. When the span was destroyed in 2009 for a replacement bridge, New York State assembled a display in the Crown Point Lake Champlain Visitors Center as a tribute to the bridge and its history. One item on display there is a section of a diagonal chord or brace from the bridge that also has *Pencoyd* stamped into the steel. This piece of the old bridge can be viewed and enjoyed by visitors to this area, along with much additional information about the bridge and region.

In 1899, Pencoyd built a pony truss bridge across the Mustang Creek near Sadler, Texas. In 2010, shortly after this bridge was replaced, the Old American Golf Club in The Colony, Texas, had the opportunity to acquire

Top: (12.1) Newly refurbished Pencoyd Bridge, which reopened as part of the Cynwyd Heritage Trail in 2016. *Author's collection.*

Bottom: (12.2) Pieces of the original Amarube viaduct, built in 1911, left on display beneath the new concrete structure. *Google Street View.*

this bridge. The club moved it from the Sadler area to The Colony and incorporated it into the design of the golf course and proudly features this bridge at the golf club. It is a striking sight in the middle of a golf course and a unique tribute to Pencoyd and all those involved in bridge design and production there over a hundred years ago.[669]

The last example is the Amarube viaduct—built on the north coast of Honshu, Japan, in 1911.[670] It was in service for nearly 100 years but was shut down in 2009 and replaced in 2012. Structures remaining from the original bridge were left on display beneath the viaduct (Figure 12.2). In addition to the remaining steel structures being used as a sky station for observation, some of the steel from the bridge was sent to universities to provide test pieces to understand the effect of aging and exposure to sea air for 100 years.[671]

Bridges are not the only structures that have been re-furbished. The 1905 Altman department store, which closed in 1985, was refurbished in 1996 and is now utilized by the City University of New York as the CUNY Graduate Center.

There may be other examples of Pencoyd bridges and buildings that have been refurbished, but these are the examples this author could locate. There are many surviving and relocated bridges from the era of iron and steel truss bridges in the nineteenth century. Perhaps these few examples will encourage the interested reader to take notice and appreciate all the detailed and specialized design and production and skill that went into their fabrication and construction.

Appendix 1

List of Bridges International

Japanese bridge information is taken from The Steel Structure Committee of the Japan Society of Civil Engineers Historic Steel Bridge Survey, http://library.jsce.or.jp/jscelib/committee/2003/bridge/brtop.htm#top.

1 T2-011; Niigata railway bridge Yahiko Line, 1898
2 I1—Chihuahua Pacific Railroad (CPRR), Santa Isabel, 1898
3 I2—CPRR, Viaduct 1, 1898
4 I3—CPRR, Viaduct 2, 1898
5 T2-010-Miyoshi, 1898
6 T1-005-Yodogawa, 1899
7 Hozugawa, Kyoto, (moved to Aichi-ken Nagoya in 1953), 1899
8 I5 - Atbara Bridge, Sudan, 1899
9 T2-012; Tarumi Railway Line Bridge Gifu, 1900
10 T1-009-Jusenji, 1900
11 T1-006; Wakayama, 1902
12 I6 - Uganda Railway 1, 1902–1903 (can be located in satellite images)
13 I7 - Uganda Railway 2, 1902–1903
14 I8 - Uganda Railway 3, 1902–1903
15 I9 - Uganda Railway 4, 1902–1903
16 I10 - Uganda Railway 5, 1902–1903
17 I11 - Uganda Railway 6, 1902–1903
18 I12 - Uganda Railway 7, 1902–1903

19 I13 - Uganda Railway 8, 1902–1903
20 I14 - Uganda Railway 9, 1902–1903
21 I15 - Uganda Railway 10, 1902–1903
22 I16 - Uganda Railway 11, 1902–1903
23 I17 - Uganda Railway 12, 1902–1903
24 I18 - Uganda Railway 13, 1902–1903
25 I19 - Uganda Railway 14, 1902–1903
26 I20 - Uganda Railway 15, 1902–1903
27 I21 - Uganda Railway 16, 1902–1903
28 I22 - Uganda Railway 17, 1902–1903
29 I23 - Uganda Railway 18, 1902–1903
30 I24 - Uganda Railway 19, 1902–1903
31 I25 - Uganda Railway 20, 1902–1903
32 I26 - Uganda Railway 21, 1902–1903
33 I27 - Uganda Railway 22, 1902–1903
34 I28 - Uganda Railway 23, 1902–1903
35 I29 - Uganda Railway 24, 1902–1903
36 I30 - Uganda Railway 25, 1902–1903
37 I31 - Uganda Railway 26, 1902–1903
38 I32 - Uganda Railway 27, 1902–1903
39 T6-004, 1903
40 T6-005-Fujimi, 1903
41 T1-008-Kumamoto, 1906
42 T1-010-Toyama, 1907
43 T3-023; Yokohama, 1907
44 T3-024; Yokohama 2, 1907
45 T1-011-Kitakata, 1908
46 T2-017; Gifu, 1910
47 T2-018-Ono, 1911
48 T2-019-Gujo, 1911
49 T2-020-Ichihara, 1911
50 T2-021-Oguni, 1911
51 T2-022 (removed), 1911
52 G4-003; Amarube Viaduct, 1911
53 T1-018-Ogino, 1911
54 T1-020-Nishiaizu, 1911
55 T1-015-Kyoto, 1911
56 T1-021-Tokusawa, 1912
57 T1-022-Kanose, 1912

58 T1-023-Toyomi, 1912
59 T2-023-Kitaazumi, 1912
60 T1-017-Minamisuita-Osaka, 1912
61 T2-027; Toyodacho Station, Nagoya, 1912
62 I4 - Iron Bridge Kaoping River, 1913
63 T2-024; Chichibu, 1913
64 T2-025; Urayamaguchi, 1913
65 T2-026-Chichibu, 1913
66 T1-024-Fuji, 1914
67 T2-015-Mukawa, 1922

Appendix 2

List of Buildings for which Pencoyd Provided Structural Iron or Steel

1875–76	Centennial Exposition buildings—Main and Memorial Hall
1880–81	Office building, Pencoyd Iron Works
1886	Philadelphia B&ORR depot
1887	Brooklyn Elevated Railway
1887, 1899	U.S. Navy Yard Shop
1891	Jersey City terminal
1892	Hotel Walton (later John Bartram Hotel), Philadelphia
1893	Metropolitan Life Insurance Company, New York City
1893	Broad Street Station, Philadelphia
1894	Manhattan Life Insurance Company, New York City
1895	Guaranty building, in Buffalo, New York
1895–96	Fisher building on Dearborn Street in Chicago
1895–96	General Electric Machine Shop Schenectady, New York (Building 16)
1896	Girard Estate Building, Philadelphia

1896	America Baptist Publishing House, Philadelphia
1896	Central Syndicate Building, New York City
1897	Land Title and Trust Building, Philadelphia
1897	Vincent Building, New York City
1897	Gillender Building, New York City
1897	The Franklin Building, New York City
1897	Randolph/Wabash Street station on the Loop Elevated railway, Chicago
1898	West End Trust Bldg., Philadelphia
1898	Beaman-Smith Mill Building, Providence, Rhode Island
1898	UGI Building, Philadelphia
1898	U.S. Mint Building, Indian Garden Street, Philadelphia
1898	The National Export Exposition buildings for the 1899 exposition, Philadelphia
1898	Fourteenth Street viaduct, Denver
1898	White Star Line pier shed in New York City
1898	Back Bay Station in Boston
1898–99	Ellis Island Immigration Station, New York City
1899	Real Estate Trust building, Philadelphia
1899–1900	Wanamaker Building Philadelphia
1899–1900	Boston Elevated railway
1900–1901	Richmond train station, train shed, viaducts and James River elevated rail line
1903	Atlantic Avenue Viaducts
1905	General Electric Machine Shop, New Jersey

1905	Marion Power Station, New Jersey
1905	Newark Viaducts
1905	Bellevue-Stratford Hotel, Philadelphia
1905	B. Altman Department Store building, New York City
1906	Market Street Elevated Railway near City Hall in Philadelphia
1906	Pennsylvania State Capitol Building in Harrisburg
1907	The United Express Company Building, New York City
1909	Trenton Avenue Elevated Railway Kensington Philadelphia
1909	Hudson Terminal Buildings in Manhattan
1909	Racquet Club House, Philadelphia
1910	Seventh Regiment Armory, New York
1910	New Theater, New York
1911	Structural elements of the Polo Grounds stadium after the fire of 1911
1912	Guaranty Trust Building, New York City
1912	Bonwit-Teller Department store building
1914	"House of Morgan," or Morgan Building at 23 Wall Street
1929	John Rodgers Airport, Hangar No. 2. at Honolulu, Hawaii airport

International

1902	Kalgoorlie carbarn, western Australia
1905	Mutual Life Insurance Company in Mexico City (today Banco Mexico building)
1909	Plaza Hotel in Buenos Aires, Argentina

Notes

Chapter 1

1. *Steel*, August 15, 1940, page 28.
2. American Bridge Company, *Successful American* 3, no. 5 (1901) 248–78.
3. D. Loth, *Pencoyd and the Roberts Family* (New York: n.p., 1961), 38.
4. Phyllis C. Maier and Mary Mendenhall Woods, eds. *Lower Merion: A History* (Ardmore, PA: Lower Merion Historical Society [hereafter LMHS], 1988), 90–91.
5. Richard B. Righter, "A Brief Historical Narrative of the Friedrich Groh, Henry Grow and Elizabeth Grow Lentz Genealogical Line of Lower Merion, Montgomery County, Pennsylvania," 2010, 15 pp., page 6, in the collection at Historical Society of Pennsylvania (HSP).
6. Percival Roberts obituary, *Iron Age*, April 7, 1898, 18.
7. Maps showing Percival Roberts land; *Atlas of the Main Line*, 1920, plate 8, http://lowermerionhistory.org/?page_id=802.
8. Maier and Woods, *Lower Merion*, 90–91.
9. Ibid, 91.
10. "Our 275th Year," *The Review*, Special Supplement, (newspaper) (Roxborough, PA: Intercounty Publishing Co., June 1965), 2.
11. R.B. Righter, *Genealogy & History of Peter Righter (Richter)*, 2006, item #288314, HSP.
12. *Review*, "Our 275th Year," 2.
13. Ibid., 2.
14. Ibid., 10.

15. Ibid., 2.
16. Ibid., 2, 10.
17. Ibid., 4.
18. Ibid.
19. Ibid.
20. Charles Francis Jenkins, *Washington in Germantown: Being an Account of the Various Visits of the Commander-in-Chief and First President to Germantown, Pennsylvania* (Philadelphia: William J. Campbell, 1905), 436 pages.
21. Find A Grave, genealogy record for Esther Righter Jones, www.findagrave.com.
22. An 1816 purchase of land of George Righter's by Stritzell showing Gates as owner of adjacent parcel.
23. W.J. Buck, *History of Montgomery County Within the Schuylkill Valley* (Norristown, PA: E.L. Acker, Norristown, PA, 1859), 32.
24. Ibid.
25. F.G. Hobson, J.W. Bickel, J.H. Hendricks and A.R. Place, A.R. *Montgomery County Law Reporter*, vol. 16, *Containing Chiefly Reports of Cases Decided by the Courts of Montgomery County for the Year 1900*, "In Re: Vacation of Part of Schuylkill River Road, and Part of Righter's Ferry Road, in Lower Merion Township" (Norristown, PA: Norristown Bar Association, 1900), 66–70.
26. E. Sloane, *A Reverence for Wood* (Mineola, NY: Dover Publications, 1965).
27. Hannah Tunis married John Righter (Righter, *Genealogy & History*).
28. Edwin Tunis, *Colonial Craftsman and the Beginnings of American Industry* (New York: World Publishing Company, 1965), 170 pages.
29. Edwin Tunis, *The Tavern at the Ferry* (New York: Thomas Y. Crowell, 1973).

Chapter 2

30. *Celebrating William Penn's Vision and the First Welsh Settlement in Lower Merion and Narberth 1682–2007* (Ardmore, PA: LMHS, 2007), 16 pages; Carl E. Doebley, *Lower Merion: A Portrait from the Welsh Tract to the Present* (Philadelphia: Philadelphia Letter Shop, Inc., 1976).
31. Christopher Hill, *The Century of Revolution: 1604–1714* (New York: W.W. Norton & Company), 201.
32. "Pencoyd Farm," The Roberts Estate Historic American Buildings Survey [hereafter HABS] No. PA-1087, 22 pp., Library of Congress.
33. Loth, *Pencoyd and the Roberts Family*, 21.
34. Ibid., v.

35. Ibid., 1–3; J.A. Christie, "Percival Roberts Jr.," *Cassier's Magazine* 23, no. 5 (March 1903): 679–80.
36. Loth, *Pencoyd and the Roberts Family*, 35–46.
37. HSP, Roberts Family Collection, diary of Algernon Roberts, 1846–1848.
38. Loth, *Pencoyd and the Roberts Family*, 38.
39. *Van Nostrand's Eclectic Engineering Magazine*, November 1869, 1,044.
40. Percival Roberts obituary, *Iron Age*, April 7, 1898, 18.
41. Loth, *Pencoyd and the Roberts Family*, 40.
42. *The Pennsylvania Railroad Company, Corporate, Financial, and Construction History of Lines Owned Operated and Controlled to December 31, 1945*, 2 volumes (New York: Coverdale and Colpitts, 1947), 671; William Bender Wilson, *History of the Pennsylvania Railroad Company with Plan of Organization, Portraits of Officials and Biographical Sketches* (Philadelphia: Henry T. Coates & Company, 1895), 543 pages.
43. D.H. Wakelin and J.A. Ricketts, "The Nature of Ironmaking," in *The Making, Shaping & Treating of Steel, Ironmaking* (Pittsburgh, PA: AISE Steel Foundation, 1999), 1–35.
44. *Map of the Pennsylvania, Reading, and Lehigh Valley Railroads, and Their Connections*, Library of Congress, https://www.loc.gov/resource/g3791p.rr005210.
45. Ellwood Roberts, "Algernon B. Roberts," in *Biographical Annals of Montgomery County, Pennsylvania* (N.p., 1903), 512.
46. Ibid.
47. Ibid.
48. *The First 300: The Amazing and Rich History of Lower Merion* (Ardmore, PA: LMHS, 2000); Kathy O'Loughlin, "George Roberts: Pa. Railroad President with Deep Roots on the Main Line," *Lower Merion Times*, August 25, 2013.
49. Roberts, "Algernon B. Roberts," 512.
50. Ibid.
51. Ibid.
52. Nicholas Phillippi, "Tracing the Chinese Wall in Center City," Hidden City, October 2, 2013, http://hiddencityphila.org.
53. Roberts, Algernon B. Roberts," 512.
54. Ibid.
55. *Railway World*, August 31, 1889, 822.
56. Ibid.
57. Ibid.; *Iron Age*, August 29, 1889, 322.
58. T.W. Bean, ed. *History of Montgomery County, Pennsylvania*, vol. 1 (Mt. Vernon, IN: Windmill Publishing, 1884), 613.

59. Ibid.
60. *Van Nostrand's Eclectic Engineering Magazine*, November 1869, 1,044; Bean, *History of Montgomery County*, 613.
61. Pencoyd Iron Works graphic, Library Company of Philadelphia. https://digital.librarycompany.org.
62. *Iron Age*, January 23, 1902, 20–21; January 30, 1902, 1–12.
63. J.D. McCabe, *The Illustrated History of the Centennial Exhibition: Held in Commemoration of the One Hundredth Anniversary of American Independence* (Toronto: J.B. Magurn, 1876), 874 pages.
64. K. Barraclough, *Steelmaking: 1850–1900* (London: Institute of Materials, 1990), 27–35; Pencoyd Iron Works, *Hexamer General Surveys*, vol. 7 (Philadelphia: A.&P. Roberts, 1872), plates 654–55. This survey and others in the Map Collection of the Free Library of Philadelphia
65. *Engineering Record*, March 25, 1893, "Pencoyd Iron and Bridge Works, Part I—General Description, History, Development, Maps, Location of Tools, Characteristic Building Construction," 334–36.
66. J.M. Swank, *History of the Manufacture of Iron in all Ages and Particularly the United States from Colonial Times to 1891* (New York: Burt Franklin, 1892), 53–54.
67. Barraclough, *Steelmaking*, 27–35.
68. Ibid., 5.
69. Bean, *History of Montgomery County, Pennsylvania*, 613.
70. W. Barnet Le Van, "Biographical Notice of John W. Murphy, C.E.," *Proceedings of the Franklin Institute* 68, no. 1 (July 1874), 304.
71. F. Griggs Jr., "Squire Whipple," *Structure Magazine*, September 2005, 58–60.
72. Ibid., 58.
73. Ibid.
74. Ibid.
75. Ibid.
76. Ibid., 60.
77. Ibid.
78. Ibid.
79. Francis E. Griggs Jr., "Preservation and Restoration of 19th Century Cast and Wrought Iron Bridges," *Practice Periodical on Structural Design and Construction* 14, no. 4 (November 2009): 159–75.
80. Percival Roberts obituary, *Iron Age*, April 7, 1898, 18.
81. Francis E. Griggs Jr., "Whipple Double Intersection Cast and Wrought the Iron Truss," *Structure Magazine*, May 2015, 39–41.

82. E. DeLony, "Surviving Cast- and Wrought-The Iron Bridges in America," In *Structural The Iron and Steel 1850–1900*, ed. Robert Thorne (New York: Ashgate Publishing, 2000), 150; Theodore Cooper, "American Railroad Bridges," *Transactions of the American Society of Civil Engineers* 21, no 2 (1889): 1–58.
83. V. Darnell "Directory of American Bridge Companies 1840–1900," Society for Industrial Archeology, *Occasional Publication No. 4* (1984), 63.
84. "An Early American Pin-Connected Truss Bridge," *Engineering News*, May 9, 1907, 511.
85. Historic American Engineering Record [hereafter HAER], Photos 3, 4 and 5, NJ-29, Morris Canal, Library of Congress.
86. Le Van, "Biographical Notice," 305; Correspondence from Rob J. Sayer to Theodore Cooper, December 6, 1888, https://hdl.handle.net/1813/56183.
87. *Illinois Central Magazine*, August 1921, 42–43.
88. Larry B. Maier, Rough and Regular: A History of Philadelphia's 119th Regiment of Pennsylvania Volunteer Infantry, the Gray Reserves (Shippenburg, PA: Burd Street Press, 1997), 359 pages.
89. "A Celebration at Pencoyd," *Iron Age*, January 23, 1902, 20–21; "The Pencoyd Works," *Iron Age*, January 30, 1902, 10–12.
90. *Van Nostrand's Eclectic Engineering Magazine*, November 1869, 1,044
91. Pencoyd Iron Works, *Hexamer General Surveys*, vol. 7, plates 654–55.
92. *Van Nostrand's Eclectic Engineering Magazine*, November 1869, 1,044.
93. Loth, *Pencoyd and the Roberts Family*, 45.
94. From "A General Chronology of Pennsylvania Railroad," Pennsylvania Railroad Technical and Historical Society, www.prrths.com.
95. "Celebration at Pencoyd," *Iron Age*; "Pencoyd Works," *Iron Age*.
96. "The Pencoyd Steam Hammer," *Railroad and Engineering Journal* 63, no. 12 (December 1889): 568–70.
97. *Iron Age*, January 17, 1889, 82–83.
98. *Van Nostrand's Eclectic Engineering Magazine*, November 1869, 1,044.
99. Henrik V. von Z. Loss, "The Art of Manufacture of Railway Car Axles," *Journal of the Franklin Institute* 163, no. 1 (January 1907): 1–30.
100. F. Griggs, "Kentucky River High Bridge," *Structure Magazine*, August 2015, 22–24.
101. Kentucky River Bridge paper, *Engineering News* 53, no. 12 (March 1905): 312–14.
102. Advertisement from *Railway World*, February 3, 1877, 119.

Chapter 3

103. "Celebration at Pencoyd," *Iron Age*; "Pencoyd Works," *Iron Age*.
104. Museum photo, LMHS, http://ajourneyintothepast.blogspot.com/2005/12.
105. "Celebration at Pencoyd," *Iron Age*; "Pencoyd Works," *Iron Age*.
106. McCabe, *Illustrated History*.
107. Ibid.
108. Ibid., 433–56.
109. Ibid., 589–94.
110. Ibid., 337–38.
111. Nicholas Wainwright, Russell Weigley and Edwin Wolf, *Philadelphia: A 300-Year History* (New York: W.W. Norton & Company, 1982), 462.
112. Ibid., 463.
113. "Celebration at Pencoyd," *Iron Age*; "Pencoyd Works," *Iron Age*.
114. Christie, "Percival Roberts Jr.," 679–80.
115. Ibid.
116. *A Souvenir of a Reception Tendered to Mr. Percival Roberts Jr. at the Pencoyd Club, Wissahickon, Philadelphia, January 18, 1902, by the Employees of the Pencoyd Iron Works* [hereafter Roberts souvenir booklet] (Philadelphia: E.A. Wright Press, 1902), 16 pages.
117. Pencoyd Iron Works, *Hexamer General Surveys*, vol. 7 (1872), plates 654–55; "Industrial Plants XI, The Pencoyd Iron and Bridge Works, Part I. General Description, History, Development, Map, Location of Tools, Characteristics Building Construction," *Engineering Record*, March 25, 1893, 334–36.
118. Mick Ricereto, "Pencoyd Bridge Reopens in Manayunk, As Redevelopment of Foundry Site Begins," *Hidden City*, January 11, 2017, http://hiddencityphila.org; "Pencoyd Farm," Roberts Estate HABS No. PA-1087.
119. Richard Jones, ed., *The First 300: The Amazing and Rich History of Lower Merion* (Ardmore, PA: LMHS, 2000), 284 pages.
120. "Celebration at Pencoyd," *Iron Age*; "Pencoyd Works," *Iron Age*.
121. Ibid.
122. Ibid.
123. Ibid.
124. "The Plant of the Pencoyd Iron Works, Pencoyd, PA," *Engineering News Record*, September 29, 1898, 194–97.
125. J.A. Christie, *Wrought Iron and Steel in Construction* (New York: John Wiley, 1884), 256 pages, followed by twelve editions (later called *Steel in Construction*).
126. Ibid.

127. James Christie, "Experiments on the Strength of Wrought—The Iron Struts," *Transactions of the American Society of Civil Engineers* 13, no. 1 (1884): 85–122.
128. James Christie, "Experiments on the Strength and Elasticity of Structural Steel," *Transactions of the American Society of Civil Engineers* 13, no. 1 (1884): 254–300.
129. James Christie obituary, *Iron Age*, August 31, 1911, 461.
130. Ibid.
131. Ibid.
132. Ibid.
133. "James Christie," *Transactions of the American Society of Mechanical Engineers* 33 (1911): 1,180–1,181.
134. Accessed from ASCE webpage, June 7, 2017, www.asce.org/templates/award-detail.aspx?id=1498.
135. *Engineering News*, July 21, 1898, 43.
136. "Merchant Steamers: Sir Henry Bessemer and Sir William Siemens," *Journal of the American Society of Naval Engineers* 8 (1896): 649–50.
137. "The Pencoyd Iron Works New 18" Beams," *Engineering News* 35, no. 17 (April 1896): 279.
138. "Manufacturing and Business," *Railroad Gazette*, March 17, 1893, 212–13.
139. C. Macdonald, C. (1887) "The Six-Hundred Ton Testing Machine at the Works of the Union Bridge Company at Athens, PA," *Transactions American Society of Civil Engineers* 16, article 349 (January 1887): 1–8; Frank Alfred Randall, "The 600,000-lb. Testing Machine for the Laboratory of Applied Mechanics" (Bachelor of Science in Civil Engineering thesis, College of Engineering, University of Illinois, June 1905).
140. J.A.L. Waddell, "Nickel Steel for Bridges," *Transactions of the American Society for Civil Engineering* 63, paper no. 1103 (1909): 101–387.

Chapter 4

141. P. Roberts, "The Puddling Process, Past and Present," *Journal of the Franklin Institute* 110, no. 1 (1880): 49–56.
142. James Christie, "Experiments on the Strength of Wrought-Iron Struts," *Transactions of the American Society of Civil Engineers* 13, no. 1 (1884): 85–122.
143. James Christie, "Experiments on the Strength and Elasticity of Structural Steel," *Transactions of the American Society of Civil Engineers* 13, no. 1 (1884): 254–300.

144. Ibid.
145. Ibid.
146. D. Carnegie and S.C. Gladwyn, *Liquid Steel: Its Manufacture and Cost* (London: Longmans, Green and Company, 1913), 116–17.
147. T.J. Misa, *A Nation of Steel: The Making of Modern America 1865–1935* (Baltimore: Johns Hopkins University Press, 1995), 367 pages.
148. Ibid.
149. Ibid.
150. Carnegie and Gladwyn, *Liquid Steel*, 271–73.
151. Ibid., 272.
152. Ibid., 271–73.
153. Ibid., 124.
154. Ibid., 125.
155. "Celebration at Pencoyd," *Iron Age*; "Pencoyd Works," *Iron Age*.
156. "Celebration at Pencoyd," *Iron Age*; "Pencoyd Works," *Iron Age*.
157. B. Talbot, Lining for metallurgical furnaces, U.S. patent 628288, July 4, 1899.
158. "Celebration at Pencoyd," *Iron Age*; "Pencoyd Works," *Iron Age*.
159. Ibid.
160. Plate XXVI, *Journal of the Iron and Steel Institute* 88, no. 2 (1913): 234–56.
161. "The Talbot Continuous Open-Hearth Steel Process," *Iron Age*, February 8, 1900, 5–7; "Increasing Prominence of the Open-Hearth Process," *Iron Age*, May 24, 1900, 22.
162. B. Talbot, "The Open-Hearth Continuous Steel Process," *Engineering*, June 22, 1900, 832–36; B. Talbot, "The Continuous Process for Open-hearth Steel," *Engineering*, May 11, 1900, 623–24.
163. G.L. Norris, "A Rapid Method for Phosphorus in Iron and Steel, Modified from a Method Proposed by Dr. Thos. N. Brown," *Journal of the Franklin Institute* 129, no. 1 (January 1890): 72–74.
164. Talbot, "Open-Hearth Continuous Steel Process."
165. Allen, Manufacture of Open-Hearth Steel, U.S. Patent 870921, 1907; Allen, Protecting Furnaces, U.S. Patent 918941, 1909.
166. N. Thomas and A.W. Allen, Open-Hearth Furnace, U.S. Patent 1217367, 1917; H.C. Ryding and A.W. Allen, Manufacture of Open-Hearth Steel, U.S. Patent 1289057, 1918; H.C. Ryding and A.W. Allen, Manufacture of Open-hearth Steel, U.S. Patent 1423031, 1922.
167. J. Christie, "Structural Steel," *Journal of the Franklin Institute* 141, no. 1 (January 1896): 33–47.

168. "Scientific Brevities," *Journal of the Franklin Institute* 144, no. 3 (September 1897): 236–38.
169. "Continuous Trusses of Silicon Steel Feature New Allegheny River Bridge," *Engineering News Record*, May 2, 1918, 848–54.
170. Waddell, "Nickel Steel for Bridges."
171. Carnegie and Gladwyn, *Liquid Steel*, 388–96.
172. Talbot, "Open-Hearth Continuous Steel Process."
173. Grace's Guide to British Industrial History, "Benjamin Talbot," www.gracesguide.co.uk/Benjamin_Talbot; *The Engineer* 184 (1947): 603.
174. *The Engineer* 184 (1947): 603.
175. H.H. Campbell, *Manufacture & Properties of Iron & Steel* (New York: Engineering and Mining Journal, 1902); H.H. Campbell, "The Open-Hearth Process," *Transactions of the AIME* 22 (1894): 345–511, 679–96.
176. Campbell, "Manufacture & Properties of Iron & Steel," 310, 319; B. Talbot, "On the Open-Hearth Continuous Steel Process (and Discussion)," *Journal of the Iron and Steel Institute* 57, no. 1 (1900): 33–108.
177. Ibid., 92–93.
178. Ibid.
179. Ibid.
180. "Celebration at Pencoyd," *Iron Age*; "Pencoyd Works," *Iron Age.*
181. First Annual Report of the United States Steel Corporation for the fiscal year ended December 31, 1902, 40 pages, to Twenty-Second Annual Report of the United States Steel Corporation for the fiscal year ended December 31, 1923, 52 pages.
182. Wellman biography in *Iron Age*, July 17, 1919, 204.
183. Wellman biography in the *Iron Trade Review*, July 17, 1919, 184–86.
184. Wellman biography, in *The National Cyclopedia of Biography*, vol. 13 (New York, James T. White Company, 1906), 37–38.
185. Wellman biographies in *Iron Age*, July 17, 1919, 204; *The Iron Trade Review*, July 17, 1919, 184–86; *National Cyclopedia of Biography*, 37–38.
186. Wellman biographies in *Iron Age*, July 17, 1919, 204; *The Iron Trade Review*, July 17, 1919, 184–86; *National Cyclopedia of Biography*, 37–38
187. Wellman biographies in *Iron Age*, July 17, 1919, 204; *The Iron Trade Review*, July 17, 1919, 184–86; *National Cyclopedia of Biography*, 37–38.
188. "Manufacture of Bridge and Building Structural Shapes," *Scientific American* 89, no. 24 (December 1903): 421–40.
189. Carnegie and Gladwyn, *Liquid Steel.*
190. Ibid.
191. Ibid.

192. "Celebration at Pencoyd," *Iron Age*; "Pencoyd Works," *Iron Age*.
193. "Hughes Mechanically-Poked Continuous Gas Producer," *Industrial World*, March 23, 1907, 341–44; advertisement for Hughes Gas producers, *Industrial Management*, March 1918, 79.
194. Pencoyd Iron Works, *Hexamer General Surveys*, vol. 21 (Philadelphia: A.&P. Roberts, 1887), plates 2054–55; Pencoyd Iron Works, *Hexamer General Surveys*, vol. 25 (Philadelphia: A.&P. Roberts, 1891), plates 2420–423.
195. "Metallurgie. Installations Americaines De Fours Siemens-Martin," *Le Genie Civil* 41, no. 2 (September 1902): 345.
196. "Celebration at Pencoyd," *Iron Age*; "Pencoyd Works," *Iron Age*.
197. Ibid.
198. Ibid.
199. Ibid.
200. Ibid.
201. "Plant of the Pencoyd Iron Works," *Engineering News Record*.
202. *National Cyclopedia of Biography*, vol. 13, 37–38.
203. Pencoyd Iron Works, "Convenient Rules, Formula and Tables for the Strength of Steel Shapes Used as Beams, Strust, Shafts, etc.," panorama in *Steel in Construction*, 10th ed. (Philadelphia: A.&P. Roberts Company, 1898), 346 pages with 35 plates.
204. T. Matthias, "Progress in Roll Design," *Monthly Bulletin of the American Iron and Steel Institute* 1, no. 10 (1913): 285.
205. H.L. James, "Progress in Roll Design," *Monthly Bulletin of the American Iron and Steel Institute* 1, no. 10 (1913): 286.

Chapter 5

206. "The Pencoyd Works," *Iron Age*, January 30, 1902, 10–12.
207. Ibid.
208. Pencoyd Iron Works, *Hexamer General Surveys*, vol. 7, plates 654–55.
209. Ibid.
210. "Pencoyd Iron and Bridge Works. Part I. General Description, History, Development, Map, Location of Tools, Characteristic Building Construction," *Engineering Record*, March 25, 1893, 334–36.
211. Pencoyd Iron Works, *Hexamer General Surveys* 1872, 1883, 1887, 1891—see previous endnotes.
212. McCabe, *Illustrated History*.
213. "Celebration at Pencoyd," *Iron Age*; "Pencoyd Works," *Iron Age*.

214. "Scientist of the Day, George Corliss," Linda Hall Library, www.lindahall.org/george-corliss.
215. George H. Corliss, Steam Engine, U.S. Patent 6162, March 10, 1849.
216. "Scientist of the Day, George Corliss."
217. Ibid.
218. "Celebration at Pencoyd," *Iron Age*; "Pencoyd Works," *Iron Age*.
219. "Elihu Thomson," Engineering and Technology History Wiki, https://ethw.org/Elihu_Thomson.
220. *The Only Automatic Self-Regulating Light System in the World* (Philadelphia: Thomsen-Houston Electric Light Company, 1885), 56 pages.
221. Ibid.
222. "The Thomsen-Houston 250 HP Generator," *Electrical Engineer*, July 29, 1891, 117–18.
223. *Only Automatic Self-Regulating Light System*.
224. "Generators and Dynamos," Edison Tech Center, www.edisontechcenter.org/generators.html.
225. Ibid.
226. "The War of the Currents: AC vs. DC Power," Department of Energy, https://energy.gov/articles/war-currents-ac-vs-dc-power.
227. "Charles F. Brush," Engineering and Technology History Wiki, notes about dynamos in industry, http://ethw.org/Charles_F._Brush.
228. *Rand, McNally & Co.'s Handbook of the World's Columbian Exposition* (Chicago: Rand, McNally & Company, 1893), 224 pages.
229. "War of the Currents."
230. Ibid.
231. Ibid.
232. *Locomotive Engineering* 5, no. 9 (September 1892): 318.
233. Pencoyd Iron Works, *Hexamer General Surveys*, vol. 18 (Philadelphia: A.&P. Roberts, 1883), plates 1743–44, Map Collection, Free Library of Philadelphia.
234. "Celebration at Pencoyd," *Iron Age*; "Pencoyd Works," *Iron Age*.
235. Ibid.
236. Ibid.
237. Pencoyd Iron Works, *Hexamer General Surveys*, vol. 21, plates 2054–55; photo from frontispiece of *Wrought Iron and Steel in Construction*, 8th ed. (Philadelphia: A and P Roberts, 1892).
238. "The Pencoyd Works," *Iron Age* 69, January 30, 1902, 10–12.
239. Pencoyd Iron Works, *Hexamer General Surveys*, vol. 25, plates 2420–423.
240. "Schuyler Skaats Wheeler," in *The National Cyclopaedia of American Biography*, vol. 10 (New York: James T. White and Company, 1900), 162.

241. "Francis B. Crocker," Engineering and Technology History Wiki, http://ethw.org/Francis_B._Crocker.
242. "Schuyler Skaats Wheeler."
243. "Schuyler Skaats Wheeler."
244. "Celebration at Pencoyd," *Iron Age*; "Pencoyd Works," *Iron Age*.
245. "Plant of the Pencoyd Iron Works," *Engineering News Record*.
246. Ibid.
247. Ibid.
248. Ibid.
249. Ibid.
250. Ibid.
251. "Celebration at Pencoyd," *Iron Age*; "Pencoyd Works," *Iron Age*.
252. "Plant of the Pencoyd Iron Works," *Engineering News Record*.
253. Ibid.
254. Ibid.
255. *Steam: Its Generation and Use with Catalogue of the Manufactures of the Babcock and Wilcox Company* (London: Babcock and Wilcox, 1898), 94 and 132.
256. M.W. Buhle, *Technische Hülfsmittel zur Beförderung und Lagerung von Sammelkörpern (Massengütern): I. Teil* (Berlin: Springer, 1901), 69.
257. *Iron Age*, December 1, 1898, 36.
258. Babcock and Wilcox, "Our History," www.babcock.com/en/about/history.
259. George G. Zipf, "Babcock & Wilcox Power for Tom Edison—and the Nuclear Navy," *Nation's Business*, January 1973, 42.
260. "Plant of the Pencoyd Iron Works," *Engineering News Record*.
261. Ibid.
262. "The Pencoyd Works," *Iron Age*, January 30, 1902, 10–12.
263. "Plant of the Pencoyd Iron Works," *Engineering News Record*.
264. Ibid., 8.
265. *Iron Age*, September 22, 1898, 30.
266. Nancy Giges, "Henry R. Worthington," American Society of Mechanical Engineers, www.asme.org/engineering-topics/articles/transportation/henry-r-worthington.
267. "Plant of the Pencoyd Iron Works," *Engineering News Record*.

Chapter 6

268. Roberts souvenir booklet, 1902; "Baltimore & Ohio Railroad Station, Twenty-Fourth and Chestnut Streets, Philadelphia, Philadelphia County, Pennsylvania," HABS PA-1220, Library of Congress.
269. "Bridges," *Railroad and Engineering Journal*, 64, no. 3 (March 1890): 139.
270. "Builders and Contractors Engineering and Plant No. XXVII. 6-Ton Universal Traveling Crane for Elevated Railroad Erection," *Engineering and Building Record*, December 17, 1887, 41–43.
271. James R. Irwin, *New York City Railroads circa 1900*, May 31, 2008, https://commons.wikimedia.org/wiki/File:New_York_City_Railroads_ca_1900.png.
272. "The New Terminals of the Pennsylvania Railroad at Jersey City," *Engineering News*, September 26, 1891, 276–79, 315–16; "The Jersey City Trainshed of the Pennsylvania Railroad," *Railroad Gazette*, October 2, 1891, 681–83.
273. "Dismantle Jersey City Trainshed of Pennsylvania R. R.," *Engineering News-Record* 89, no. 7 (August 1922): 270–72.
274. Ibid.
275. John C. Trautwine, *The Civil Engineers' Pocket-Book* (New York: John Wiley & Sons, 1906); "Broad Street Station," HABS PA-51-PHILA, 341–8, Library of Congress.
276. Roberts souvenir booklet, 1902.
277. "Union Elevated Railway, Union Loop (Chicago Loop L)," HAER IL-1, (1983); "Union Elevated Railroad, Chicago, 1983, Randolph St. Station (On Wabash)," HAER IL-1D; J.A.L. Waddell, "Elevated Railway Design," *Engineering News Record* 35, no. 11 (February 1897): 227–30.
278. "Union Elevated Railway, Union Loop (Chicago Loop L)," HAER IL-1, (1983); "Union Elevated Railroad, Chicago, 1983, Randolph St. Station (On Wabash)," HAER IL-1D, 3.
279. The drawings are on microfilm in the archives of the Chicago Transit Authority (CTA Archives, Engineering Department, reviewed by Julia Schneiderman, July 1, 1994).
280. Roberts souvenir booklet, 1902.
281. Ibid.
282. *Five Alarm Fire at Back Bay Station*, Digital Commonwealth, www.digitalcommonwealth.org/search/commonwealth:05742c121.
283. *Engineering News*, May 11, 1899, 303–7.
284. "The Terminal Improvements of the Chesapeake and Ohio Railway, Richmond, Virginia," *Engineering News*, November 29, 1900, 379–80.

285. "Erection of the Atlantic Avenue Improvement Viaduct, Brooklyn," *Engineering Record*, September 5, 1903, 271–73; "The Newark Viaducts of the Lackawanna Railroad," *Engineering News Record*, July 22, 1905, 102–4; "The Market Street Elevated Railway," *Philadelphia Engineering Record*, August 11, 1906, 158–61.
286. "The Trenton Avenue Elevated Railroad," *Philadelphia Engineering News*, August 7, 1909, 153–55.
287. "The Hudson Companies Building, New York," *Engineering Record*, August 3, 1907, 121–24.
288. *New York Times*, December 23, 1906; *Singer, City Investing & Hudson Terminal Bldgs*, www.loc.gov/pictures/resource/cph.3c25895.
289. "14th Street Viaduct, Denver, Colorado," HAER-CO-218.
290. *Railroad Gazette* 31 no. 4 (1898): 64.
291. Ibid.
292. "14th Street Viaduct, Denver, Colorado," HAER-CO-218.
293. "John Rodgers Airport, Hangar No. 2, Honolulu, International Airport," HABS No. HI-575, Library of Congress.
294. Roberts souvenir booklet, 1902.
295. "Heavy Plate Girders in the Bellevue-Stratford Hotel Extension," *Engineering News Record*, July 15, 1905, 71–72.
296. Roberts souvenir booklet, 1902.
297. "Manhattan Life building: General Article Part I," *Engineering Record*, January 20, 1894, 122–25.
298. "Vincent Building; Wall Supports in a Steel Cage Building," *Engineering Record*, November 4, 1899.
299. "The Gillender Building: Design and Construction of Foundations and Framework," *Engineering News Record*, January 16, 1897, 140–45.
300. "Foundations of the Franklin building," *Engineering Record*, May 28, 1898, 566.
301. "The New Altman building, New York," *Engineering Record*, November 4, 1905, 522.
302. "Metropolitan Life Insurance Building 1909 Tower," National Register of Historic Places, 1977; *The Metropolitan Life Insurance Company; Its History, Its Present Position in the Insurance World, Its Home Office Building and Its work Carried on Therein.* (New York: Metropolitan Life Insurance Company, 1908).
303. "Enlarging and Remodeling the Manhattan Life Building," *Engineering Record*, April 4, 1903, 338–42; "Manhattan Life Insurance Building: Building Construction Details, Part 1," *Engineering Record*, January 20, 1894), 122–25; "Part 2," *Engineering Record*, August 18, 1894, 189–90; "Part 3,"

Engineering Record, November 17, 1894, 408–9; "Part 4," *Engineering Record*, November 24, 1894, 428–29; "Part 5," *Engineering Record*, December 1, 1894, 5–6; "Part 6," *Engineering Record*, January 26, 1895, 152–53; "Part 7," *Engineering Record*, April 27, 1895, 388–90.

304. "The Manhattan Life Building," *Scientific American*, December 22, 1894, 392–93.

305. Joseph Korom, *The American Skyscraper, 1850–1940: A Celebration of Height* (Minneapolis, MN: Branden Books, 2008), 199.

306. "The Gillender Building: Design and Construction of Foundations and Framework," *Engineering News Record*, January 16, 1897, 140–45.

307. New York Architecture, www.nyc-architecture.com/GON/GON013.htm; Korom, *American Skyscraper, 1850–1940*, 221.

308. "The United States Express Co. Building, New York City," *Engineering Record*, July 28, 1906, 108–11.

309. "Girders and Trusses in the Guaranty Trust Building, New York," *Engineering Record*, August 31, 1912, 244–45.

310. R. Gabrielan, *Along Broadway* (Charleston, SC: Arcadia Publishing, 2007), 35.

311. "Special Steelwork in the Morgan Building, New York City," *Engineering Record*, October 17, 1914, 423–25.

312. "Eliminating Columns by a Heavy Girder," *Engineering Record*, March 16, 1912, 290–91.

313. "Prudential (Guaranty) Building, 28 Church Street, Buffalo, Erie County, NY," HABS, NY-5487, Library of Congress.

314. "Buildings" note that Guaranty Building steel work goes to Pencoyd, *Engineering News Record*, April 4, 1895, 108.

315. "Fisher building," HABS IL-1082, Library of Congress.

316. Roberts souvenir booklet, 1902.

317. Ibid.

318. "The Cresson Medal for the Pencoyd Iron Works," *Railway Age* November 2, 1900, 354.

319. "Ellis Island Structural Steel," *Engineering*, September 8, 1899, 293; "Convention of the ASCE," *Engineering Record*, July 8, 1899, 132–34.

320. Ruthann Hubbert-Kemper and Jason L. Wilson, eds., *Literature in Stone: The Hundred Year History of Pennsylvania's State Capitol* (Harrisburg, PA: Pennsylvania Capitol Preservation Committee, 2006).

321. Roberts souvenir booklet, 1902; *Annual Report of the Navy Department for the Year 1899: Report of the Secretary of the Navy, Miscellaneous Reports* (Washington, D.C.: U.S. Government Printing Office, 1899), 706.

322. "Steelwork of the New General Electric Machine Shop.—II," *Engineering News Record*, September 2, 1905, 267–68; "Steelwork of the Marion Power Station, Public Service Corporation of New Jersey," *Engineering News Record*, August 19, 1905, 210–12.
323. "New York's Tribute," *Sporting Life* 57, no. 26 (September 1911).
324. Beaman and Smith Company Mill, Providence County, RI, United States Department of the Interior, National Park Service, National Register of Historic Places (2005).
325. "A Pier Shed and Pavilion," *Engineering and Building Record*, July 19, 1890, 102.
326. Trautwine, *Civil Engineers' Pocket-Book*.
327. F.L. Castleman, U.S. Patent No. 1,519,292, 1923.
328. F.L. Castleman, U.S. Patent No. 1,259,488, 1918.
329. "Merchant Steamers," *Journal of the American Society of Naval Engineers* 5, no. 1 (February 1893): 240.
330. Cruising the Great Lakes and Inland Waterways, https://riverandlakescruising.wordpress.com/2011/08/17/a-brief-history-and-introduction-to-great-lakes-cruising.
331. Alpena County George N. Fletcher Public Library, http://greatlakeships.org/results?q=101232.
332. Alpena County George N. Fletcher Public Library, http://greatlakeships.org/results?q=101718.
333. *Annual Report of the Navy Department for the Year 1899*, 706.
334. NavSource Naval History, www.navsource.org/archives/05/tb/05032905.jpg; "Annual Report of the Engineer-in-Chief," *Journal of the American Society of Naval Engineers* 11, no. 4 (November 1899): 872.
335. The Sachem Project, www.the-sachem-project.org.
336. *Real Estate Record and Builders' Guide* 109, no. 25 (June 1922): 790.

Chapter 7

337. Henry Petroski, *Engineers of Dreams: Great Bridge Builders and the Spanning of America* (New York: Vintage Books, 1996); F.W. Skinner, *Types and Details of Bridge Construction, Part III. Specifications and Standards for Short Railroad Spans* (New York: McGraw Publishing, 1908); Theodore Cooper, *American Railroad Bridges* (New York: Engineering News Publishing Company, 1889); J.A.L. Waddell, *De Pontibus: A Pocket-Book for Bridge Engineers* (New York: John Wiley and Sons, 1898), 5–7.

338. C.C. Schneider, "Movable Bridges," *Proceeding of the American Society of Civil Engineers* 33, no. 1 (1907): 153–90.
339. Percival Roberts obituary, *Iron Age*, April 7, 1898, 18.
340. Correspondence from Percival Roberts to Theodore Cooper, December 17, 1888, Cornell University Library; correspondence from Percival Roberts to Theodore Cooper, December 10, 1888, Cornell University Library.
341. Joseph Gies, *Of Bridges and Men* (New York: Doubleday Books, 1963), 108.
342. *Report of the Committee of the Pacific Railroad to Investigate the Causes of the Accident at Gasconade Bridge, St. Louis* (Philadelphia: Republican Book and Job Office, 1855).
343. "Railroad Accident," *Janesville (WI) Gazette*, August 10, 1871.
344. John A.L. Waddell, *Bridge Engineering*, vol. 2 (New York: John Wiley & Sons, 1916), 1,541.
345. "Charles Conrad Schneider," *Engineering News* 75, no. 2 (January 1916): 90–91; F. Griggs, "Charles Conrad Schneider," *Structure Magazine*, January 2011, 44–45; "Paul L. Wolfel Obituary," *Engineering News Record*, January 6, 1921, 45.
346. Schneider, "Movable Bridges," 153–90; C.C. Schneider, "The Structural Design of Buildings, Paper No. 997," *Transactions of the American Society of Civil Engineers* 54 (1905): 371–412.
347. "Charles Conrad Schneider," *Engineering News*, 90–91; Griggs, "Charles Conrad Schneider," 44–45; "Paul L. Wolfel Obituary," *Engineering News Record*, 45.
348. "Charles Conrad Schneider," *Engineering News*, 90–91; Griggs, "Charles Conrad Schneider," 44–45; "Paul L. Wolfel Obituary," *Engineering News Record*, 45.
349. "Charles Conrad Schneider," *Engineering News*, 90–91; Griggs, "Charles Conrad Schneider," 44–45; "Paul L. Wolfel Obituary," *Engineering News Record*, 45.
350. "Charles Conrad Schneider," *Engineering News*, 90–91; Griggs, "Charles Conrad Schneider," 44–45; "Paul L. Wolfel Obituary," *Engineering News Record*, 45
351. "Charles Conrad Schneider," *Engineering News*, 90–91; Griggs, "Charles Conrad Schneider," 44–45; "Paul L. Wolfel Obituary," *Engineering News Record*, 45.
352. Roberts souvenir booklet, 1902.
353. Ibid.

354. "Paul L. Wolfel Obituary," *Engineering News Record*, 45.; "Charles Conrad Schneider," *Engineering News*, 90–91.
355. Petroski, *Engineers of Dreams*.
356. "Charles Conrad Schneider," *Engineering News* 75, no. 2 (January 13, 1916): 9–91.
357. "Memoir of Paul Ludwig Wolfel," *Transactions of the American Society for Civil Engineers* 84 (1920): 940–42. "Paul L. Wolfel Obituary," *Engineering News Record*, 45; "Paul Wolfel," in *History of Pittsburgh and Environs by Special Contributors and Members of the Editorial Staff* (New York: American Historical Society, 1922), 117–19. 1922.
358. "Memoir of Paul Ludwig Wolfel," *Transactions*, 940–42; "Paul L. Wolfel Obituary," *Engineering News Record*, 45.
359. "Memoir of Paul Ludwig Wolfel," *Transactions*, 940–42; "Paul L. Wolfel Obituary," *Engineering News Record*, 45.
360. "Memoir of Paul Ludwig Wolfel," *Transactions*, 940–42; "Paul L. Wolfel Obituary," *Engineering News Record*, 45.
361. "Memoir of Paul Ludwig Wolfel," *Transactions*, 940–42; "Paul L. Wolfel Obituary," *Engineering News Record*, 45.
362. "Memoir of Paul Ludwig Wolfel," *Transactions*, 940–42; "Paul L. Wolfel Obituary," *Engineering News Record*, 45.
363. "Memoir of Paul Ludwig Wolfel," *Transactions*, 940–42; "Paul L. Wolfel Obituary," *Engineering News Record*, 45.
364. "Memoir of Paul Ludwig Wolfel," *Transactions*, 940–42; "Paul L. Wolfel Obituary," *Engineering News Record*, 45.
365. "Memoir of Paul Ludwig Wolfel," *Transactions*, 940–42; "Paul L. Wolfel Obituary," *Engineering News Record*, 45.
366. O.A. Ammann, "Obituary for F.C. Kunz," *Engineering News*, May 11, 1917, 919.
367. Ibid.
368. "Waddell 'A' Truss," HAER MO-8, 2016.
369. Ibid.
370. "Waddell 'A' Truss," HAER MO-8, 2016; George F. W. Hauck, "Waddell 'A' Truss Bridge," National Register of Historic Places Nomination Form (Washington, D.C.: U.S. Department of the Interior, National Park Service, 1989).
371. Hauck, "Waddell 'A' Truss Bridge."
372. Ibid.
373. Ibid.
374. Ibid.

375. Ibid.
376. Ibid.
377. J.A.L. Waddell, *Bridge Engineering*, 2 vols. (New York: John Wiley and Sons, 1916).
378. John A.L. Waddell ASCE biography, www.asce.org/templates/person-bio-detail.aspx?id=11229.
379. F. Griggs, "Leffert Lefferts Buck—Bridge Maker, ASCE Paper No. 21817," *Journal of Bridge Engineering* 5, no. 4 (November 2000): 271–83.
380. H. Reissner, "Nordamerikanische Eisenbauwerkstatten," *Dinglers Polytechnische Journal* 87, 321 Band, 5 Heft (February 1906): 9–21.
381. C.C. Schneider,"General Specifications for Railroad Bridges," issued by the Pencoyd Iron Works, 1887.
382. Agreement No. 1728, "A. & P. Roberts Co., with the Penna. R. R. Co. for Selinsgrove Bridge Four Spans over Eastern Channel Susquehanna River, Dated Dec. 29,1891," located in file: Bridges—Lewistown Division 1888–1891, Box 746, Construction Contracts, Engineering Department, Pennsylvania Railroad Company records, Ace. 1807, Hagley Museum and Library, Greenville, Delaware. A&P. Roberts had bid $0.0365 per pound.
383. "Selinsgrove bridge," HAER PA-554, April 2000.
384. Roberts souvenir booklet, 1902.
385. Emily Morry, "Platt Street Bridge," http://media.democratandchronicle.com/retrofitting-rochester/platt-street-bridge.
386. Griggs, "Leffert Lefferts Buck," 271–83.
387. "Philadelphia and Reading Railroad, Mule Bridge," HAER PA-3763, April 2000.
388. A. Oviatt-Lawrence, "To Engineer Is to Sustain: Gustav Lindenthal's Smithfield St. Bridge, Pittsburgh, PA, 1883," *Structure Magazine*, October 2012, 11–13.
389. Ibid.; "Smithfield Street Bridge," HAER PA-2, 1974.
390. Roberts souvenir booklet, 1902.
391. "Widening a Pittsburg Bridge," *Engineering News*, April 11, 1912, 676–80.
392. "Bellefontaine bridge," HAER MO-26; "Nebraska City Bridge," HAER NE-42, October 1986.
393. C. Latrobe, B.H. Bollman, W. Wernwag, L. Lester and J. Brown, "Baltimore and Ohio Railroad Harpers Ferry Bridge," HAER No. MD-16, 1968.
394. "Engineering Notes from Buffalo and Niagara Falls" *Engineering News* February 10, 1898, 102–3; F.C. Kunz, "Die Neue Straßenbrücke über

den Niagara-Fluss," *Zeitschrift Des Oesterr. Ingenieur und Architekten Vereines* 30 (1899) 465–74.

395. Niagara Falls Info, "Honeymoon Steel Arch Bridge," www.niagarafallsinfo.com.
396. Ibid.
397. Ibid.
398. Ibid.
399. Waddell 'A' Truss," HAER MO-8, 2016.
400. Ibid.
401. Ibid.
402. R. Quinn, "Mahoning Creek Trestle, Buffalo, Rochester & Pittsburgh Railway," HAER PA-266, 1993.
403. National Park Service, www.nps.gov/neri/learn/historyculture/prince.htm.
404. "Bridge Building" *Railroad Gazette,* January 11, 1901, 31.
405. "Joshua Falls Bridge, *Spanning James River at CSX Railroad, Lynchburg, VA,"* HAER VA-93, 1968.
406. Ibid.
407. John C. Trautwine Jr., "The Philadelphia and Columbia Railroad of 1834," *Philadelphia History* 2, no. 7 (1925), in folder "Railroads in Park–General," Fairmount Park Commission Archives, Philadelphia, Pennsylvania; Coverdale & Colpitts, Consulting Engineers, *The Pennsylvania Railroad Company, Description of Important Bridges and Stations* (New York, 1945), 18; located in file PRR Office of Secretary, Studies by Consultants and Published Reference Materials, 1855–1958, Box 1, Penn Central Railroad Records, Manuscript Group 286, Pennsylvania State Archives, Harrisburg, Pennsylvania.
408. "The Pennsylvania R.R. Bridge at Fifty-second Street, Philadelphia," *Engineering Record*, October 25, 1902, 398.
409. T. Allan Comp and Donald Jackson, "Bridge Truss Types: A Guide to Dating and Identifying, Technical Leaflet No. 95," *History News* 32, no. 5 (May 1977).
410. "The Approach to the PA RR bridge at 52nd St, Philadelphia," *Engineering Record*, February 14, 1903, 174–77.
411. "The Erection of the Thebes Bridge Super Structure," *Engineering Record*, September 16, 1905, 330–35.
412. Ibid.
413. "The Thebes Bridge," *Engineering News Record*, November 12, 1904, 566–67; "Expansion Joints of the Thebes Bridge," *Engineering News Record*, December 24, 1904, 752–53.

414. "The Erection of the Thebes Bridge Super Structure," *Engineering Record*, September 16, 1905, 330–35.
415. Ibid.
416. Ibid.
417. "Rebuilding the Rondout Viaduct," *Engineering Record*, April 7, 1906, 440–44.

Chapter 8

418. Schneider, "Moveable Bridges," 258–95.
419. Ibid.
420. Ibid.
421. "Charles Conrad Schneider," *Engineering News*, 90–91.
422. C.H. Cartlidge, "Design of Swing Bridges from a Maintenance Standpoint (with Discussion by W. H. Finley, and Others)," *Journal of the Western Society of Engineers* 12, no. 1 (1907): 13–80.
423. Ibid.
424. Ibid.
425. Edward Heite, "Seaford Station Complex," Application for National Register of Historic Places, May 1977).
426. Ibid.
427. Cumberland River Swing Bridge, https://bridgehunter.com/tn/montgomery/bh43622.
428. Cartlidge, "Design of Swing Bridges," 13–80.
429. "Dutch Kills Creek Bridge," *Railroad Gazette*, January 6, 1893, 9.
430. F.C. Kunz, "Die Bruecke der Pennsylvania Eisenbahn Uber den Delaware bei Philadelphia," *Allgemetne Bauzeitung I* (1901): 5–15; Justin Spivey, "Pennsylvania & New Jersey Railroad, Delaware River Bridge," HAER PA-54; "The Delaware River Bridge at Bridesburg," *Engineering Record*, November 25, 1899, 594–97; Paul L. Wolfel, "Superstructure of the Delaware-River Bridge at Bridesburg, Philadelphia, for Pennsylvania and New Jersey RR Company," *Proceedings of the Engineers Club of Philadelphia* 14, no. 22 (1897): 155–65.
431. Kunz, "Die Bruecke der Pennsylvania Eisenbahn," 5–15; Spivey, "Pennsylvania & New Jersey Railroad," HAER PA-545; "Delaware River Bridge at Bridesburg," *Engineering Record*, November 25, 1899, 594-597; Wolfel, "Superstructure of the Delaware-River Bridge," 155–65.
432. Spivey, "Pennsylvania & New Jersey Railroad," HAER PA-545, April 2001.

433. Ibid.
434. Ibid.
435. Ibid.
436. P. Harshbarger, "New Bedford Fairhaven Middle Bridge," HAER MA-101, August 1990.
437. Ibid.
438. Ibid.
439. Ibid.
440. Ibid.
441. Ibid.
442. Ibid.
443. "A Long Double-Track Plate Girder Span," *Engineering Record*, October 21, 1899, 474–75; "New York Central & Hudson River, at Albany, N.Y.," *Railroad Gazette*, December 16, 1898, 890; "New York Central Improvements at Albany," *Railroad Gazette*, November 10, 1899, 774–75.
444. "Long Double-Track Plate Girder Span," *Engineering Record*, 474–75; "New York Central & Hudson River," *Railroad Gazette*, 890; "New York Central Improvements," *Railroad Gazette*, 774–75.
445. "Long Double-Track Plate Girder Span," *Engineering Record*, 474–75; "New York Central & Hudson River," *Railroad Gazette*, 890; "New York Central Improvements," *Railroad Gazette*, 774–75.
446. "Long Double-Track Plate Girder Span," *Engineering Record*, 474–75.
447. "All About Railroads," https://penneyandkc.wordpress.com/castleton-selkirk-and-hudson-valley.
448. "The 8-Track Railway Drawbridge," (4 parts) *Engineering News*, April 7, 1898, 231; October 20, 1898, 241; November 10, 1898, 289; March 1, 1900, 137; "Eight-Track Rolling-Lift Drawbridge Over the Chicago Drainage Canal," *Engineering News*, May 24, 1900, 338–39.
449. C. Scott, F. Alexander and J. Nicolay, "Pennsylvania Railroad, 'Eight-Track' Bascule Bridge, Cook County, Illinois," HAER No. IL-99, 1986.
450. "The Eight-Track Scherzer Rolling Lift Bridge at Chicago," *Engineering Record*, May 26, 1900, 491–92.
451. Scott, Alexander and Nicolay, "Pennsylvania Railroad," HAER No. IL-99.
452. "Louisville and Nashville," *Railway Age*, March 16, 1900, 274.
453. *The Following Illustrations Represent a Few Typical Railway and Highway Bridges Built by the American Bridge Company* (New York: American Bridge Company, 1908).
454. "The Havre de Grace Bridge of the Pennsylvania Railroad," *Railway Age*, October 6, 1905, 420–22.

455. Ibid.
456. "The Replacement of the Broadway Bridge over the Harlem Ship Canal," *Engineering Record*, August 4, 1906, 116.
457. Erie Shin Hollow Bridge, www.railfan.net/lists/erielack-digest/201202/msg00508.html.
458. Railroad Turntable, http://portjervisny.com/turntable.htm.
459. Stephen E. Drew, *Nevada's Virginia and Truckee Railroad* (Charleston, SC: Arcadia Press, 2014).
460. "American Mining in Cuba," *Railroad Gazette*, April 1, 1892, 243.
461. R.P. Porter, *Commercial and Industrial Condition of the Island of Cuba* (Washington, D.C.: U.S. Government Printing Office, 1898): 281–82.
462. "Notes by Rail in the Southwest," *Engineering News*, January 5, 1899, 11.
463. "Manufactures-Supplies: Iron and Steel," *Railway Age*, May 11, 1900, 494.
464. "The Recent Pan-American Exposition. The Railway Building," *Engineering*, December 20, 1901, 827.

Chapter 9

465. Roberts souvenir booklet, 1902.
466. "The New Bridge Shop at Pencoyd Part I—General Plans, Elevations, Diagrams, and Description," *Engineering and Building Record*, July 27, 1889, 118–19; "The New Bridge Shop at Pencoyd Part II—Details of Construction," *Engineering and Building Record*, August 3, 1889, 133.
467. "Industrial Plants No. XII. The Pencoyd Iron and Bridge Works. Part I.— General Description, History, Development, Map, Location of Tools, Characteristics Building Construction," *Engineering Record*, March 25, 1893, 334–38; "Industrial Plants No. XIII. Pencoyd Iron and Bridge Works. Part II.—General Description, Plans and Details of Characteristic Hoisting and Transfer Apparatus," *Engineering Record*, April 1, 1893, 354–56; "Industrial Plants No. XIV. The Pencoyd Iron and Bridge Works. Part III.—Special Bridge Shop Tools," *Engineering Record*, April 8, 1893, 375–78.
468. "Celebration at Pencoyd," *Iron Age*; "Pencoyd Works," *Iron Age*.
469. Roberts souvenir booklet, 1902.
470. H.V. Loss, "The Loss Hydraulic Packing," *Iron Age*, April 20, 1893, 902.
471. H.V. Loss, "Hydraulic Packing," Patent No. 492218, February 21, 1893.
472. H.V. Loss, "Machine for Shearing Metal," Patent No. 891,626, June 23, 1908.
473. Loss, "Loss Hydraulic Packing," 902.

474. "Trusses: A Study by the Historic American Engineering Record," poster (Washington, D.C.: U.S. Government Printing Office, 1976).
475. "Plant of the Pencoyd Iron Works," *Engineering News Record.*
476. Ibid.
477. Ibid.
478. H.V. Loss, "The Forging of Eye-Bars and the Flow of Metal in Closed Dies," *Railroad Gazette*, November 24, 1893, 847; "The Forging of Eye-Bars and the Flow of Metal in Closed Dies: Steel Eye-Bars," *Railroad Gazette*, December 1, 1893, 868; "The Forging of Eye-Bars and the Flow of Metal in Closed Dies: c. Die Construction," *Railroad Gazette*, December 15, 1893, 903.
479. Loss, "Forging of Eye-Bars," *Railroad Gazette*, 5; "Forging of Eye-Bars and the Flow of Metal," *Railroad Gazette*, 43–45.
480. "Plant of the Pencoyd Iron Works," *Engineering News Record.*
481. Ibid.
482. Ibid.
483. "The Ambridge Plant of the American Bridge Company. Part IV.-Eye-Bar Plant," *Engineering Record*, December 12, 1903, 720–24.
484. Tennessee Department of Transportation, *Tennessee's Survey Report for Historic Highway Bridges* (Nashville, TN: Ambrose Printing Company, 2008), 161.
485. Kenneth Bjork, *Saga in Steel and Concrete: Norwegian Engineers in America* (Oslo: Norwegian-American Historical Association, 1948), www.naha.stolaf.edu.
486. Joseph Wickham Roe, *English and American Tool Builders* (New Haven, CT: Yale University Press, 1916), 246–52.
487. Bjork, *Saga in Steel.*
488. Loss, "Forging of Eye-Bars," *Railroad Gazette*, 847; "The Forging of Eye-Bars and the Flow of Metal in Closed Dies: Steel Eye-Bars," *Railroad Gazette*, December 1, 1893, 868; "The Forging of Eye-Bars and the Flow of Metal in Closed Dies: c. Die Construction," *Railroad Gazette*, December 15, 1893, 903;. "The Forging of Eye-Bars and the Flow of Metal in Closed Dies: d. Forms and Sizes of Eyes," *Railroad Gazette*, January 5, 1894, 5; "The Forging of Eye-Bars and the Flow of Metal in Closed Dies: e. Motors and Machines," *Railroad Gazette*, January 19, 1894, 43–45.
489. Bjork, *Saga in Steel.*
490. Ibid.
491. H.V. Loss, "The Forging of Eye-Bars and the Flow of Metal in Closed Dies: e. Motors and Machines," *Railroad Gazette*, January 19, 1894, 43–45.

492. H.V. Loss, "The Pressing of Steel; with Especial Reference to Economy in Transportation," *Journal of the Franklin Institute*, December 1899, 461–73; *Journal of the Franklin Institute* 149 (January 1900): 26–40; H.V. Loss, "The Flow of Metal," *Journal of the Franklin Institute* 151 (June 1901): 456–64.
493. Loss, "Pressing of Steel," 461–73; *Journal of the Franklin Institute* 149 (January 1900): 26–40.
494. Loss, "Flow of Metal," 456–64.
495. Bjork, *Saga in Steel.*
496. "Systems of Rivet Signs," *Engineering and Building Record* 19, no. 14 (March 1889): 174.
497. "A Discussion of the Riveting Pressures Required for Bridge and Boiler Work," *Proceedings of the Engineers Club of Philadelphia* 40, no. 1 (January 1894): 1–13.
498. Roberts souvenir booklet, 1902.
499. "Bridge Building and Bridge Works in the United States. No. VII., Pencoyd Bridge Works," *Engineer*, March 6, 1903, 238.
500. "Industrial Plants No. XIV. The Pencoyd Iron and Bridge Works. Part III - Special Bridge Shop Tools," *Engineering Record*, April 8, 1893, 376; G. Barkhausen, "Mitteilungen von einer Studienreise nach den Vereinigten Staaten von Nordamerika," *Zeitschrift des Vereines deutsche Ingenieure* 37 (December 1893): 1,512–521.
501. "Pneumatic Riveting Tools for Bridge Work," *Railroad Gazette*, February 10, 1899, 100.
502. "Miscellanea," *Engineering*, November 24, 1899, 661.
503. W. Sellers, *A Treatise on Machine Tools* (Philadelphia, PA, J.B. Lippincott and Company, 1877).
504. "Manufacture of Bridge and Building Structural Shapes," *Scientific American*, December 12, 1903, 432–33; H. Reissner, "Nordamerikanische Eisenbauwerkstatten," *Dinglers Polytechnisches Journal* 86, no. 46 (1905): 726–31.
505. J.T. Scharf and T. Westcott, "William Sellers," in *History of Philadelphia*, 2,263–66 (Philadelphia, PA: L. Leveretts & Co., 1884).
506. Ibid.
507. Ibid.
508. D. Vitiello, *Engineering Philadelphia: The Sellers Family and the Industrial Metropolis*. (Ithaca, NY: Cornell University Press, 2013) 51–55.
509. Ibid., 53.
510. Ibid., 55–70.
511. Scharf and Westcott, "William Sellers."

512. Ibid.
513. "Death of William Sellers," *Iron Trade Review*, February 2, 1905 89.
514. Scharf and Westcott, "William Sellers."
515. H. Reissner, "Nordamerikanische Eisenbauwerkstatten," *Dinglers Polytechnisches Journal* 86, no. 46 (1905); no. 38, 593–98; no. 39, 609–13; no. 40, 628–32; no. 41, 643–49; no. 42, 662–66; no. 46, 726–31; no. 47, 741–46; H. Reissner, "Nordamerikanische Eisenbauwerkstatten," *Dinglers Polytechnisches Journal* 87 (321) (1906) no. 3, 33–35; no. 4, 54–59; no. 5, 65–70; no. 6, 88–92; no. 7, 97–100; no. 9, 131–35; no. 10, 145–49; no. 11, 164–68; no. 12, 182–85; no. 14, 214–18; no. 15, 230–34.
516. Roberts souvenir booklet, 1902.
517. "Brownhoist Cranes," Brown Hoisting Machinery Company catalogue (New York: Casman and Winchell, 1901), 58.
518. Ibid., 64.
519. "Manufacture of Bridge and Building Structural Shapes," *Scientific American*, December 12, 1903, 432–33.
520. H.B. Molesworth, "American Workshop Methods in Steel Construction," *Minutes of the Proceedings of the Institution of Civil Engineers* 168 (1902): 58–73, with plate.
521. "Industrial Notes: Bridges," *Railway Review*, October 17, 1896, 588.
522. "Cramp's Shipyard," *Engineering*, September 8, 1899, 293.
523. "Of Interest to the Building Trades," *Real Estate Record and Builders Guide* 67, no. 1729 (May 1901): 793.
524. "Bridge building, Notes," *Railroad Gazette*, January 27, 1899, 71.
525. "The Machine Shop and Foundry of the Pencoyd Iron Works—I," *American Machinist*, June 25, 1903, 897–901; "The Machine Shop and Foundry of the Pencoyd Iron Works—II," *American Machinist*, July 9, 1903, 980–81.
526. Roberts souvenir booklet, 1902.
527. "Amount of Work Done Per Man in a Large Bridge Works," *Engineering-Contracting*, October 14, 1908, 247.
528. "The American Bridge Company," *American Architect and Building News* 69, no. 1280 (July 1900): 1–2.
529. V. Darnell, "Directory of American Bridge Companies 1840–1900," *Society for Industrial Archeology, Occasional Publication* 4 (1984) 77–81.
530. "The American Bridge Company," *Successful American* 3, no. 5 (1901): 248–78.
531. "The American Bridge Company" *American Architect and Building News* 69, no. 1280 (July 1900): 1–2.

532. "American Bridge Company," *Successful American*, 248–78.
533. Ibid.
534. C. Weygandt, *The Plenty of Pennsylvania* (New York: H.C. Kinsey & Company, 1942).

Chapter 10

535. *New York Journal and Advertiser*, December 2, 1897.
536. *Boston Evening Transcript*, December 13. 1897.
537. "Waddell 'A' Truss", HAER MO-8, 2016.
538. J.A.L. Waddell, "A System of Iron Railroad Bridges for Japan," in *Memoirs of Tokyo Daigaku*, 11 (Tokyo: Tokyo Daigaku, 1885).
539. "American versus English Bridges in Japan," *Engineering News and American Contract Journal* 14 (October 1885): 216–17.
540. "Waddell 'A' Truss," HAER MO-8, 2016.
541. Ibid.
542. J. Konishi, "Breakthrough in Japanese Railways 8: Railways and Bridges," *Japan Railway & Transport Review* no. 57 (March 2011): 50–57.
543. Ibid.
544. Konishi,"Breakthrough in Japanese Railways 8," *Japan Railway & Transport Review*, 50–57.
545. Y. Matsuda, "Maintenance of Railway Structures with Aging Deterioration and Amarube Bridge Reconstruction," *Japan Railway and Transport Review*, no. 62 (October 2013): 32–40.
546. Ibid.
547. http://library.jsce.or.jp/jscelib/committee/2003/bridge/T2-017.htm.
548. "New York: Finished Iron and Steel," *Iron Age*, April 28, 1904, 38.
549. "Erection of the Atbara River Bridge," *Railway and Engineering Review*, January 13, 1900, 18–20; "The Atbara Bridge," *Engineering Record*, November 4, 1899, 524–28; R. Khuen, "The Atbara River Bridge," *Proceedings of the Engineers Club of Philadelphia* 16 (1899): 324–45.
550. Khuen, "Atbara River Bridge," *Proceedings*, 324–45.
551. Ibid.
552. Ibid.
553. Ibid.
554. M. Linder, *The Imperialist Origins of the International Operations of U.S. Construction Firms* (Westport, CT: Greenwood Press, 1994), 95–118.
555. "The Atbara Bridge," *Engineering Record*, November, 4, 1899, 524–28.

556. Ibid.
557. Ibid.
558. Ibid.
559. Ibid.
560. Ibid.
561. Ibid.
562. Khuen, "Atbara River Bridge," *Proceedings*, 324–45.
563. "Another British Explanation of the Atbara Contract," *Engineering Record*, June 24, 1899, 74.
564. Ibid.
565. Khuen, "Atbara River Bridge," *Proceedings*, 341.
566. Lower Merion Historical Society Library Collections, http://lowermerionhistory.org/?p=144518.
567. "Personal," *Iron Age*, October 19, 1899, 30a.
568. "Manufactures-Supplies," *Railway Age*, April 29, 1898, 304; F. Lavis, "The Construction of the Chihuahua & Pacific Railroad," *Engineering Record, Building Record and Sanitary Engineer*, March 2, 1907, 241–43; "Industrial Notes: Bridges," *Railway and Engineering Review*, May 14, 1898, 266.
569. "Manufactures-Supplies," *Railway Age*, April 29, 1898, 304.
570. Lavis, "Construction of the Chihuahua & Pacific Railroad," 241–43.
571. Ibid.
572. Ibid.
573. Ibid.
574. Ibid.
575. G. Molesworth, G. "The Uganda Railway," in *Proceedings of the International Engineering Conference, Glasgow*, 1–11 (London: William Clowes and Sins, 1902).
576. "The Bridge Contracts for the Uganda Railway," *Engineering*, February 15, 1901, 215; "American Bridge Building in Equatorial Africa.—I," *Engineering Record*, September 3, 1904, 276–78; "American Bridge Building in Equatorial Africa.—II," *Engineering Record*, September 10, 1904, 310–12; A.B. Lueder, "Experience in the Erection of American Viaducts on the Uganda Railway," *Engineering News*, April 14, 1904, 345–47.
577. "The Bridge Contracts for the Uganda Railway," *Engineering*, February 15, 1901, 215.
578. Ibid.
579. Ibid.
580. Ibid.
581. Ibid.

582. Ibid.
583. Ibid.
584. "Manufactures-Supplies: Bridges and Buildings," *Railway Age*, May 4, 1900, 474; "Our Foreign Trade," *Bulletin of the American Iron and Steel Association* 34, no. 10 (April 1900): 76.
585. "American Steel Frame Buildings Abroad," *Far Eastern Review* 8, no. 1 (July 1911): 52.
586. "American Steel Frame Buildings Abroad," *Far Eastern Review* 8, no. 2 (July 1911): 49–55.

Chapter 11

587. Deborah Del Collo, *Roxborough* (Charleston, SC: Arcadia Publishing, 2011).
588. Laura Catalano and Kurt D. Zwikl, *Along the Schuylkill River* (Charleston, SC: Arcadia Publishing, 2009); Del Collo, *Roxborough*.
589. John Charles Manton, *Bygones: A Guide to Historic Roxborough-Manayunk* (York, PA: Maple Press Company, 1990), 87.
590. *Conshohocken Recorder*, January 24, 1890.
591. *Conshohocken Recorder*, October 2, 1891.
592. *Conshohocken Recorder*, February 15, 1901.
593. *Lehighton Press*, October 27, 1892.
594. *Conshohocken Recorder*, October 15, 1907
595. Ibid.
596. *Conshohocken Recorder*, January 28, 1902.
597. *Conshohocken Recorder*, February 7, 1902.
598. *Conshohocken Recorder*, May 10, 1898.
599. *Public Ledger Almanac*, 1901, page 64.
600. "The Week," *Iron Age*, August 8, 1889, 207.
601. *Conshohocken Recorder*, February 28, 1908.
602. Raymond J. Robertson, *Ironworkers 100th Anniversary 1895–1996: A History of the Iron Workers Union*, (Washington, D.C.: International Association of Bridge, Structural and Ornamental Iron Workers, 1996).
603. Ibid.
604. Ibid.
605. *Conshohocken Recorder*, April 10, 1891.
606. "Manufacturing: Iron and Steel," *Iron Age*, May 7, 1891, 883.
607. *Conshohocken Recorder*, May 15, 1891.
608. "Industrial Notes," *Engineering and Mining Journal* 52, no. 4 (July 1891): 103.

609. "Manufacturing: Iron and Steel," *Iron Age*, May 21, 1891, 979.
610. "Industrial Notes," *Engineering and Mining Journal*, 103.
611. J. Rees, "Homestead in Context: Andrew Carnegie and the Decline of the Amalgamated Association of the Iron and Steel Workers," *Pennsylvania History: A Journal of Mid-Atlantic Studies* 64, no. 4 (Autumn 1997): 509–33.
612. *Conshohocken Recorder*, April 8, 1902.
613. Charles P. Kindleberger, *Manias, Panics and Crashes: A History of Financial Crises*, 5th ed. (New York: John Wiley & Sons, 2005), 137.
614. "New York: Finished Iron and Steel," *Iron Age*, April 28, 1904, 38.
615. *Conshohocken Recorder*, April 26, 1904.
616. "American Institute of Mining Engineers—The Philadelphia Meeting," *Engineering and Mining Journal* 31, no. 9 (February 1881): 143–44.
617. Ibid.
618. "American Engineers in Germany," *Iron Age*, August 8, 1889, 160–61.
619. "The Convention of the American Society of Civil Engineers," *Engineering Record*, July 8, 1899, 132–34.
620. "The Newark Viaducts of the Lackawanna Railroad," *Engineering News*, July 22, 1905, 102–4.
621. "The Erection of the Thebes Bridge Super Structure," *Engineering Record*, September 16, 1905, 330–35.
622. "Rebuilding of the Pennsylvania Railroad Bridge at Colombia, PA," *Railway and Engineering Review*, July 17, 1897, 415.
623. Stephen H. Smith, "How a Mile Long River Bridge Was Built in 21 Days," www.yorkblog.com.
624. J.W. Snyder, "South Fork Trinity River Bridge, California State Highway 299, at South Fork of Trinity River, Salyer Vicinity of Humboldt and Trinity Counties, California," HAER No. CA-29, 1985; "Industrial Notes: Bridges," *Railway Review*, October 17, 1896, 588.
625. "Erection of the Atbara River Bridge," *Railway and Engineering Review*, January 13, 1900, 18–20; "The Atbara Bridge," *Engineering Record*, November, 4, 1899, 524–28; Khuen, "Atbara River Bridge," *Proceedings*, 324–45; "American Bridge Building in Equatorial Africa.—I," *Engineering Record*, September 3, 1904, 276–78.
626. C.-C. Fu, "From Political Governance and Spatial Restructure to Urban Transformation and Architectural Achievements: Discourse on Architecture in the Japanese Colonial Period, 1895–1945," in *Constructing the Colonized Land: Entwined Perspectives of East Asia around WWII*, edited by I. Kuroishi, 125 (Burlington, VT: Ashgate Publishing, 2014), 126.

627. "Erection of the Atbara River Bridge," *Railway and Engineering Review*, January 13, 1900, 18–20; "Atbara Bridge," *Engineering Record*, 524–28; Khuen, "Atbara River Bridge," *Proceedings*, 324–45.
628. "American Bridge Building in Equatorial Africa.—I," *Engineering Record*, September 3, 1904, 276–78; "American Bridge Building in Equatorial Africa.—II," *Engineering Record*, September 10, 1904, 310–12; A.B. Lueder, "Experience in the Erection of American Viaducts on the Uganda Railway," *Engineering News*, April 14, 1904.
629. "American Bridge Building in Equatorial Africa.—I," *Engineering Record*, September 3, 1904, 276–78.
630. "American Bridge Building in Equatorial Africa.—II," *Engineering Record*, September 10, 1904, 310–12.
631. Ibid.
632. Ibid.
633. Ibid.
634. Ibid.
635. Ibid.
636. Ibid.
637. Ibid.
638. Ibid.
639. Ibid.
640. Lavis, "Construction of the Chihuahua & Pacific Railroad," 241–43.
641. Ibid.

Chapter 12

642. First Annual Report of the United States Steel Corporation for the fiscal year ended December 31, 1902, to 22nd Annual Report of the United States Steel Corporation for the fiscal year ended December 31, 1923.
643. "The United States Naval Railway Batteries in France," *Navy Department Office of Naval Records and Library Historical Section. Publication Number 6* (Washington D.C.: U.S. Government Printing Office, 1922).
644. Ibid.
645. Ibid.
646. Ibid.
647. Ibid.
648. "Two Carnegie Mills to Be Improved" *Steel* 100, no. 8 (February 1937): 16.
649. "Pencoyd Plant Inactive" *Steel* 106, no. 16 (April 1940): 28.

650. "The Ambridge Plant of the American Bridge Company. Part I.—Arrangement, Operation, Power, Transportation, and Buildings," *Engineering Record*, November 21, 1903, 620–25.
651. Penn Group, "Pencoyd Iron Works Office," www.pennrealestategroup.com.
652. Sikora Wells Appel, www.sikora-wa.com.
653. Ken Finkel, "June 11, 1923: Fiery Destruction at Broad Street Station," www.phillyhistory.org.
654. "Train Accidents in April," *Railway Age Gazette*, June 5, 1914.
655. "12 Killed When Tank of Molasses Explodes," *New York Times*, January 16, 1919.
656. Ronald Smothers, "Dozens Are Killed in Wreck of Train in Alabama Bayou," *New York Times*, September 23, 1993, www.nytimes.com.
657. F. Griggs Jr., "Preservation and Restoration of 19th Century Cast and Wrought the Iron Bridges," *Practice Periodical on Structural Design and Construction* 14, no. 4 (November 1, 2009) 159–75.
658. "Freight House Pedestrian Bridge," www.bnim.com.
659. Ibid.
660. "Koya-Kosenkyo Bridge," http://kikuko-nagoya.com/html/Koya-kosenkyo.html
661. http://tenere.blog.shinobi.jp.
662. "Waddell 'A' Truss," HAER MO-8, 2016.
663. Roberts souvenir booklet, 1902.
664. "Philadelphia's Schuylkill River Trail," www.cynwydtrail.org.
665. Sikora Wells Appel, "Pencoyd Landing," www.sikora-wa.com
666. Seashore Trolley Museum, https://collection.trolleymuseum.org.
667. Leslie Newell Peacock," The Clinton Bridge Opens," www.arktimes.com.
668. "Bridge Building, Notes" *Railroad Gazette*, April 14, 1899, 269.
669. Old American Golf Club, www.theoldamericangolfclub.com.
670. Y Matsuda, "Maintenance of Railway Structures with Aging Deterioration and Amarube Bridge Reconstruction," *Japan Railway and Transport Review*, no. 62 (October 2013): 32–40.
671. Ibid.

Index

A

B

Y

About the Author

Kevin Righter was born in Pittsburgh, Pennsylvania, attended Haverford and Bryn Mawr Colleges, University of Michigan and University of California at Berkeley, where he received degrees in geology and geological science. His family is from the Philadelphia area dating back to 1680s (he is the ninth generation). Interest in the family history and the Philadelphia area was spurred by his parents, who started nearly from scratch and researched remarkable detailed history that even includes records in Europe. His great-grandfather Walter Righter worked at Pencoyd for fifty years from 1882 to 1932, first as a mechanic, then as a supervisor and finally as superintendent of motive power. Righter is a planetary scientist and lives with his family in Houston.